DISNEYLAND™

&

SOUTHERN CALIFORNIA

with Kids

10th Edition

MICHAEL & TRISA KNIGHT

Authors: Michael and Trisa Knight
Editors: Mike Nalepa, Linda Cabasin
Editorial Production: Carolyn Roth
Production/Manufacturing: Angela L. McLean
Design: Guido Caroti
Cover Photo: © The Disneyland® Resort

www.fodors.com

All products mentioned in this book are trademarks of their respective companies.

Every effort has been made to make this book complete and accurate as of the date of publication. In a time of rapid change, however, it is difficult to ensure that all information is entirely up-to-date. Although the publisher and authors cannot be liable for any inaccuracies or omissions in this book, they are always grateful for corrections and suggestions for improvement. Please feel free to send your comments and corrections to editors@fodors.com or Michael and Trisa Knight c/o Fodor's at 1745 Broadway, New York, NY 10019.

This book is available at special discounts for bulk purchases for sales promotions or premiums. Special editions, including personalized covers, excerpts of existing books, and corporate imprints, can be created in large quantities for special needs. For more information, write to Special Markets/Premium Sales, 1745 Broadway, MD 6-2, New York, New York 10019 or e-mail specialmarkets@randomhouse.com.

Tenth Edition

ISBN: 978-1-4000-0427-0

PRINTED IN THE UNITED STATES OF AMERICA

10 9 8 7 6 5 4 3 2 1

To our children,
Beth, Sarah, Connor,
Tanner, Paige, and Nathan.
Through their eyes,
the magic of the
world comes alive.

Contents

List of Maps and Quick Guide Reference Tables

MAPS

QUICK GUIDES

Helpful Phone Numbers and Web Sites

Airport Bus	800-828-6699 or 714-978-8855 www.graylineanaheim.com
Alpine Motel	800-772-4422 or 714-535-2186 www.alpineinnanaheim.com
AMC Theatres (Downtown Disney)	714-781-4560
The Anabella Hotel	800-863-4888 or 714-905-1050 www.anabellahotel.com
Anaheim Carriage Inn	800-345-2131 or 714-740-1440 www.anaheimcarriageinn.com
Anaheim Camelot Inn and Suites	800-828-4898 or 714-635-7275 www.camelotinn-anaheim.com
Anaheim Desert Inn and Suites	800-433-5270 or 714-772-5050 www.anaheimdesertinn.com
Anaheim Fairfield Inn by Marriot	800-228-2800 or 714-772-6777 www.marriot.com
Anaheim–Orange County Visitors and Convention Bureau	714-765-8888 www.anaheimoc.org
Anaheim Resort Transportation System	www.rideart.org
Audiences Unlimited	www.audiencesunlimited.com
Autry National Center of the American West	323-667-2000 www.autrynationalcenter.org

Best Western Mission Bay Inn	800-457-8080 or 619-275-5700 www.bestwestern.com
Best Western Park Place	800-854-8177 or 714-776-4800 www.stovallshotels.com
Best Western Raffles Inn and Suites	800-308-5278 or 714-750-6100 www.bestwesternrafflesinn.com
California Science Center	323-724-3623 www.californiasciencecenter.org
Candy Cane Inn	800-345-7057 or 714-774-5284 www.candycaneinn.net
Carousel Inn and Suites	800-854-6767 or 714-758-0444 www.carouselinnandsuites.com
Castle Inn and Suites	800-227-8530 or 714-774-8111 www.castleinn.com
Catal and Uva Bar	714-774-4442 or 714-781-DINE www.patinagroup.com/catal.htm
CityPass	888-330-5008 or 208-787-4300 www.citypass.com
Comfort Suites Mission Valley	800-433-0452 or 619-881-4000 www.comfortsuitesmv.com
The Dana on Mission Bay	800-445-3339 or 619-222-6440 www.thedana.com
Del Sol Inn	888-686-1122 or 714-234-3411 www.delsolinn.com
Desert Palm Hotel and Suites	888/788-0466 or 714-535-1133 www.desertpalmshotel.com
Disney Resort Map Requests	714-781-4560
Disney Resort Restaurant Reservations	714-781-DINE
Disney's Grand Californian Hotel	714-956-6425 or 714-635-2300 www.disneyland.com
Disney's Paradise Pier Hotel	714-956-6425 or 714-999-0990 www.disneyland.com
Disneyland Hotel	714-956-6425 or 714-778-6600 www.disneyland.com
Disneyland Information	714-781-4565 www.disneyland.com

Disneyland Merchandise Ordering	800-362-4533
Disneyland Resort Guest Relations	714-781-4400
Disneyland Resort Lost and Found	714-817-2166
Disneyland Tickets	714-781-4043 www.disneyland.com
Disneyland Weather	www.disneyland.com
Doubletree Club Hotel	800-489-9671 or 619-881-6900 www.doubletreeclubsd.com
El Capitan Theatre	800-DISNEY6 www.elcapitantickets.com
ESPN Zone Reservations and Event Schedule	714-300-3776 www.espnzone.com/anaheim
Gibson Amphitheater	818-622-4440 www.livenation.com/venue/ gibson-amphitheatre-tickets
Hilton Anaheim	800-445-8667 or 714-750-4321 www.hilton.com
Holiday Inn Carlsbad by the Sea	800-465-4329 or 760-438-7880 www.carlsbadhi.com
Holiday Inn SeaWorld	800-383-5430 or 619-881-6100 www.himb.com
House of Blues Reservations	714-778-2583 or 714-781-DINE www.houseofblues.com/venues/ clubvenues/anaheim
House of Blues Tickets	714-778-2583 www.houseofblues.com
Howard Johnson Hotel in the Anaheim Resort	800-422-4228 or 714-776-6120 www.hojoanaheim.com
Jolly Roger Inn	888-296-5986 or 714-782-7500 www.jollyrogerhotel.com
Knott's Berry Farm	714-220-5200 www.knotts.com
Knott's Berry Farm Hotel and Resort	866-752-2444 or 714-995-1111 www.knottshotel.com

La Brea Bakery	714-490-0233
	www.labreabakery.com
La Brea Tar Pits	323-934-7243
	www.tarpits.org
LEGOLAND	760-918-LEGO
	www.legoland.com
Long Beach Aquarium	562-590-3100
of the Pacific	www.aquariumofpacific.org
Los Angeles Zoo	323-644-6400
	www.lazoo.org
Medieval Times	888-935-6878 or 714-521-4740
	www.medievaltimes.com
Naples Ristorante e Pizzeria	714-776-6200 or 714-781-DINE
	www.patinagroup.com/naples.htm
Natural History Museum	213-763-3466
of Los Angeles County	www.nhm.org
NBC Studio Tours	818-840-3537
Park Vue Inn	800-334-7021 or 714-772-3691
	www.parkvueinn.com
Pinocchio's Workshop	714-635-2300
(Child Care)	
Pirates Dinner Adventure	866-439-2469 or 714-690-1497
	www.piratesdinneradventure.com
Portofino Inn and Suites	800-511-6907 or 714-782-7600
	www.portofinoinnanaheim.com
Queen Mary	800-437-2934
	www.queenmary.com
Rainforest Café	714-956-5260 or 714-781-DINE
	www.rainforestcafe.com
Ralph Brennan's Jazz Kitchen	714-776-5200 or 714-781-DINE
	www.rbjazzkitchen.com
Ramada Inn Maingate	800-854-6097 or 800-422-4402
	www.ramadamaingate.com
Ramada Limited Suites	800-272-6232 or 714-971-3553
	www.ramada.com
San Diego Zoo	619-231-1515
	www.sandiegozoo.org

San Diego Zoo's Wild Animal Park	760-747-8702 www.sandiegozoo.org/wap
SeaWorld	800-257-4268 or 619-226-3901 www.seaworldsandiego.com
Six Flags Magic Mountain	661-255-4100 www.sixflags.com/magicmountain
Sony Pictures Studios Tours	310-244-8687 www.sonypicturesstudiostours.com
Studio Disney 365 Reservations	714-781-7895
Super Shuttle	800-258-3826 www.supershuttle.com
Tortilla Jo's	714-535-5000 www.patinagroup.com/tortillajos
Tropicana Inn	800-828-4898 or 714-635-4082 www.tropicanainn-anaheim.com
Universal CityWalk	818-622-4455 www.citywalkhollywood.com
Universal Studios Hollywood	818-622-3801 universalstudioshollywood.com
Walt Disney Travel Company	866-279-7165 or 714-520-5050 www.disneyland.com
Warner Bros. Studio (VIP Tour)	818-972-8687 wbsf.warnerbros.com

Key to Icons

 Knight Choice

 Helpful Hint

 Insider's Secret

 Money-Saving Tip

 The Scare Factor

 Time-Saving Tip

 Fun Fact

Acknowledgments

We would like to thank Michael Nalepa at Fodor's for making this book a reality in the first place. We also appreciate all of our friends for sharing their vacation memories with us, as well as the countless families at Disneyland and other Southern California attractions with whom we spoke for their personal tips, experiences, and observations. We would also like to acknowledge all of the cast members at the Disneyland Resort and the staff at other attractions for their inside information, as well as the public relations specialists for their help.

We also want to offer a huge thanks to Barbara Knight (Grandma) and David and Jamie Knight (Michael's brother and sister) for vacationing at Disneyland with us.

Introduction

Get Ready for a Great Family Vacation!

For 55 years, families have been making pilgrimages to the most universally known and loved theme park in the world—Disneyland. Since the park first opened in July 1955, many things have changed both at Disneyland as well as throughout Southern California. In fact, this evolution in the family vacation continues to this very day and promises to evolve right on into the future.

In the past, many families just loaded up the station wagon and drove to Disneyland to spend a day at the park. If time allowed, they might also visit another attraction in the area. No real planning was needed: just hop in the car and head to Disneyland for a day of fantasy and adventure.

Since those days, things have changed. Disneyland has become its own resort. Anaheim and the surrounding areas of Southern California have become the family playland of the West. To enjoy as much of it as possible, today's family must do a bit more planning and preparation for a vacation to Disneyland. No longer can you see all of Disneyland in just one day, and with the opening of Disney's California Adventure, you will want to take at least a couple of days, if not more, to experience it all.

Why This Book Is Special

This book has many important and unique features to make your family vacation a big success. We take you from the early stages of planning your vacation all the way to what to do just before you leave the park. In fact, this book offers just about everything you need to ensure a fun-filled family getaway.

Visiting Disneyland as an adult can be an exhilarating experience. The joy and excitement increase as you see the wonders and magic through the eyes of your children. Therefore, we target much of the information in this book toward children as well as parents. To help keep kids happy and parents sane, this book contains information on the suitability of attractions for children of various ages, including height requirements as well as just how scary an attraction may be. We also include information about parent-swaps and the FAST-PASS system.

Not only did we write this book for families, but we also wrote it with the help of families. We have taken numerous vacations at Disneyland with our children, at various ages from 4 months old and up. In addition, we have talked to dozens of other families to get their personal insights as well as tips from their experiences, such as the best place to sit for the parades or the best place to dine with the Disney characters.

Not every family wants the same type of vacation. Therefore, you can find information here not only to fit the time frame for your trip but also to fit your budget. It takes at least three to four days to fully see the Disneyland Resort, but your family can still have a great time in just a couple of days. Also, no matter how thrifty you may be, a vacation to the Disneyland Resort will cost you. However, with some planning, you can maximize your fun while minimizing the cost.

This book has three sections. The first section covers all the preparations you need to make a great vacation. It includes chapters on planning, choosing hotels, and even packing. The second section covers the Disneyland Resort, with chapters on the Magic Kingdom, Disney's California Adventure, Downtown Disney, and Disney dining. The third section covers other attractions in Southern California. Here you can find chapters on Knott's Berry Farm, Universal Studios Hollywood, Six Flags Magic Mountain, LEGOLAND, and much, much more.

In addition to the usual travel guide information, this book contains hints, tips, and strategies for getting the most out of your vacation. Because there is so much to do, and often not enough time to do it in, every time-saving tip helps make your vacation that much better.

Disneyland & Southern California with Kids goes beyond planning, strategy, and hints. We wrote it for you to take along on your vacation and into the parks and attractions. While you are waiting in line for a ride, read up on some interesting facts or trivia, as well as things to look for during the ride—such as Hidden Mickeys and other fun things. This enrichment can add a lot of new excitement for even the most veteran Disneyland visitors.

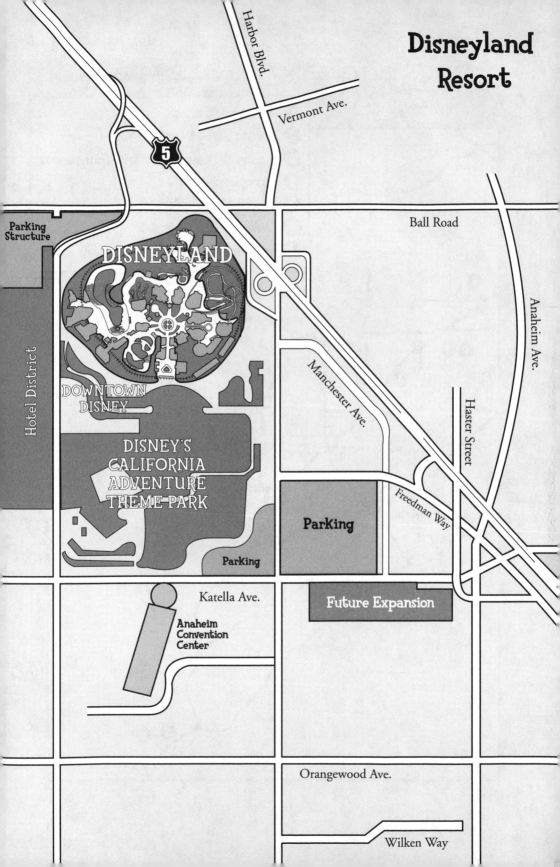

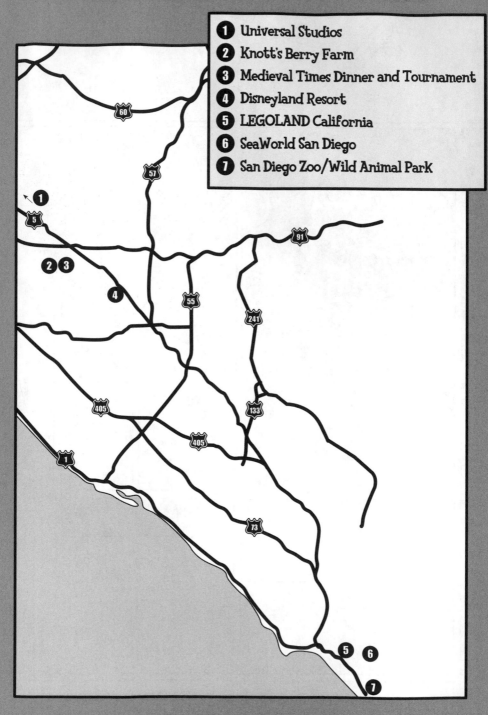

Southern California Attractions

1. Universal Studios
2. Knott's Berry Farm
3. Medieval Times Dinner and Tournament
4. Disneyland Resort
5. LEGOLAND California
6. SeaWorld San Diego
7. San Diego Zoo/Wild Animal Park

CHAPTER

1

Planning the Trip

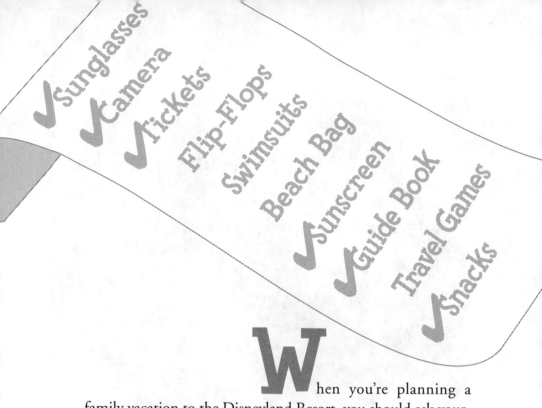

Sunglasses ✓ Camera ✓ Tickets ✓ Flip-Flops Swimsuits Beach Bag Sunscreen ✓ Guide Book Travel Games Snacks ✓

When you're planning a family vacation to the Disneyland Resort, you should ask yourself three main questions: "When should we go?" "What do we want to do?" and "How long should we stay?" The answers to these questions can help you put together a plan for a family vacation that will be memorable and a whole lot of fun. The first part of this chapter deals with these three questions. The remainder of the chapter deals with putting your plan into action and booking your vacation. Now let's get started.

When Should You Go?

The first question you need to ask yourself is, "When should we go?" To answer it, look at three main factors: work schedules, school schedules, and how busy the resort will be at the time.

The least crowded time to visit the Disneyland Resort is usually the first week of January to mid-February, the last week of April to Memorial Day week (in May), the end of Labor Day week (in early September) to mid-October, and after Thanksgiving week in November to a week before Christmas. The busiest times are Presidents' Day week (in February), the week before and the week after Easter, the second week of June to the last week of August (summer vacation), Thanksgiving week, and Christmas Day through New Year's Day.

Although spring break and summer are probably the most convenient times for your family to vacation at the Disneyland Resort, everyone else will be there, too. Try to avoid the busiest times if at all possible. However, if you must vacation then, we have included several tips to help make your stay more enjoyable and help you get the jump on the crowds.

The downside to visiting the resort during the least crowded times is that the resorts' hours are shorter and the parades and shows may be running only on the weekends, if at all.

Mid-May and the last two weeks of September are usually pretty good times to go. They offer a balance between small crowds, on the one hand, and shows and parades running, on

Insider's Secret
The days of the week also matter. Saturday is always the busiest day throughout the year. Tuesday, Wednesday, and Thursday are usually the slowest, though of course relative to the time of year.

the other. If you want to see all of the holiday decorations and activities, try the first two weeks of December.

Weather can also be a factor. Southern California tends to get most of its rainfall from the latter half of December through the first couple of weeks in March. However, even during these months there are still dry days.

Should You Take the Kids Out of School?

If your work allows you some flexibility in taking vacation time, then the limiting factor is school. Because many schools have the same or similar holidays, these are usually the times when the parks are at their busiest. So consider taking the kids out of school for a few days. The older the kids, the harder it is for them to miss school: there's usually a lot more schoolwork to make up. No matter what age your kids are, you should speak with their teachers beforehand. Ask if you can get assignments in advance for the days they will miss. You might also ask if your children could do a special project or report while on the trip to make up for work missed. Several educational places to visit in Southern California may even fit in with your child's course of study. (For more tips on making your vacation educational, *see* Chapter 15.) Some school districts offer independent study programs for students who will be absent for a week or more. You need to check into this at least a week or even two before you leave. Talking to your children's teachers can also help you avoid missing important tests and exams. If you do decide to have your kids miss a few days of school, be sure to have them start the makeup work before you leave. (They will want to do it even less when they return.)

Helpful Hint

To keep down the amount of instruction your child misses, plan your vacation around school days off for in-service or teacher development and "minimum" or half days. Unlike Christmas and spring break, these dates vary from school to school, which means not everyone will be hitting the park at the same time.

What Do You Want to Do?

Once you have figured out a time frame for your vacation, you must decide what you want to do while you're in Southern California. In addition to the Disneyland Resort, which includes both Disneyland and Disney's California Adventure, a number of other attractions are in the area: Knott's Berry Farm, Universal Studios, Six Flags Magic Mountain, LEGOLAND, Hollywood, the beaches, and much more. Unless your vacation will last a couple weeks, you will have to decide which things you want to do most.

To help you decide, take a look at the later chapters in this book, covering the various theme parks and attractions in Southern California. There truly is something for everyone.

How Long Should You Stay?

The third question goes hand in hand with the second. You need to know what you will be doing to determine how long to stay—at the same time, you need an idea of how long you will stay so that you can figure out how many things you can do.

For most families, the Disneyland Resort is their main reason for vacationing in the area. Although Disneyland can be seen in a single day, you will be very rushed and may not get to do everything you want to do. Two days is a bit better, but you're still going to be somewhat rushed to do everything. Three days is ideal, though some families could stay a fourth or fifth day as well. California Adventure can be covered in a single day. You may not get to do every single attraction there, but two days is probably too long. For the other theme parks in this area, plan on a day for each. Smaller attractions such as water parks or museums take about half a day each.

As a family, piece together the places you plan on going, as well as how long you can spend at each, to come up with a total number of days you'll be in Southern California. Once you have this information, you're ready to start putting your plan into action.

Making Reservations and Travel Plans

While making reservations and travel plans, you must take care of three main things: choose and make reservations at a hotel, arrange for tickets, and book transportation. Chapter 2 covers finding a hotel and contains several important guidelines for choosing one that meets your family's needs. Chapter 2 also lists a few hotels in the Anaheim area that are good choices. Remember: when considering hotels, location is an extremely important factor—just as important as price. We recommend a hotel within easy walking distance of the Disneyland Resort, especially if you're not taking your own vehicle or renting one.

Package Deals

You can get several types of package deals through travel clubs such as AAA (Automobile Association of America), the Walt Disney Travel Company, travel agents, individual hotels, and airlines. These packages include hotel accommodations and tickets for the Disney theme parks and possibly other Southern California attractions. Some packages also include transportation.

Package deals are often a great way to save money and to get everything you need at once. However, be cautious. Some packages can be expensive or include things you don't really want to do. We suggest you look at several packages and then compare them to getting everything separately. Check with the Walt Disney Travel Company. You can get a quick quote for a package deal at its Web site at www.disneyland.com or by calling 714/520–5050. Also check with AAA (if you're a member) or with a travel agent. Finally, see what kinds of deals you can get on your own, especially if you'll be flying, because you can sometimes get cheaper airfares separate from packages. Compare the various packages, and choose the one that best fits your price range and includes everything you want and nothing you don't.

For more information on package deals, *see* Chapter 2.

Insider's Secret

Many packages include additional tours or attractions and may refer to them as "bonuses." Although they may seem to be included at no extra charge, their cost is already factored into the price of the package. If you don't want these add-ons, ask if you can remove them. Doing so usually lowers the price of the package. Although the agent usually does not tell you that you can delete options, always ask. Each bonus you delete can save you up to $50 per person.

Tickets

If you get a package deal, your tickets are usually included. However, if you're not using a package, you can get your tickets elsewhere. The key is to get your tickets in advance. You do not want to have to wait in line at the ticket booths. On some days, the wait for tickets can be more than an hour.

You can order tickets directly from Disneyland either through its Web site or by calling 714/781–4043. You can also purchase them at the Disney Stores, through AAA, and at some hotels. Some club stores, like Sam's Club or Costco, and even supermarkets carry tickets for Disneyland. However, the types of tickets are usually limited. Prices at the gate at this writing are listed next. Some tickets are cheaper to purchase online from the Disneyland Web site: if this is the case, the online prices are listed in parentheses. Children under age 3 are free.

One-Day Ticket
Regular: $69
Child (ages 3–9): $59

Note: This ticket is valid either at the Disneyland Park *or* California Adventure. You cannot visit both on the same day with a single ticket. This ticket is not available for purchase online.

One-Day Park Hopper Ticket
Regular: $94
Child (ages 3–9): $84
   Note: This ticket allows you back-and-forth admittance to both Disneyland and Disney's California Adventure on the same day.

Two-Day Park Hopper Ticket
Regular: $143
Child (ages 3–9): $123
   Note: Park Hopper tickets allow you back-and-forth admittance to both Disneyland and Disney's California Adventure for the number of days purchased. This ticket is valid for 13 days after first use.

Three-Day Park Hopper Ticket
Regular: $199 ($179)
Child (ages 3–9): $169 ($149)

Four-Day Park Hopper Ticket
Regular: $224 ($194)
Child (ages 3–9): $194 ($164)

Five-Day Park Hopper Ticket
Regular: $244 ($204)
Child (ages 3–9): $214 ($174)

Six-Day Park Hopper Ticket
Regular: $249 ($209)
Child (ages 3–9): $219 ($179)

Insider's Secret
If you plan on staying for three or more days, be sure to order your tickets online and save from $20 to $40 per ticket. Specials sometimes include 1–2 days of free admission.

Money-Saving Tip

Specially priced Disneyland Resort tickets for U.S. military service personnel and Department of Defense employees and their families are available at MWR ticket offices throughout the United States.

Annual Passports

If you plan on visiting more than once in a year's time, we highly recommend getting Annual Passports, which are available at the parks or via Disney's Web site. They're a lot less expensive than buying Two-Day Park Hopper tickets twice and allow access to both parks. The nice thing about Annual Passports is that you do not feel rushed. If you arrive in Anaheim during the afternoon, you can hit one of the parks for a few hours and not feel as if you are wasting one of your days on the ticket.

A few months before your passports expire, Disney will send out a renewal form for each person in your family. When you renew by mail, you can save at least $20 per person and usually get some special offers or discounts as well. However, if you will not be returning for a while after your passports expire, it's usually cheaper to let them lapse and buy tickets next time you go—then cash them in for Annual Passports later.

Deluxe Annual Passports
All ages: $269

This passport allows you to visit both parks as many times as you wish during 315 particular days of the year. There are 50 blackout days (most Saturdays, Memorial Day weekend, Thanksgiving Thursday and Friday, and from Christmas Eve to New Year's Day). You can also get a 10% discount at park and Disney hotel restaurants, special rates for Disneyland hotels, and discounts in Downtown Disney. For $59 more, you can

Insider's Secret

You can cash in your tickets while inside the Disney-land Park and apply the value to an Annual Passport. For example, if you purchased the Three-Day Park Hopper ticket, you would only have to pay an additional $70 per adult and $100 per child for an entire year of fun. The only requirement is that you must purchase the Annual Passports at the park while your tickets are still valid. Currently Annual Passports can be purchased at the Bank of Main Street. At times, an additional processing location is set up for this purpose. Your annual passes are valid for one year from the first day of use of your ticket, and you can use them immediately if you want to stay a few more days.

add unlimited parking (add this parking provision to one of the adult passes). Parking is normally $12 a day. You can still visit the parks on blackout days, but you'll pay a reduced rate, around $40 per person per day.

Premium Annual Passports
All ages: $389

This passport has no blackout days and includes free parking as well as 10% off merchandise throughout the resort, a 15% discount at the restaurants in the parks as well as those at Disney hotels, and a 10% discount on accommodations at the Disney hotels. Since blackout days are usually busy, it's best to go for the Deluxe Annual Passport and save $120 per passport. With that savings, you can spend more money on food, souvenirs, or other things—even the $20 per day for visiting on blackout days.

Southern California CityPass
Regular: $259
Child (ages 3–9): $219

If you're planning to visit other Southern California attractions in addition to Disneyland, consider purchasing the Southern California CityPass. For one low price, you get a Three-Day Park Hopper ticket for Disneyland and California Adventure and One-Day Tickets to Universal Studios Hollywood, SeaWorld in San Diego, and *either* the San Diego Zoo or San Diego Wild Animal Park. These can be purchased online at the Disneyland Web site or the CityPass Web site (www. citypass.net) as well as at the parks' ticket booths. At $60 more than an adult Three-Day Park Hopper Ticket and $50 more than a child's ticket, this is a really good deal. You'll still save money even if you skip one of the additional attractions.

Transportation

There are two main ways to get to the Disneyland Resort: by plane or car. Depending on your budget and the distance you must travel to the resort, the choice is up to you. If you're more than 300–400 miles away, it's usually faster to fly. Remember to consider the extra time it takes to check in because of increased security restrictions. However, driving provides more flexibility and is often cheaper.

By Car
The Disneyland Resort is quite easy to find by car. You should get a map of Southern California as well as a city map of Anaheim and Orange County. Members of AAA can get free maps as well as TripTiks, which are custom-made routings for your trip, showing you exactly how to get from your home to Disneyland. The main part of driving is getting to Interstate 5. Once you're there, the I–5 freeway will take you directly to Disneyland.

If you're traveling southbound on I–5, take the Disney-land Drive exit. If you want to go to the park, follow the signs to the parking structure. If you want to go to the Disney hotels, continue on Disneyland Drive. For the Disneyland Hotel, turn right on Magic Way and follow the signs. For the Paradise Pier Hotel and the Grand Californian Hotel, continue down Disneyland Drive past the Disneyland Hotel, and the entrances are on the right and left, respectively.

If you're traveling northbound on I–5, exit on Katella Avenue and turn left. For the Disney parks, turn right on Harbor Boulevard and then left on Disney Way into the park-ing lot. For the hotels, continue on Katella Avenue and turn right on Disneyland Drive. The Paradise Pier and Grand Cal-ifornian hotels are on your left and right, respectively. To get to the Disneyland Hotel, continue down Disneyland Drive and turn left on Magic Way. Follow the signs to the hotel entrance.

California Traffic Laws

If you're traveling from out of state and will be either driving to the Disneyland Resort or renting a car, there are a few laws you should know. All passengers in front and rear seats must wear safety belts. Also, all children must be in a child safety seat or booster until they are either 6 years old or 60 pounds. It is also illegal to talk on a cell phone without a hands-free device or to text while driving. If you do not obey these laws, you risk being pulled over and ticketed.

Insider's Secret

You can get directions from your house to the Disneyland Resort at www.disneyland.com.

By Plane

If you'll be flying into South-ern California, you must first decide at which airport to ar-rive. Unfortunately, there's no Disneyland international air-port, so you'll have to choose from the ones in the area: LAX in Los Angeles, John Wayne in Santa Ana, and Long Beach.

LAX is the largest airport in the area, but it's not the closest. Check the rates into each of these airports and see which has the best price. You'll also need to arrange ground transportation from the airport to the resort. There are several options. You can rent a car, take the Airport Bus, or take the SuperShuttle. The Airport Bus picks you up at the airport and then makes several stops around the Anaheim area, including the main entrances of the Disney hotels. From LAX, the one-way fare is $22 for adults and $19 for children 3–11 (round-trip prices are $30 and $23, respectively). From John Wayne, the fares are $15 for adults and $12 for children one way ($25 and $16 round-trip, respectively). To find the Airport Bus, look for the red signs as you leave the baggage claim area at the airport. Take a bus with Anaheim-Disneyland as its destination. For more information, call 800/828–6699 or 714/978–8855, or visit the Web site at www.graylineanaheim.com.

The SuperShuttle is a van shuttle that carries your family from the airport directly to your hotel. The one-way fare from LAX is $16 per person and $10 from John Wayne. Children under 3 are free. You can also get a private van that will hold up to nine people. These vans cost $107 from LAX and $67 from John Wayne. You'll need to reserve a shuttle in advance. For more information and to make reservations, call 800/258–3826 or visit www.supershuttle.com. Cabs are also an option, but rates are higher than both shuttles. If you have a large group, you may want to consider hiring a limousine.

The bus or van can be expensive—a family of four may have to pay $80 or more round-trip. With that in mind, you may want to consider renting a car. If you can use discounts (such as those in *Entertainment Books* or for AAA members), renting a car can be cheaper than riding a bus or van and can

Helpful Hint
Some of the nicer, non-Disney hotels in the area offer airport shuttles. Check with your hotel about this option.

give you flexibility in getting around the area. If you'll be visiting other attractions in the area, especially those in Los Angeles or San Diego, then a rental car is a good idea. Although you can often include transportation to these other attractions as part of a package, the costs add up and you must conform to a shuttle's schedule rather than your own. Some packages also include a rental car or offer it at an additional price. Keep in mind that with a rental car you may have to pay for parking. At theme parks in the area, parking is usually $12. Although many hotels offer free parking, some charge. Be sure to ask about parking costs when you're making reservations.

Budgeting Your Trip

Families with all types of budgets can enjoy a wonderful vacation at the Disneyland Resort and in Southern California. The key is determining how best to spend your money. Listed below are hints and tips for three different budgets. These budgets are only examples of what you can expect to spend during a vacation. *Note*: The budgets do not include travel expenses, transportation, rental car, or souvenirs, and are estimated for a family of four with two adults and two children under age 17.

As Inexpensive as Possible

Even if you don't have a lot of money to spend, you can still have a great time. You just have to maximize the amount of fun for your dollar.

ℯ If you can drive your own car, this is usually the cheapest way to get to the Disneyland Resort. However, if you must drive for more than a day and have to spend money for lodging on the way there and the way back, compare the cost of driving to flying.

@ Look for all the discounts you can. If you don't belong to AAA, consider getting a membership. Not only does it include free roadside assistance and towing, but you can also get reduced rates on tickets, lodging, and airfare.

@ Travel during the off-season, when rates are cheapest.

@ Find the least expensive hotels you can that are within walking distance of the resort.

@ Choose a hotel with a microwave and refrigerator, or even a kitchenette, so you can prepare some of your own meals.

@ Choose a hotel that serves complimentary breakfasts or where kids eat free.

@ Spend all of your vacation at the Disneyland parks. A Three-Day Park Hopper ticket is cheaper than one day at each of the two parks and a third day somewhere else.

@ Eat only one meal per day in the park.

Here is a sample low-cost budget for a family of four:

@ Lodging for two nights and Three-Day Park Hopper tickets in a package: $900.

@ Meals at $18 per day per person at the park, supplemented by snacks you bring in, for three days (breakfast provided by hotel): $216.

The total for three days at the resort is $1,116. You could cut it even further by eating dinner at a fast-food place outside the parks and by taking a sack lunch. (You can leave these lunches in lockers outside the parks at the picnic area.)

The Moderate Budget

This budget features a vacation with more amenities while saving money at the same time:

- If you want to stay on-site, stay at the Paradise Pier Hotel during the off-season or with a special discounted rate from a travel club.

- To save money at the parks, eat only two meals there. A late lunch and a light dinner are usually best, with a complimentary breakfast at the hotel or light breakfast. Or have a large, late breakfast and then an early dinner.

- Carry snacks with you at the park and take your own drinks (water bottles or juice boxes in backpacks).

- Buy souvenirs that the entire family can share, such as videos or CDs, instead of souvenirs for each person. Mickey antenna balls for your car are a great idea.

Here is a sample moderate-cost budget for a family of four:

- Three nights at the Paradise Pier Hotel, off-season, with package including Southern California CityPass (three days Disneyland + Universal Studios + SeaWorld + San Diego Zoo: $1,780).

- Meals at $25 per day per person for four days: $400.

Adding an extra day, a nicer hotel, more money for food, and three more attractions increases the cost to $2,180—about double the previous budget.

The Luxury Budget

If money is not a limiting factor and you want to experience the Disneyland Resort in all of its glory, and even hit a few off-site attractions, here is what you can expect to pay:

- Five nights at the Grand Californian, regular but not peak season, concierge level with theme-park view, with Five-Day Park Hopper tickets, plus tickets to Universal Studios Hollywood and Knott's Berry Farm as part of a package deal: $5,100.

- Meals at $45 per person per day at the park: $900.

This very nice package would cost a family of four $6,000 and would include every amenity available at the Disneyland Resort as well as three nice meals a day.

Insider's Secret

If you book a package deal through the Disneyland Web site, you can schedule a call from Mickey, Minnie, or Goofy as a way to announce your trip to the family. Packages also often include souvenirs such as pins and lanyards.

As you can see from looking at these three different budgets, the amount that families can spend on their vacation can vary greatly. When budgeting your vacation, separate the things you really want from the things that would be nice to have. Once you calculate how much the things you want will cost, start adding the things that would be nice, until you reach your spending limit.

CHAPTER

2

Where to Stay

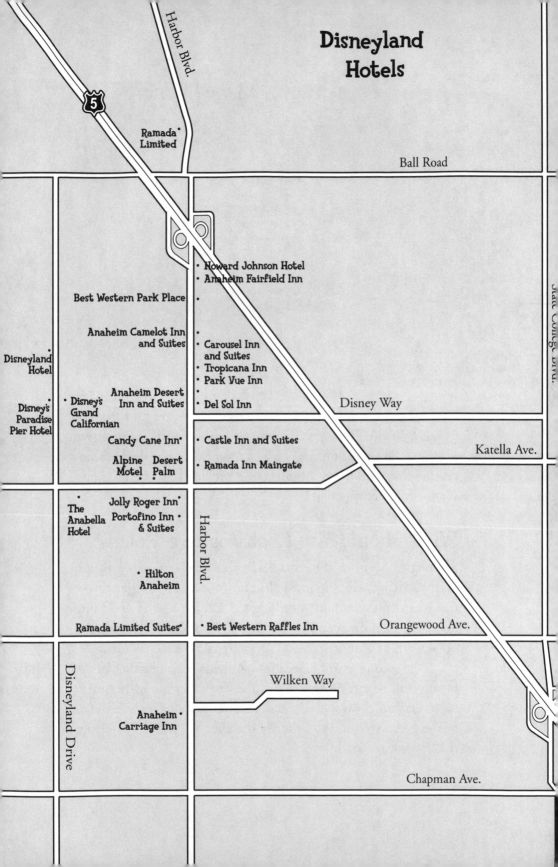

Disneyland
Hotels

Harbor Blvd.

State College Blvd.

5

Ramada
Limited

Ball Road

• Howard Johnson Hotel
• Anaheim Fairfield Inn

Best Western Park Place
•

Anaheim Camelot Inn
and Suites

• Carousel Inn
and Suites
• Tropicana Inn
• Park Vue Inn

Disneyland
Hotel
•

Anaheim Desert
Inn and Suites

• Disney's
Grand
Californian

• Del Sol Inn

Disney Way

Disney's
Paradise
Pier Hotel

Candy Cane Inn•

• Castle Inn and Suites

Katella Ave.

Alpine   Desert
Motel   Palm
         •

• Ramada Inn Maingate

•
The
Anabella
Hotel

Jolly Roger Inn•
Portofino Inn
& Suites   •

• Hilton
Anaheim

Harbor Blvd.

Ramada Limited Suites•

• Best Western Raffles Inn

Orangewood Ave.

Disneyland Drive

Wilken Way

Anaheim •
Carriage Inn

Chapman Ave.

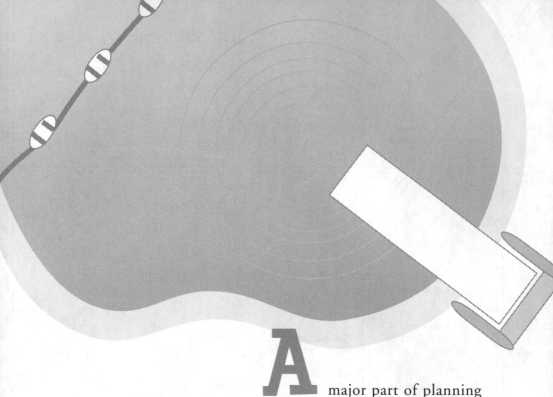

A major part of planning your vacation is deciding where to stay. There are hundreds of places near the Disneyland Resort, ranging from inexpensive motels to luxurious resorts. This chapter helps you decide what type of place will fit your budget and provide the amenities and services your family needs.

What Should You Look for in a Hotel?

Although a number of factors determine where you stay during your vacation, the biggest is likely to be your budget. How much can you spend on your lodging? On average, after adding hotel tax, plan on spending about $150 per night. During the off-season, or with discounts, you may be able to pay less.

The second factor is location. Some hotels are either in the Disneyland Resort or right across the street from it. Others may be several miles away. It's usually a good idea to be as close as possible, to save time and money traveling back and forth from the hotel to the parks.

Other things to consider might include the amenities the hotel offers and whether there's an on-site or nearby restaurant.

Be Sure to Ask . . .

The best way to find out just what a hotel offers is to call and ask a lot of questions. Travel guides, advertisements, and Web sites can be vague and often do not include vital information you need to know. Once you have narrowed down your list of hotels to a few, begin calling. We find it's good to have a list of questions you want to ask in front of you, so you don't forget any. Also, be sure to write down the answers from each hotel so you can refer to them later. Not all these questions will apply to your family's vacation. Just ask the ones that do, and customize them to fit your circumstances.

Helpful Hint
Be sure to talk to friends and relatives who have recently taken a vacation to the Disneyland Resort. Ask where they stayed and how they liked it. We have found some great hotels—and avoided some bad ones—from the experiences of others.

What are the hotel's rates for when you'll be there? Are there any discounts or specials? Do children stay free?

Hotels do not always offer you their cheapest rates to begin with. Because many customers just take what the hotels offer first, they might as well start high. Ask about seasonal discounts, *Entertainment Book* discounts, or rates for travel clubs, such as AAA, if you belong to such an organization. These often save you at least 10%. If traveling with grandparents, be sure to check senior-citizen rates. At the Disneyland Hotels, senior citizens can save up to 35%, which can make these hotels comparable in price to off-site hotels.

How close is the hotel to the Disneyland Resort?

Most hotels say they are close, but ask just how close. Can you walk, or will you need to take a shuttle?

Does the hotel offer shuttle service to the resort? If so, how often does it run?

Although most hotels advertise shuttle service, the shuttles run at different intervals, and some run only twice a day. Also be sure to ask if there's a fee for the shuttle or if it's included with the room.

Does the hotel include a breakfast buffet or continental breakfast? If so, what type of food is served?

Most hotels offer a continental breakfast. However, that usually means just sweet rolls, juice or coffee, and maybe some fruit. Others have buffets where you can get eggs, potatoes, toast, and more. Also, be sure to ask the hours when breakfast is served. Make sure it starts before you plan to leave for the park, especially in summer when the park opens earlier.

Is there a charge for parking?

Some hotels in the area add from $5 to $10 a day if you want to leave your car in their parking lot.

Money-Saving Tip

When comparing hotel rates, be sure to factor in any additional fees. The Disneyland Hotels charge a resort fee of $12 per night (however, this includes parking, Internet access, and other amenities). Off-site hotels can have separate fees for parking, Internet access, and even for mini-fridges and microwaves. When in doubt, check the hotel's Web site or call the property directly to ask about any potential extra charges.

❧ *Does the hotel have rooms with kitchenettes or at least a microwave and a refrigerator?*

You'll usually need at least a refrigerator when traveling with children. A fridge lets you keep drinks cool and store snacks from home or leftovers from meals. What the kids couldn't eat for dinner makes a good lunch the next day. And a microwave is nice to have, too.

❧ *Is there an on-site restaurant or one nearby? Do kids eat free? Does the hotel offer room service?*

Some hotels with an on-site restaurant offer free meals for kids when you buy an adult meal. Even if you eat only one meal a day at the restaurant, these savings can add up.

❧ *Is there airport pickup from the hotel? Does the hotel have shuttles to other attractions?*

If you'll be flying into Southern California, having a hotel van pick you up is nice and can save you money. Also, if you plan on going to other attractions, you'll need either a shuttle or rental car.

❧ *What programs does the hotel offer for children? For what ages? When do the programs run? What are the activities? Are there any costs? Is there a swimming pool? Spa? Fitness center?*

Not many hotels in the area have children's programs. However, it doesn't hurt to ask. A swimming pool is about all most places offer for recreation.

❧ *Can arrangements be made for in-room babysitting? What are the qualifications of the sitters? What is the cost? How far in advance do you need to make reservations?*

If you would like an evening out for just the adults, be sure to see if child care is available and what reservations you need to make.

℮ *Does the hotel have rollaway beds or cribs? Is there a charge for them?*

Sometimes a rollaway can keep you from having to get a bigger room or suite and can save you money. If traveling with a baby, you may need a crib.

℮ *Is there a laundry room at the hotel?*

Several hotels have coin-operated washing machines and dryers. These can come in handy if you get caught in the rain or just need to clean a few clothes.

℮ *Is there a car-rental agency on-site?*

If you need to rent a car, this can be handy. Some agencies will pick you up at the airport and drive you back to their office at the hotel.

℮ *Does the hotel sell tickets to Disneyland and other attractions?*

You do not want to have to buy your tickets at the main gate. Therefore, if you don't get them before you leave on your vacation, purchase them at your hotel.

℮ *Does the hotel offer package deals?*

Several hotels offer packages that include the room along with tickets for Disneyland and possibly other attractions. Some also include meals. Packages are often less expensive than hotel and theme-park tickets purchased separately.

Insider's Secret

Not only can vacation packages save you money, they also make planning your vacation easier because they usually include everything you'll need.

Vacation Packages

Unless you have an Annual Passport for Disneyland, it's usually a good idea to consider package deals. Basic packages include lodging and tickets; others may include meals and other bonuses.

Disney Packages

Some of the best packages are put together by the Walt Disney Travel Company. These include stays at any of the three Disneyland Resort hotels as well as at nearly 40 other hotels in the area. Although these packages change from year to year, here's a sampling of what might be offered.

- Hotel accommodations
- Park tickets
- One early entry into the Disneyland park
- A morning interactive guest and character experience in Mickey's Toontown
- Preferred seating at select attractions in Disney's California Adventure park
- A Downtown Disney District Fun Card (for discounts and specials in Downtown Disney)
- A lanyard for pin trading

Money-Saving Tip

AAA offers a number of Disneyland Resort packages that are similar to those offered by the Walt Disney Travel Company. They usually include extras such as travel kits, free parking at the resort, coupon books, and discounts on the lodging part of the package during certain times of the year.

You can also add a dining package that includes meals and snacks. Tickets to other attractions can be included as well. Furthermore, you can include air travel and transportation from the airport to your hotel all within your package.

To get a price quote for these packages, either call the Walt Disney Travel Company at 866/279–7165 or 714/520–5050 or visit the Disneyland Web site at www.disneyland.com. This lets you enter all your selections, gives you a price quote, and allows you to book your vacation. You can also arrange for plane reservations and other transportation.

Off-Site Packages

If you plan on staying at an off-site hotel and the Disney packages don't fit your needs, look into packages offered by the individual hotels themselves. Several in the area offer deals that include lodging, tickets to the Disneyland Resort parks, and possibly some meals and/or a rental car. When you call about rates, just ask if the hotel offers any package deals.

Insider's Secret

Be wary of tours to other places in Southern California. These include bus tours of the Los Angeles area, harbor cruises, and shopping spree trips to Mexico. These can last all day, and there's usually no way to get back to the hotel during the middle of the trip. That usually makes them a bad idea for families with young children. Before you agree to these types of tours, ask how long they last and exactly what will happen during the tour, including contingency plans for returning to the hotel early. Although such trips are usually part of a package, you're still paying for them. If you don't really want to go on these optional tours, then don't get them. Cutting them from the package often lowers the price of the package and saves you money.

Travel Agents

Many travel agencies offer packages to the Disneyland Resort. They're usually similar to those offered by the Walt Disney Travel Company or AAA, but you usually pay more for the package and do not get all the extras. However, a travel agent may be able to get you better prices on airline fares or be better at arranging other transportation to the resort and back home for your family. Just be sure you're getting a good hotel that meets your needs. If the hotel offered is not listed in this book, be sure to check its Web site and find out just how far away from Disneyland it really is. We know of families that were promised a nice hotel with great amenities and a shuttle to the resort. However, the hotel was 10 miles away, and the shuttle ran only once in the morning and once in the evening. They ended up having to drive back and forth between the hotel and the resort, paying for both parking and gas.

Money-Saving Tip

By making reservations early, such as several months in advance, you have a better chance of getting cheaper rates. Many hotels have a limited number of rooms they offer at lower prices as promotions. However, these fill up quickly—especially the suites. If you know when you'll be on vacation, there's no reason not to make reservations early. You can cancel them later if you have to change plans. Just be sure to check the cancellation policy before booking a hotel. Some online specials offer incredible rates that can be up to half off the regular rates—but these offers usually do not allow for any cancellations and require that you pay the entire amount up front. Since kids get sick and unexpected events do come up, it can be risky to book these rates too far in advance (or at all).

Discounts and Specials

Always try to take advantage of some type of discount when choosing a hotel. Almost all hotels offer reduced rates during the off-season. Ask about discounts for members of particular groups you may belong to, such as AAA or those with ties to the military. The *Entertainment Book* offers discounts of 50%, but these are usually off the high-rack rates and only about 10% off the regular rate. Don't expect huge savings. You may also be able to get coupon books offering hotel discounts from your employer or credit union. When calling to check rates, be sure to mention you belong to a travel club or have a discount. Even if you don't have a discount of your own, ask if the hotel is running any specials or has lower rates. It never hurts to ask.

On-Site Versus Off-Site

When deciding whether to stay at one of the Disneyland hotels or an off-site hotel, there are a few factors you should consider.

Benefits of Staying On-Site

1. Staying at the Disneyland hotels saves time. If you'll be vacationing during the summer, holiday, or other busy season, or if you have only a day or two, you can definitely see more of the resort by staying at one of the hotels.

2. It's easy to return to the hotel during the day. If you have small children who need to nap or rest, a quick trip on the monorail will take you right back to the hotel in a matter of minutes. Hotel guests have Express Priority Boarding for the monorail. Just show your room key and avoid the lines, which can get quite long—especially at night. You can then return to the park the same way. This is also important if your family will be split up. Dad may want to take some of the younger kids back for a swim while Mom stays with the older kids at the park.

3. If you won't be driving to the resort and plan on spending all of your time there, there's no need to rent a car. Everything is within walking distance, and you can also use the monorail.

4. You're guaranteed admission to the Disney theme parks. When the parks are extremely full, usually on days near holidays such as Thanksgiving, Christmas, or New Year's, they stop letting people in, even those with valid tickets. However, guests of the Disney hotels are always admitted.

Benefits of Staying Off-Site

1. Off-site hotels are almost always less expensive. If you're trying to save money or would rather spend it on parts of your vacation other than lodging, stay off-site.

2. Many off-site hotels offer complimentary breakfasts or have deals where kids eat free at their restaurant. Eating at the Disneyland Resort can be expensive. Off-site hotels are often closer to fast-food and other inexpensive restaurants.

3. The Disney hotels can be booked months in advance during the busy season. If your vacation was arranged at the last minute, you may not be able to get reservations at a Disney hotel, especially for three or more nights.

4. If Disneyland is only a part of your vacation and you'll be visiting several other attractions in Southern California, why pay a lot to stay by the Disneyland Resort when

Insider's Secret
The Disneyland hotels are often cleaner and better staffed than most of the off-site hotels. Since cast members are the staff, you can expect better service. They know the answers to almost all your questions, and if they don't they'll find out for you.

you'll also be spending time elsewhere? You may want to consider staying a couple of nights at one of the Disney hotels and then transferring to a less expensive hotel when you visit other attractions.

Getting More Information on Hotels in the Anaheim Area

The Anaheim–Orange County Visitors and Convention Bureau is a great place to get information about the Anaheim area. Check its Web site at www.anaheimoc.com. The site includes hotel and restaurant directories, and offers a hotel search: specify what you're looking for, and the site returns names of hotels in the area that match your needs. (You can also book a room directly through the Web site.) You can print coupons right off your computer for a number of hotels, restaurants, and attractions, as well as request an official visitor's guide. You can also call the bureau at 888/598–3200 and request the guide over the phone; it takes about four to six weeks to get it via mail, so be sure to request it a couple of months or more before your vacation.

What the Star Ratings Mean

The following hotels are ranked using the star rating system:

★★★★ These top-quality hotels have superior amenities and guest services. In addition, they're near the resort.

★★★ These hotels offer not only good prices for what you get but also good amenities or a location close to the resort.

★★ These hotels usually offer good value but may not be as close to the park as other hotels.

★ These hotels are basic and inexpensive but often are some distance from the park.

Knight Choice

Our family picked our favorite hotel in each category: Disneyland Resort Hotels, Off-Site Hotels, and San Diego Area Hotels. These hotels were selected on the best overall experience for everyone in the fam.

The Disneyland Resort Hotels

All of the Disneyland Resort hotels offer special amenities and guest services that make you feel as if you never left the theme parks. The employees at these hotels are some of the friendliest and most outgoing of those at any hotels in the area.

Guests here have special privileges unavailable to other tourists. Not only do they have access to the pool and fitness facilities, but they also have easy access to both parks by a short walk or, in Disneyland's case, by monorail. Disneyland Resort hotel guests also have a private entrance into Disney's California Adventure via Disney's Grand Californian Hotel. Another perk is that you can charge meals and merchandise bought anywhere in the resort to your hotel room. This saves you from having to carry around a lot of cash and provides an itemized statement of your spending. In addition, you can have purchases sent to the hotel so you do not have to carry them

Insider's Secret

If your family will need a wheelchair during your stay, guests of the Disneyland hotels can rent wheelchairs at the hotels and keep them for the length of their stay. This is much easier than renting a wheelchair after you enter the park because you can use it to get to the park in the first place. The price is the same as in the parks—$10 per day.

Quick Guide to

Hotel Name	Description	Price
Alpine Motel 715 W. Katella Avenue 800-772-4422 or 714-535-2186 www.alpineinnanaheim.com	Inexpensive; two-room units available	$–$$
The Anabella Hotel 1030 W. Katella Avenue 800-863-4888 or 714-905-1050 www.anabellahotel.com	Family suites available	$$
Anaheim Camelot Inn and Suites 1520 S. Harbor Boulevard 800-828-4898 or 714-635-7275 www.camelotinn-anaheim.com	Family suites available	$$–$$$
Anaheim Carriage Inn 2125 S. Harbor Boulevard 800-345-2131 or 714-740-1440 www.anaheimcarriageinn.com	Family suites and two-room suites available	$–$$
Anaheim Desert Inn and Suites 1600 S. Harbor Boulevard 800-433-5270 or 714-772-5050 www.anaheimdesertinn.com	Family suites and two-room suites available	$–$$$
Anaheim Fairfield Inn by Marriott 1460 S. Harbor Boulevard 800-228-2800 or 714-772-6777 www.marriott.com	Normal hotel rooms	$$–$$$
Best Western Park Place Inn 1544 S. Harbor Boulevard 800-854-8177 or 714-776-4800 www.stovallshotels.com	Standard rooms and mini suites	$–$$

$$$$ $250 and up
$$$ $150–$250
$$ $100–$150
$ $50–$100

Disneyland Resort Area Hotels

Distance from Resort	Rating	Amenities	Details On
Walking distance to Disneyland; tram available	★★	Heated pool; refrigerators available; free continental breakfast	Page 48
One block from Disneyland	★★★	2 heated pools and spa, refrigerators and coffeemakers, microwaves in some rooms, fitness center	Page 48
Across the street from the main gate	★★	Heated pool; refrigerators in all rooms, microwaves in suites	Page 49
Two blocks from resort; shuttle available	★★	Heated pool and spa; microwaves and refrigerators available; free continental breakfast	Page 49
Across the street from main gate	★★★	Heated pool and spa; microwaves, refrigerators, and coffeemakers; free continental breakfast	Page 50
Half a block from the main gate	★★	Heated pool; refrigerators in all rooms; on-site Pizza Hut and coffee shop	Page 50
Across the street from the main gate	★★	Heated pool; sauna, spa, refrigerators, and microwaves; free continental breakfast	Page 50

★★★★ Top quality with superior amenities
★★★ Good prices with good amenities
★★ Good value with few amenities
★ Basic and inexpensive

(continues)

Quick Guide to

Hotel Name	Description	Price
Best Western Raffles Inn and Suites 2040 S. Harbor Boulevard 800-308-5278 or 714-750-6100 www.bestwesternrafflesinn.com	Disneyland theme rooms and suites available	$–$$
Candy Cane Inn 1747 S. Harbor Boulevard 800-345-7057 or 714-774-5284 www.candycaneinn.net	Garden view rooms available	$$–$$$
Carousel Inn and Suites 1530 S. Harbor Boulevard 800-854-6767 or 714-758-0444 www.carouselinnandsuites.com	Family suites available	$$–$$$
Castle Inn and Suites 1734 S. Harbor Boulevard 800-227-8530 or 714-774-8111 www.castleinn.com	Family suites available; with a medieval theme, the hotel looks like a castle	$–$$
Del Sol Inn 1604 S. Harbor Boulevard 888-686-1122 or 714-234-3411 www.delsolinn.com	Inexpensive; two-room suites available	$$–$$$
Desert Palm Hotel and Suites 631 W. Katella Avenue 888-788-0466 or 714-535-1133 www.desertpalmshotel.com	Several different types of suites available	$$–$$$
The Disneyland Hotel 1150 Magic Way 714-956-6425 or 714-778-6600 www.disneyland.com	Rooms for up to five people; suites available, but expensive; many on-site restaurants	$$$$

$$$$ $250 and up
$$$ $150–$250
$$ $100–$150
$ $50–$100

Disneyland Resort Area Hotels

Distance from Resort	Rating	Amenities	Details On
Two blocks from resort; shuttle available	★★	Heated pool; microwaves and refrigerators in some rooms; free continental breakfast	Page 51
One block from main gate; shuttle available	★★	Heated pool, spa, and children's wading pool; microwaves and refrigerators in some rooms; free continental breakfast	Page 51
Across the street from main gate	★★	Rooftop heated pool; microwaves, refrigerators, and coffeemakers in all rooms; free continental breakfast	Page 52
One block from main gate; shuttle available	★★	Heated pool; microwaves and coffeemakers in all rooms; microwaves in suites	Page 52
Across the street from main gate	★★	Microwaves, refrigerators, and coffeemakers; free continental breakfast	Page 53
One block from Disneyland; located near the Anaheim Convention Center	★★★	Heated pool and spa; microwaves, refrigerators, and coffeemakers; free continental breakfast	Page 53
On site	★★★★	Large pool area; fitness center; refrigerators in all rooms	Page 40

★★★★ Top quality with superior amenities
★★★ Good prices with good amenities
★★ Good value with few amenities
★ Basic and inexpensive

(continues)

Quick Guide to

Hotel Name	Description	Price
Disney's Grand Californian Hotel 1600 S. Disneyland Drive 714-956-6425 or 714-635-2300 www.disneyland.com	Normal hotel rooms, some with bunk beds for kids; on-site restaurants	$$$$
Disney's Paradise Pier Hotel 1717 Disneyland Drive 714-956-6425 or 714-999-0990 www.disneyland.com	Normal hotel rooms; suites available, but expensive; on-site restaurants	$$$–$$$$
Hilton Anaheim 777 Convention Way 800-445-8667 or 714-750-4321 www.hilton.com	Nice hotel with several restaurants and seasonal children's program	$$$–$$$$
Howard Johnson Hotel in the Anaheim Resort 1380 S. Harbor Blvd. 800-422-4228 or 714-776-6120 www.hojoanaheim.com	Several different types of one-bedroom rooms	$–$$
Jolly Roger Inn 640 W. Katella Avenue 888-296-5986 or 714-782-7500 www.jollyrogerhotel.com	Two-room units and regular hotel rooms; restaurant on-site	$–$$
Knott's Berry Farm Hotel and Resort 7675 Crescent Avenue Buena Park 866-752-2444 or 714-995-1111 www.knottshotel.com	Family suites available; some rooms with Peanuts theme; restaurant on-site	$–$$

$$$$ $250 and up
$$$ $150–$250
$$ $100–$150
$ $50–$100

Disneyland Resort Area Hotels

Distance from Resort	Rating	Amenities	Details On
On site	★★★★	Heated pool and spa; fitness center; stocked refrigerators; empty refrigerators available; children's care center for evenings; private entrance to California Adventure	Page 43
On site	★★★★	Heated pool and spa; fitness center; refrigerators in all rooms; private entrance to California Adventure	Page 46
One block away; shuttle available	★★★	Great pool area; fitness center use for additional fee	Page 54
One block north of main gate	★★	Heated pools; kids pool area; refrigerators in all rooms	Page 54
One block from Disneyland; shuttle available	★★	Heated pool and children's wading pool; coffeemakers	Page 54
Several miles away; shuttle available; on site at Knott's Berry Farm	★★	Heated pool, spa, and children's pool; fitness center; tennis courts; packages include meals and tickets to Knott's Berry Farm	Page 55

★★★★ Top quality with superior amenities
★★★ Good prices with good amenities
★★ Good value with few amenities
★ Basic and inexpensive

(continues)

Quick Guide to

Hotel Name	Description	Price
Park Vue Inn 1570 S. Harbor Boulevard 800-334-7021 or 714-772-3691 www.parkvueinn.com	Family suites available; 24-hour restaurant on-site	$–$$
Portofino Inn & Suites 1831 S. Harbor Boulevard 800-398-3963 or 714-782-7600 www.portofinoinnanaheim.com	Family and kids' suites available; kids eat free at adjacent restaurant	$–$$
Ramada Inn Maingate 1650 S. Harbor Boulevard 800-854-6097 or 800-422-4402 www.ramadamaingate.com	Suites with two or three beds available, some with kitchenettes; on-site restaurant	$–$$
Ramada Limited Suites 2141 S. Harbor Boulevard 800-272-6232 or 714-971-3553 www.ramada.com	All units are two-room suites with TV and phones in each room	$–$$
Tropicana Inn 1540 S. Harbor Boulevard 800-828-4898 or 714-635-4082 www.tropicanainn-anaheim.com	Two-room suites available	$$

$$$$ $250 and up
$$$ $150–$250
$$ $100–$150
$ $50–$100

Disneyland
Resort Area Hotels

Distance from Resort	Rating	Amenities	Details On
Across the street from main gate	★★	Heated pool; refrigerators in all rooms; free continental breakfast	Page 55
Walking distance to main entrance; shuttle service available for a fee	★★★	Heated pool and spa; video arcade; refrigerators and microwaves in all rooms; free parking	Page 55
Across the street from main gate	★★★	Heated pool and spa; refrigerators available for fee; free continental breakfast	Page 56
Two blocks away; shuttle available	★★	Pool and spa; microwaves and refrigerators in all units; free continental breakfast	Page 56
Across the street from main gate	★★	Heated pool and spa; refrigerators and microwaves in all rooms; free continental breakfast	Page 57

★★★★ Top quality with superior amenities
★★★ Good prices with good amenities
★★ Good value with few amenities
★ Basic and inexpensive

around with you. (The purchases will be at the hotel by 1 PM on the day after your purchase, so don't do this if you'll be leaving that same day.) You can also have your packages sent to the park entrance to be picked up as you leave the park. All the hotels have quality on-site restaurants and are close to others in Downtown Disney. You can also have tickets waiting for you at the hotel when you check in. Although the Disney hotels are some of the most expensive in the area, they're worth the cost if you want the extra perks.

Note: Rates listed in the hotel descriptions are for the off-season (dates depend on hotel) and may include a discount for travel club membership or for only a limited number of rooms. Be sure to ask for the hotel's best available rate. The Disneyland hotels also charge a resort fee of $12 per night. This fee covers local phone calls, Internet connection, access to the fitness facility, a newspaper on weekdays, and parking. It's automatically included on your bill whether or not you use the services.

The Disneyland Hotel	★★★★
1150 Magic Way	**Knight Choice**
www.disneyland.com	**714/956–6425 or**
	714/778–6600

The Disneyland Hotel is one of the best places to stay during a vacation to the resort. In addition to having the amenities you would expect from a hotel of its caliber, several other perks make a family stay here extra special. The rooms are decorated with Disney-inspired art, and the soap and shampoo come in containers emblazoned with the famous mouse. The hotel also offers activities for children, such as treasure hunts and craft stations, especially during holidays or the busy season. The cast members and the hotel's ambience make you feel like you're still inside Disneyland.

Staying at the Disneyland Hotel is convenient. You can take the monorail right into Disneyland and then back to the hotel. (This hotel is the closest to the monorail station.) You can also walk through Downtown Disney straight to the main gate. These options make it easy to come back to the hotel in the afternoon for a nap or just a break.

In the center of the hotel area is the Never Land Pool, a 5,000-square-foot swimming pool done in a Peter Pan theme, with Captain Hook's pirate ship and the crocodile as a centerpiece. Adults and older children can walk up a path and across a suspension bridge to Skull Rock, where they can then ride down a 100-foot waterslide. For younger children, there's a smaller slide away from the larger one. There's also a spa and plenty of lounge chairs for the pampered set. The hotel provides towels poolside, as well as flotation vests for young children. The pool area is a great place to come during the afternoon to cool off and rest while the parks are at their busiest. The Cove Pools, smaller, shallow pools for young children, have a beach theme, with a sandy area where you can relax and a jungle gym for kids to play on. There's a net for

Insider's Secret

Although check-in time is 3 PM, you can actually register earlier and be assigned a room. If your room is ready, you can go on up to it. Otherwise, you can have the bell captain hold your luggage; then you can head over to one of the parks or Downtown Disney. When you return to the hotel, pick up your key and a bellhop will bring your luggage up to you. Registering early gives you a better chance of getting a good room. You can ask for a room with a view, and if one is not reserved, you just might get it, even if you did not pay extra to reserve one in advance. Don't plan on this happening during the busy season, though.

Insider's Secret

All of the Disneyland Resort hotels have portable cribs at no additional charge. They're already in the rooms for you to use. If you have small children, that can save you packing and bringing one from home.

beach volleyball, and you can also get a workout in the fitness center.

And as if that were not enough, the hotel includes an arcade and a pond where you can sail remote-control boats. There are also koi ponds and waterfalls, which further add to the fun. For families with both older and younger children, the older ones can find lots of things to do here while the younger siblings take a nap.

There are several shops where you can purchase souvenirs as well as toiletries, and the hotel features a number of on-site restaurants. Steakhouse 55 is an elegant restaurant serving seafood, steak, and prime rib. Hook's Pointe specializes in mesquite-grilled seafood and meats along with other favorites. Goofy's Kitchen serves a breakfast, lunch, and dinner buffet, and Goofy and other characters visit with the diners. For a quick morning bite, try the Coffee House, where you can also get java, hot chocolate, or tasty baked goods all day long. Croc's Bits 'n' Bites serves hamburgers and chicken sandwiches as well as ice cream, and the Captain's Galley is a poolside shop for sandwiches, salads, snacks, and sushi. Room service, from Steakhouse 55, is also available.

The Disneyland Hotel offers a variety of guest services, including a list of babysitters licensed and bonded by the city of Anaheim. Bellhops are full of information about not only the hotel but also the parks. Rooms are always clean, and each includes a refrigerator. A complimentary newspaper is left by your door each weekday morning.

Insider's Secret

The Disneyland Hotel offers 19 themed rooms for kids called Character Quarters. There are 12 Mickey Mouse rooms and seven Disney Princess rooms. Each features two twin beds with highly themed furniture, linens, carpets—even the TV. These kids' rooms are only available when booking an adjoining room (parents stay in a regular room while two children can stay in the Characters Quarters). These rooms tend to go fast, so be sure to book them early. Also, be aware that the rooms can be quite expensive. (The Character Quarters alone run between $635 and $750, depending on the time of year.)

The bonuses of staying at the Disneyland Hotel do come with a price. A basic room starts at about $270 a night. Make reservations early, especially if you plan on staying more than two nights. The hotel consists of three towers. The Magic Tower offers views of either the pool area or the parking area. The Dreams Tower looks out over the pool area or Downtown Disney. The Wonder Tower has views of the koi ponds and waterfalls or a parking area. We prefer the Wonder Tower with a room overlooking the waterfalls because it's a bit quieter and the sound of the waterfalls tends to drown out the noise from the pool area. Rooms with a view cost extra.

Disney's Grand Californian Hotel	★★★★
1600 S. Disneyland Drive	714/956–6425 or
www.disneyland.com	714/635–2300

Disney's Grand Californian, which opened in 2001, is the most luxurious of the Disney hotels and one of the nicest in the area.

You'll also pay for what you get, with rooms starting at about $370 per night. During the busy season, expect to pay more than $500 per night. The hotel is designed in the Arts and Crafts style, and is filled with redwood and cedar. It looks more like a Yosemite mountain chalet than something you would be likely to find in downtown Anaheim. Each room features Arts and Crafts–style furniture and marble sinks in the bathroom area.

Insider's Secret

The architecture at Disney's Grand Californian is incredible. If you're interested in this as well as the artwork around the hotel, take the Art of the Craft tour. There's no charge for this tour and you can ask the front desk for the times.

The refrigerators in the rooms come filled with snacks and drinks, but just picking up one of the items causes it to be charged to your room. Since kids could have you buying the entire contents of the fridges, have the front desk lock it electronically. You can then request that housekeeping bring up an additional refrigerator to keep your own food and drinks cool. Each room also has an iron and ironing board, a hair dryer, a coffeemaker, a lighted wardrobe, and robes for the adults (children's robes can be requested). A complimentary local newspaper is left by your door each morning. Some rooms have a bunk bed for the kids with a trundle bed under it, so that you can sleep three children in the room.

The hotel's main lobby is fantastic, with cut marble floors, lots of wood, a hearth made of large river rocks, and a grand fireplace. Children can sit in kid-size rocking chairs and listen to cast members share stories from California's history by the fire at various times during the day. The hotel has two pools (one with a waterslide) as well as a kiddie splash pool. The Eureka Springs Health Club (access is included with a stay at the hotel) has a variety of workout equipment and weights, as well as dry and steam saunas. Massages are available for an additional fee.

The hotel features several restaurants and eateries. The award-winning Napa Rose is open for lunch and dinner and serves a variety of dishes, including some standout seafood dishes. Storytellers Cafe serves a character-breakfast buffet in the morning. There's also a breakfast menu and a custom-made omelet bar. A host of entrées are served for lunch and dinner. For a quick bite, stop by White Water Snacks, which carries sandwiches, salads, desserts, and snacks. The Hearthstone Lounge serves coffees and pastries for breakfast, then mixed drinks, cocktails, and wine later in the day. Room service features Storytellers Cafe's menu.

One nice aspect about this hotel is that it has its own private entrance into California Adventure. Guests of the hotel enter the theme park near the Grizzly River Run attraction. This lets you bypass the crowds at the main gate and also provides easy access if you need to come back during the day for a rest or a swim. The hotel is also close to Disneyland and attached to Downtown Disney. If the adults would like an evening out, Pinocchio's Workshop provides supervised activities for children ages 5–12. The cost starts at $13 per child per hour, and the fee includes a snack. Dinners are also available for an additional $5. Hours are from 5 PM to midnight. Space is limited, so if you plan on using this service, make reservations up to two months in advance by calling 714/635–2300. Although there's self-parking available at the lots across from Disneyland Drive, it's usually best just to use the valet parking. The fee is about $10 per night.

Disney's Grand Californian is a great hotel for adults. However, families, especially those with young children, may be disappointed by the lack of Disney characters in the design. On the other hand, it's the closest hotel to both theme parks, making it handy for taking children back for naps during the day. If you want to feel pampered and surrounded by luxury, we recommend staying here. If you want more of a Disney-type experience, stay at one of the other Disney hotels.

Disney's Paradise Pier Hotel	★★★★
1717 Disneyland Drive	**714/956–6425 or**
www.disneyland.com	**714/999–0990**

Although not as glamorous as the Disneyland Hotel or the Grand Californian, the Paradise Pier is still a fine hotel and a bit quieter. It offers most of the same amenities and guest services as the Disneyland Hotel, and you can use the monorail for transportation into Disneyland. You also have your own private entrance into California Adventure via the Grand Californian Hotel. All rooms have refrigerators, and a newspaper will be left by your door each weekday morning.

The hotel has a rooftop pool and spa including a waterslide as well as a workout center. In addition to a few shops, the hotel has two on-site restaurants. The PCH Grill offers a variety of selections with a California and Pacific Rim theme. The upscale restaurant Yamabuki serves teriyaki, tempura, fresh sushi, and other Japanese dishes. Takeout is available if you want to eat in your room. Room service is provided from the PCH Grill. In the morning, the PCH Grill hosts the Lilo and Stitch Aloha Breakfast. The all-you-care-to-eat breakfast buffet includes an omelet bar and other morning favorites as well as a traditional Japanese breakfast. While you're eating, Lilo and Stitch sing songs and visit each table to chat and take pictures with the guests.

Rooms at the Paradise Pier are a bit less expensive than those at the other Disney hotels, but they still give you the Disney experience with a bit of savings. Rooms start at about $245.

Because the rates are a bit cheaper, you may want to spend a bit extra and go for a room on the concierge level. It includes breakfast as well as snacks and drinks in the private lounge all day long. Each room on this level also has a VCR and nightly turndown service that includes chocolates on your pillow.

The rooms at the Paradise Pier Hotel overlook either California Adventure or the pool area and parking lot. The park view is a bit more expensive but worth it. Register early, before the normal check-in time, and ask for a corner room. Because of the way they're situated, corner rooms have a bit more space than the others, which is good if you need a crib.

Off-Site Hotels

Anaheim and the surrounding area have hundreds of hotels. Some are right near the resort; others are several miles away. We have listed just a few here and have included a variety of types and styles. If you have a large family (more than five people), consider a hotel with suites.

Although some off-site hotels are right across the street from the main entrance to the Disneyland Resort, others may be a block or more away. Some hotels offer their own complimentary shuttle service. However, many use the Anaheim Re-

Money-Saving Tip
Some of the following hotels are Disneyland Good Neighbor hotels. Special packages with these hotels can be booked through the Walt Disney Travel Company, AAA, or a travel agent. These packages can reduce the rates for rooms, and they usually have several amenities. You can also view these packages online at the Disneyland Resort Web site (www. disneyland.com).

sort Transportation System (ART), shuttle buses that travel around making stops at various hotels in the area. An individual pass is $4 per adult and $1 per child (3–9) for one day, $10 per adult and $2 per child for three days, and $16 per adult and $4 per child for five days. You can ride the shuttle an unlimited number of times while the ticket is valid. Children under 3 ride free. You can use this system to get not only to Disneyland but also to other locations around the resort area. Check the ART Web site at www.rideart.org for routes and schedules or ask at your hotel. Most routes run every 10 minutes during busy hours and every 20 minutes the rest of the time. You can purchase your passes online, at kiosks near several hotels, or directly from several of the area hotels.

Alpine Motel	★★
715 W. Katella Avenue	**800/772–4422 or**
www.alpineinnanaheim.com	**714/535–2186**

This inexpensive motel is across the street from the Anaheim Convention Center and on the same block as Disneyland. Rates can go as low as $54 during the off-season, and two-bedroom units are available. Stays include a free continental breakfast, and there's an adjacent restaurant as well. Refrigerators are available in some units for an additional fee, and there's a heated pool.

The Anabella Hotel	★★★
1030 W. Katella Avenue	**800/863–4888 or**
www.anabellahotel.com	**714/905–1050**

This hotel is about a block away from the entrance to Disneyland. Rates for standard rooms that sleep four begin at $115. Deluxe rooms and suites allow for families of five and six. In addition to two pools (one for adults only) and a Jacuzzi, the hotel

Money-Saving Tip

Most off-site hotels either have an on-site restaurant or are close to places to eat. These restaurants can be cheaper than eating in the parks or at Downtown Disney. For example, on Harbor Boulevard just across the street from Disneyland are Mimi's Café, IHOP, Denny's, McDonald's, and even a Tony Roma's. Some restaurants, such as Denny's, offer discounts when you show them a room key from a neighboring hotel.

has a fitness center, a nail and hair salon, and a spa. Concierge level and room service are also available. If you plan on walking to Disneyland from this hotel, head toward the Disneyland hotels and Downtown Disney rather than walking down Katella Avenue and then north up Harbor Boulevard. You can take the monorail into Disneyland from the Downtown Disney station. It's a Disneyland Good Neighbor hotel and ART stop.

Anaheim Camelot Inn and Suites	★★
1520 S. Harbor Boulevard	800/828–4898 or
www.camelotinn-anaheim.com	714/635–7275

Disneyland is right across the street from this Good Neighbor inn. All rooms have refrigerators and microwaves. You can relax at the heated pool and spa, and there's also a video game arcade and room service. Basic rooms start at $129. Tickets are available.

Anaheim Carriage Inn	★★
2125 S. Harbor Boulevard	800/345–2131 or
www.anaheimcarriageinn.com	714/740–1440

This average hotel is two blocks away from Disneyland, and it has a heated pool and spa. Continental breakfast is included, and each room has a microwave and a refrigerator. Prices start at

$59 for a standard room and $109 for a suite. Tickets are available for sale and the hotel is less than 100 feet from an ART stop.

Anaheim Desert Inn and Suites ★★★
1600 S. Harbor Boulevard   800/433–5270 or
www.anaheimdesertinn.com   714/772–5050

This hotel is across the street from Disneyland's main gate, so you can easily walk over to the park. A stay here includes complimentary continental breakfast, and each room has a microwave, a coffeemaker, and a refrigerator. You can use the heated indoor pool and spa year-round. In the off-season, suites start at $120 and single rooms at $70. In-season prices are $200 or more for suites and at least $110 for single rooms. Several families we talked to recommended this inn for its prices, nice suites, and great location. Tickets are available here.

Anaheim Fairfield Inn by Marriott ★★
1460 S. Harbor Boulevard   800/228–2800 or
www.marriott.com   714/772–6777

About a half block north of Disneyland's main gate, this hotel features standard rooms with Disney-inspired decorations. In addition to a heated pool, there's also an on-site Pizza Hut and a coffee counter. Rates start at about $109 and package deals that include pizza and in-room movies are available. It's a Disneyland Good Neighbor hotel.

Best Western Park Place Inn ★★
1544 S. Harbor Boulevard   800/854–8177 or
www.stovallshotels.com   714/776–4800

Right across the street from the Disneyland main gate, this Disneyland Good Neighbor hotel has an attractive location. Standard rooms start at $90; minisuites that sleep up to five begin at $115. All rooms contain microwaves and refrigerators. This hotel has a heated pool, sauna, and spa. You receive a complimentary continental breakfast. Check for seasonal specials, when kids eat free at the on-site restaurant.

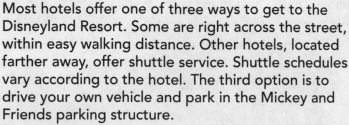

Helpful Hint
Most hotels offer one of three ways to get to the Disneyland Resort. Some are right across the street, within easy walking distance. Other hotels, located farther away, offer shuttle service. Shuttle schedules vary according to the hotel. The third option is to drive your own vehicle and park in the Mickey and Friends parking structure.

Best Western Raffles Inn and Suites	★★
2040 S. Harbor Boulevard	800/308–5278 or
www.bestwesternrafflesinn.com	714/750–6100

Two blocks from Disneyland, this inn offers shuttle service to the park. Microwaves and refrigerators are available in some rooms. Amenities here include an exercise room, a heated pool and spa, Internet access, and a complimentary continental breakfast. Rates start at $80 for regular rooms and $115 for suites. There are three different suite floor plans to choose from. Tickets are available. It's a Disneyland Good Neighbor hotel and ART stop.

Candy Cane Inn	★★
1747 S. Harbor Boulevard	800/345–7057 or
www.candycaneinn.net	714/774–5284

Beautiful gardens surround this boutique-style hotel, which makes this place quite a bit different from the other nearby options. Although the walk to the Disneyland Resort is a bit longer than from some of the other hotels, there's a complimentary shuttle service. A continental breakfast is included, and each deluxe room has a refrigerator. There's a heated pool and spa as well as a children's wading pool. Rates for a basic room start at $130. The hotel also has 10 premium rooms, which include a microwave, complimentary movie rentals, daily newspaper, and in-room breakfast service. These premium rooms are about $40 more than the standard rooms and go quickly. Be sure to ask for a room with a garden view. Tickets are available. It's a Disneyland Good Neighbor hotel.

Carousel Inn and Suites	★★
1530 S. Harbor Boulevard	800/854–6767 or
www.carouselinnandsuites.com	714/758–0444

This Disneyland Good Neighbor inn is across the street from the Disneyland Resort and within easy walking distance. All units have refrigerators, microwaves, and coffeemakers. There's a heated pool on the rooftop, which allows a view of the fireworks at Disneyland. Basic rooms start at $120, and suites start at $210. There is also a view suite on the top floor, with a large family room which looks out toward Disneyland and three separate bedrooms. If you're interested in booking this popular unit, be sure to make reservations early since.

Castle Inn and Suites	★★
1734 S. Harbor Boulevard	800/227–8530 or
www.castleinn.com	714/774–8111

With its turrets and towers, the Castle Inn is hard to miss. In addition to basic rooms, which start at $90, there are suites for families of up to six people, starting at $110. Each unit has a refrigerator and a coffeemaker, but only the suites have microwaves. The inn is a block away from the Disneyland Resort, and complimentary shuttle service is available. You can enjoy the heated pool and spa, and there's a children's wading pool. Tickets are available.

Del Sol Inn ★★
1604 S. Harbor Boulevard   888/686–1122 or
www.delsolinn.com   714/234–3411

This inn is across the street from the Disneyland Resort and a short walk to the main gate. Larger families can reserve two adjoining rooms as a suite. All rooms contain microwaves, refrigerators, and coffeemakers. A continental breakfast is included. Rates are around $100 off-season for single rooms and start at $180 for two-room suites. Disneyland tickets are available for sale at the front desk. Vacation packages are also available. Coin-operated laundry is on-site. The Del Sol also has a 24-hour on-site restaurant.

Desert Palms Hotel and Suites ★★★
631 W. Katella Avenue   888/788–0466 or
www.desertpalmshotel.com   714/535–1133

Remodeled in 2004, this inn offers good value and has a variety of suites for larger families. It's across the street from the Anaheim Convention Center, on the same block as Disneyland. Each room has a microwave, a coffeemaker, and a refrigerator. A few rooms with kitchenettes are also available, and there's a heated outdoor pool. Single rooms start as low as $100, and suites start at $135. A Quiznos sandwich shop and a bar and grill are on-site. Tickets are available, and this is a Disneyland Good Neighbor hotel and ART stop.

Hilton Anaheim   ★★★
777 Convention Way   800/445–8667 or
www.hilton.com   714/750–4321

Renovated in 2007, this hotel is one block from the Disneyland
Resort and has complimentary shuttle service. The hotel has a
heated pool, a summer children's program, and several restaurants, including a buffet and a sushi bar, as well as a Starbucks.
Guests can use the fitness center for an additional fee. This is a
nice hotel, and although it has a children's program, it seems
designed more for businesspeople and adults than for families.
Rooms start at $199. It's a Disneyland Good Neighbor hotel
and ART stop.

Howard Johnson Hotel in the Anaheim Resort   ★★
1380 S. Harbor Boulevard   800/422–4228 or
www.hojoanaheim.com   714/776–6120

The Howard Johnson Hotel is about a block away from
Disneyland and located just south of Interstate 5. In addition
to two pools, it also has a children's wading pool and a fountain
sprayground. Rates start at $89 for a basic room. It's a Disney-
land Good Neighbor hotel and ART stop.

Jolly Roger Inn   ★★
640 W. Katella Avenue   888/296–5986 or
www.jollyrogerhotel.com   714/782–7500

The Jolly Roger is near the Anaheim Convention Center; from
the center you can take a complimentary shuttle to the Disneyland Resort. The inn has a heated pool and children's wading
pool. Rates start at $79, with suites starting at $100. Mini-
fridges and microwaves are available upon request for an addi-

tional fee. You can also purchase packages that include tickets. It's a Disneyland Good Neighbor hotel and ART stop.

Knott's Berry Farm Hotel and Resort ★★
7675 Crescent Avenue, Buena Park   866/752–2444 or
www.knottshotel.com   714/995–1111

Several miles away from Disneyland, this hotel is right next to Knott's Berry Farm. Rooms start at $80, and the hotel offers package deals that include meals and admission to Knott's. There's a complimentary shuttle to the Disneyland Resort, and the hotel has a pool, a spa, a children's pool, a fitness center, and lighted tennis courts. There are a limited number of Peanuts-theme rooms, which include a nightly Snoopy turndown service. Refrigerators are available in some rooms.

Park Vue Inn ★★
1570 S. Harbor Boulevard   800/334–7021 or
www.parkvueinn.com   714/772–3691

This inn is across the street from the Disneyland main gate and within easy walking distance. There are refrigerators and microwaves in all units, a heated pool, and complimentary continental breakfast. A 24-hour restaurant is on-site, too. Basic rooms start at $86, and family suites start at $130. Tickets are available.

Portofino Inn & Suites ★★★
1831 S. Harbor Boulevard   Knight Choice
www.portofinoinnanaheim.com   800/398–3963 or
**   714/782–7600**

The Portofino Inn & Suites offers two floor plans. The Kids Suites have bunk beds, a sofa sleeper, and an activity table as well as the standard amenities, including refrigerator and microwave. The kids' area can be closed off from the parents with French doors. Our kids love having their own room with their own television. The King Suite, on the other hand, has a king-size bed in one room and a sofa sleeper in the other. We've found rooms here are cleaner than any of the other off-site hotels in which we have stayed. The hotel has a pool and spa, a sundeck, a video arcade, and a fitness center. This hotel is within walking distance of the parks. Shuttle service is offered for a small fee. Packages are available through the hotel. The Kids Suites, which sleep six, start at $140, and the King Suites begin at $119. It's a Disneyland Good Neighbor hotel and ART stop.

Ramada Inn Maingate	★★★
1650 S. Harbor Boulevard	800/854–6097 or
www.ramadamaingate.com	800/422–4402

This inn is directly across the street from the main gate of Disneyland, making it a short walk to the resort and back. In addition to basic rooms, which start at $90, the inn offers two- and three-bed suites, some with a kitchenette. The suites start at around $130. A continental breakfast is included. There's an on-site restaurant as well as a heated pool and spa. It's a Disneyland Good Neighbor hotel.

Ramada Limited Suites	★★★
2141 S. Harbor Boulevard	800/272–6232 or
www.ramada.com	714/971–3553

What's unique about this hotel is that all of the rooms are two-room suites. Each suite has a microwave, a refrigerator, two telephones, and two televisions. A complimentary continental breakfast is included, and a covered swimming pool and spa are available for guest use. What's more, the Disneyland Resort is two blocks away, and the hotel offers a complimentary shuttle. The suites begin at $69, and the hotel offers Disneyland package deals as well as tickets.

Tropicana Inn   ★★
1540 S. Harbor Boulevard   800/828–4898 or
www.tropicanainn-anaheim.com   714/635–4082

This inn is across the street from the Disneyland Resort and is a five-minute walk away from the main gate. Two-room suites are available for large families. Each room features a microwave and a refrigerator. A few kitchen suites are also available. A complimentary continental breakfast is included, and there's a heated pool and spa for guests to enjoy. Basic rooms start at $109. Tickets are available, and it's a Disneyland Good Neighbor hotel.

San Diego Area Hotels

Best Western Mission Bay Inn   ★★
2575 Clairemont Drive, San Diego   800/457–8080 or
www.bestwestern.com   619/275–5700

The Mission Bay Inn is a mile from SeaWorld and is within walking distance of the Mission Bay beaches. A few minutes' drive and you'll find yourself at the San Diego Zoo. The hotel has an outdoor pool and spa, and each room has a coffeemaker, a refrigerator, a microwave, and cable TV. A continental breakfast is available every morning. Hotel prices start at $99 for the off-season. Tickets for SeaWorld and the zoo are available at a discount through the hotel.

Comfort Suites   ★★
631 Camino del Rio S., San Diego   800/433–0452 or
www.comfortsuitesmv.com   619/881–4000

Mission Valley Comfort Suites offers a standard suite and a kids' suite. The kids' suite has bunk beds and is separated by French doors. This hotel has a heated pool and spa, a fitness

Quick Guide to

Hotel Name	Description	Price
Best Western Mission Bay Inn 2575 Clairemont Drive San Diego, CA 92117 800-457-8080 or 619-275-5700 www.bestwestern.com	Family suites available, some with bunk beds	$–$$$
Comfort Suites 631 Camino del Rio S. San Diego, CA 92108 800-433-0452 or 619-881-4000 www.comfortsuitesmv.com	Standard suites or kids' suites available	$$–$$$
The Dana on Mission Bay 1710 W. Mission Bay Drive San Diego, CA 92109 800-445-3339 or 619-222-6440 www.thedana.com	Rooms with views of bay or marina available	$$$–$$$$
Doubletree Club Hotel 1515 Hotel Circle S. San Diego, CA 92108 800-489-9671 or 619-881-6900 www.doubletreeclubsd.com	Family suites available; private balconies	$$–$$$
Holiday Inn Carlsbad by the Sea 850 Palomar Airport Road Carlsbad, CA 92008 800-465-4329 or 760-438-7880 www.carlsbadhi.com	Standard rooms and 2 suites available	$$–$$$
Holiday Inn Sea World 3737 Sports Arena Boulevard San Diego, CA 92110 800-383-5430 or 619-881-6100 www.himb.com	Two-room suites and kids' suites available	$–$$$

$$$$ $250 and up
$$$ $150–$250
$$ $100–$150
$ $50–$100

San Diego Area Hotels

Distance from Resort	Rating	Amenities	Details On
Close to SeaWorld, zoo, and beaches	★★	Pool and spa; microwaves and refrigerators; continental breakfast	Page 57
5 minutes from SeaWorld	★★	Pool and spa; fitness center and game room; microwaves and refrigerators; continental breakfast	Page 57
Closest hotel to SeaWorld	★★★	2 pools and 2 spas; refrigerators; microwaves in some; fitness room; private marina	Page 60
Close to SeaWorld	★★★	Pool and spa; fitness center and game room; refrigerators and microwaves	Page 60
Less than 1 mile to Legoland	★★	Pool and spa; microwaves; refrigerator; kids eat free at on-site restaurant	Page 61
Close to SeaWorld	★★	Pool and spa; health club and game room; refrigerators and microwaves; kids eat free at on-site restaurant	Page 61

★★★★ Top quality with superior amenities
★★★ Good prices with good amenities
★★ Good value with few amenities
★ Basic and inexpensive

center, a game room, and cable TV. A continental breakfast buffet is served daily. Passes for SeaWorld can be bought at the hotel. Suite prices start at $110.

The Dana on Mission Bay	★★★
1710 W. Mission Bay Drive,	**Knight Choice**
San Diego	**800/445–3339 or**
www.thedana.com	**619/222–6440**

Although it can be expensive, especially for the bay view rooms, The Dana on Mission Bay is our favorite hotel in the San Diego area. There are two pools and two spas in tropical garden surroundings, and you can rent bicycles, paddleboats, canoes, and other watercraft at the private marina. The resort atmosphere will beg you to stay an extra day just to take in the activities available here and to relax by the ocean. (The hotel is right on Mission Bay.) There are two on-site restaurants, one fine dining and the other casual. All rooms have refrigerators and some also have microwaves. Pool view rooms start at $125, marina view rooms at $139, and bay view rooms at $160. This is the closest hotel to SeaWorld—within easy walking distance. They also offer a shuttle. Package deals are available as well as discounted tickets. This is a good place for some down time after visiting theme parks and other Southern California attractions.

Doubletree Club Hotel	★★★
1515 Hotel Circle S., San Diego	**800/489–9671 or**
www.doubletreeclubsd.com	**619/881–6900**

This upscale hotel offers regular rooms as well as family suites that start at $119 and $169, respectively. Features include a heated pool and spa, an on-site restaurant, a video game center, and a gift shop. The hotel also has a fitness center where you can work off the famous Doubletree fresh-baked cookies they give you on arrival. Each room has a refrigerator, a microwave, cable TV, and a coffeemaker. Packages are available for SeaWorld and the San Diego Zoo, and discounted tickets are also available.

Holiday Inn Carlsbad by the Sea ★★
850 Palomar Airport Road, Carlsbad   888/465–4329 or
www.carlsbadhi.com   760/438–7880

This is one of the closest hotels to LEGOLAND. Most of its rooms are standard, with rates beginning at $139. There are two suites, each of which contains a spa tub and kitchenette, starting around $327. The hotel has a heated pool and spa, fitness center, and an adjacent Ruby's Diner where kids eat free. The hotel provides a shuttle to LEGOLAND, and LEGOLAND packages are available.

Holiday Inn SeaWorld ★★
3737 Sports Arena Boulevard,   800/383–5430 or
   San Diego   619/881–6100
www.himb.com

Near SeaWorld and the beaches of Mission Bay, this hotel offers two different suites for families. The Kids Mini Suite has bunk beds and gives kids their own space. A standard two-room suite is also available. Rates range from $79 for a standard room to $95 for a standard suite. The hotel has a heated pool and spa, a Baker's Square Restaurant & Pie Shop where kids eat free, a sports bar, and a video game room, and you can have free use of an adjacent health club. The hotel sells tickets to SeaWorld.

CHAPTER

3

Before You
Leave Home

You already have your hotel reservations, arrangements for tickets, and your transportation is booked. This chapter covers some of the other things you should do before you leave home.

Getting the Latest Info

A week or two before your vacation, you may want to check on ride closures, special happenings, park operating hours, and the weather forecast. Even though you checked on these when first planning your trip, some may have changed. There are a couple of ways to check these things. Visit the Disneyland Web site at www.disneyland.com for the latest listing of rides and attractions scheduled to be closed for refurbishment. Knowing ahead of time which rides will not be up and running will keep you from being surrounded by disappointed faces at the park. The Web site also lists show and parade times. The other route to this information is via telephone, by dialing 714/781–4565. Local weather information in the Anaheim area is available by visiting the Disneyland Web site at www.disneyland.com.

What to Take with You

Whether you're an expert traveler or a novice, vacationing with children can be challenging. To help make things easier, we have provided some hints and tips on what you should take with you.

Clothing and Other Necessities

A well-planned packing list will make preparations much easier for everyone. Make a list for each member of the family. If you're traveling with older children, let them help compile their own list. Each list should include clothing that is weather appropriate (remember, Southern California days can be hot, and evenings can be quite cool), shoes that fit comfortably (now is not the time to break in those new tennies), toiletries, a swimsuit, sunglasses, sunscreen, and so on. Remember also to list special-needs items such as medications. If you're traveling during the rainy season, you might want to pack inexpensive ponchos for each family member. Don't try to include everything and the kitchen sink. Pack lightly; if something more is needed, it can most likely be found at the resort. Children can purchase T-shirt souvenirs that can double as either swim cover-ups or pajamas. If the weather changes drastically, sweatshirt souvenirs can also be purchased. (If you're on a tight budget, be sure to prepare for weather changes so that you won't be tempted to overspend.) Many of the hotels have laundry service or laundry facilities for your use. No matter what time of year you travel, be sure to include sunscreen. The Southern California sun can be deceiving in fall and spring, and a nasty sunburn can result even when it's cloudy. Parents and older children can bring along fanny packs to carry money, room keys, snacks, and so forth. If you're traveling with children requiring a diaper bag, you may want to switch to a backpack for the trip. A backpack will free up your arms while also allowing you to tote all your baby-care and family necessities. A basic first-aid kit should also be included as a group item.

Helpful Hint

Break in your walking shoes weeks before your trip. The Disneyland Resort is a large place, so expect to walk several miles a day. Be sure to bring your most comfortable walking shoes as well as good socks. Several weeks before your trip you may want to begin a walking regimen with your family so that your body (mainly your feet) is prepared to traverse the Disneyland Resort in tip-top condition. Hi ho, hi ho, it's off to walk you go!

Family First-Aid Kit

Here's a list of first-aid items that may prove useful while traveling. This list is a basic guideline. Customize your kit according to your family's needs.

- Pain reliever
- Infant's and/or children's acetaminophen, such as Tylenol
- Teething medicine (if needed)
- Band-Aids
- First-aid antibiotic
- Diarrhea medication
- Insect sting relief
- Sunscreen
- Sunburn relief
- Thermometer
- Allergy and/or cold medication

Instead of lugging a large first-aid kit around all day with these items, leave it at the hotel and just take a few of the items, primarily Band-Aids, in a small container or a Ziploc bag. All of the theme parks we include in this book have first-aid centers with basic first-aid supplies. A few of the theme parks, including Disneyland, also carry pain relievers. The staff will administer them to you and document the time and the dose so that you may return later to receive a second dose if needed.

Helpful Hint

Take this opportunity to get rid of old toothbrushes. Instead of making the common mistake of forgetting to pack your toothbrush, buy new toothbrushes for everyone several days before and immediately pack them. Young children really enjoy getting a new toothbrush, especially if it's Disney-themed.

Communication

If you know your family will be splitting up for some of the time while at the Disneyland Resort, and you don't have two cell phones, you may find it useful to invest in a pair of walkie-talkies, which let you stay in contact with each other even when at opposite ends of the park. Try to find walkie-talkies that have several different channels; chances are you'll find your family using the same frequency as another family and have to change to another frequency. Since these are not secure forms of communication (other people may be listening in), avoid giving personal information over these walkie-talkies, such as your hotel and room number or credit card numbers.

Capture the Memories

The one thing you're sure to see everyone toting along is a camera or video camera. Make sure you have plenty of memory card space or film and batteries for both your camera and video

Helpful Hint

The Disneyland parks offer a unique service called PhotoPass. When you have your first photo taken by a Disneyland photographer, he or she will give you a PhotoPass card. Then each time your photo is taken again, the photographer will scan the card and assign your photos to that card's account number. These photos can be viewed and purchased at the parks or through the Web site disneyphotopass.com. At the Web site, you can customize your photos by cropping them or even adding Tinkerbell and other art. One of the options is to purchase all of the photos taken during your visit on a CD, which runs about $60—regardless of the number of photos you have taken at the parks (so strike a pose whenever you see one of Disney's professional photographers). You can also visit the Web site to set up an account before your trip; it contains a lot of information about the service as well as maps of where PhotoPass photographers are located throughout the parks. Your PhotoPass account will store your photos for 30 days . . . so be sure to order the CD or photos soon after you return home.

recorder. There are several spots throughout the park where professional pictures with the characters can be taken. The photographers will also be happy to take your family's picture with your camera, too, or if you choose not to be in the picture and just want a cute shot of the kids, you can take it yourself. Either way you'll be capturing the memories and saving a bundle. Film and batteries are available at the park; however, buying them here is more expensive than purchasing them in advance at home.

Video cameras are a great way to record your trip, but after a while you might get tired of lugging it around. We suggest you choose one day as your video day and leave the camera at the hotel on all other days. Shows and parades are great to record because children will love to watch them over and over again at home. Also, be sure to get shots of your family on various attractions. Filming inside some attractions can be difficult because they're dark—although you're free to try. Note that using lights or flashes in these attractions is not allowed.

I'm Hungry!

During your stay at even the fanciest hotel, you may find you do not have all the comforts of home, especially if you're traveling with small children. While packing for your trip, you may want to include nonperishable snack foods and drinks such as juice boxes. These will be useful when someone has a craving late in the evening. Small snacks can also be placed in fanny packs for midday munchies at the park. Remember to bring individual bottled water as well. It's important to stay hydrated, especially in the hot summer months. Bottled water is available within the park but at a premium price. It's also worthy to note that tap water always tastes different when you travel, so if you have a sensitive palate, you might want to bring some extra water along to refill your water bottles. Most hotels have in-room coffeemakers. These come in handy if you're on a tight budget. Use the coffeemaker to heat up some hot water to make instant oatmeal, noodle soups, hot cocoa, and so on. Some hotels may not have a coffeemaker in the room to begin with, so try requesting one from housekeeping. If a microwave is also included in your hotel room, be sure to pack a few bags of microwave popcorn for those late-night munchies.

Mom, I'm Bored!

You may find small children become bored rather quickly in the hotel room—that is, if they haven't already collapsed from exhaustion. Most hotels around Disneyland offer the Disney

Helpful Hint

Don't worry if you left something behind! There's a Wal-Mart not far from Disneyland. Here you can buy almost anything you may have forgotten without having to pay inflated prices within the resort. The store is right off I–5 (Santa Ana) at the Euclid exit. If you're coming from the Disneyland Resort, take the freeway northbound to Wal-Mart and then southbound back to the resort.

Channel; however, bringing along a few activities may ward off boredom. For infants, be sure to take a few of their favorite toys. Preschool and young school-age children will enjoy coloring or playing with a special toy as well as being read to or quietly looking at a picture book. A few containers of Play-Doh are often a welcome treat for small children. Have older children choose a book or two to bring along. The Compass Books bookstore in Downtown Disney is great for new books and offers several about Disneyland and other Disney-related topics.

Should You Bring Play Yards, Cribs, and Strollers?

If you're traveling with an infant, you'll have more needs than those traveling with older children. Disneyland and most hotels are able to meet those needs, but other options are available. Most hotels have portable cribs available for your use. If you're uncomfortable using someone else's crib, you can bring along a play yard. Most play yards today can double as a bassinet for newborns and a crib for older babies. During waking hours, the play yard can be used to keep your infant safe in your hotel room, which may not be childproof.

A stroller is a necessity when traveling with infants and small children. If you do not already have one or would rather not bring yours, strollers are available to rent for about $12 at the front entrance of Disneyland as well as at most other area theme parks. The ones at Disneyland look much like a single-child jogging stroller. If you're staying for more than one day or visiting other attractions, you may be better off purchasing an inexpensive umbrella stroller. (Renting one every day can add up quickly.) Umbrella strollers can be found at baby stores or discount department stores before your trip. These strollers are easily collapsible for travel and maneuverability. Because you can take the stroller with you rather than having to return it as you would a rented stroller, they also allow you to transport an exhausted child between the park and your hotel.

Helpful Hint

If your family is going to LEGOLAND, you might consider buying a small set of LEGOs to entertain your children at the hotel and as a souvenir. There's also a large LEGO store at Downtown Disney that has all the latest sets—and some you may not be able to find at stores back home.

Preparing the Kids–Building Up the Excitement

As exciting as it is just knowing you will soon be visiting the Disneyland Resort, the excitement can be multiplied by learning more about the park and its attractions. Bring the family together and explore the Disneyland Web site at www.disneyland. com. Also, discuss and plan the trip together using this book as your guide. Talk about and watch the movies that inspired some of the rides, such as *Dumbo, Peter Pan,* or *Toy Story.* You can even make a "countdown to Disneyland" chain or calendar.

Height Checks

Some of the rides at the Disneyland Resort and other places have height requirements. About a week before your trip, line up the kids and measure their height with the shoes they'll be wearing at the parks. If a child is just barely under the height requirement for some rides, consider shoes with a higher heel or sole (as long as they're comfortable) to get the child above the height limitation. The height restrictions at Disneyland and other parks are strictly enforced, and your child may be measured more than once for the same ride. *See* the Quick Guides to rides and attractions in chapters 5 and 6 for all height requirements.

Planning the Fun

A successful and memorable trip takes some amount of planning. Gather together for a family night to get organized. Grab a pad of paper, anything you may have received from your hotel or travel agent, this book, and anything you may have printed out from the Disneyland Web site, and have a planning session. List the number one priority for each family member to accomplish while at the park, and put those at the top of your "to do" list. Continue making the list of things to do, ride, see, or eat in order

Helpful Hint

Make a "countdown to Disneyland" chain to enhance the anticipation of the trip. To make a chain, cut 1-inch by 8-inch strips of colored paper (8-inch by 10-inch sheets of construction paper work great) and loop them around each other, securing with tape or staples. At the top of the chain, attach a cutout of a castle or a Mickey Mouse silhouette to represent the day of arrival at Disneyland. Pull off a link for each day that the trip gets nearer. You can make it as far ahead of time as you like; however, two weeks is usually sufficient.

of how important they are for the family. Use the map provided in this book to arrange a logical, time-sensitive plan. If your children do not know what they would like to do, you can read them the ride descriptions in chapters 5 and 6. With younger children, remember to keep in mind height requirements and scare factors.

Special Needs

Illness

No matter how much planning anyone does, an illness cannot be predicted. Disneyland is a popular place, attracting people from all over the world. Everyone comes to Disneyland with enthusiasm and excitement as well as germs! As unpleasant as it may sound, people do come down with stomach ailments or the common cold. Be prepared for someone in your family to come down with something while at Disneyland. Bring along medications just in case. The best prevention is to wash your hands often. Throw a few antibacterial wet wipes or hand wash into each person's bag to use when hand washing is inconvenient. Remember, an ounce of prevention is worth a pound of cure. Listed below are a few local hospitals, if things get serious.

Anaheim Area Hospitals
Anaheim General Hospital
3350 W. Ball Road, Anaheim, CA 92804
714/827–6700

Anaheim Memorial Hospital
1111 W. La Palma Avenue, Anaheim, CA 92801
714/774–1450

Kaiser Foundation Hospital
441 N. Lakeview Avenue, Anaheim, CA 92807
714/978–4000

Disabilities

Disneyland and other theme parks offer special services and/or ride accommodations for guests with disabilities. Disneyland also has programs for blind and hearing-impaired guests. Portable tape players are available for those with visual impairments. There are also volume-controlled telephones available for the hearing impaired. Visit City Hall at Disneyland and Guest Relations in California Adventure to find out further information on disability assistance. You can also call Guest Relations for further information or log onto Disneyland.com and click on guest services. Wheelchairs are available to rent at the stroller rental stand near the front entrance for $12 a day. Electric convenience vehicles are also available for about $45 a day. Remember: Disneyland is frequented by guests with illnesses and disabilities. Disneyland cast members will assist you in any way they can to make your visit enjoyable, but they cannot transfer guests to or from their wheelchair onto an attraction.

Pregnancy

If you're traveling while pregnant, remember that you have special needs. Drink plenty of water and take care not to overheat. There are many shady areas where you can take a load off your feet and cool down. Another place to take a break is in the Baby Care Centers on Main Street at Disneyland and behind the Mission Tortilla Factory at California Adventure. Note that many of the more turbulent rides at Disneyland and at other parks do not allow pregnant women to ride.

Babies and Young Children

When traveling with babies and young children, you'll always have extras to worry about. Don't forget the baby food. If your infant is on formula, be sure to bring bottled water with which to prepare it. Little tummies can be sensitive to water from a different source. Diapers may be bulky to pack, but be sure to bring along plenty of them—they're expensive within the park. Young children can be messy, so don't forget extra clothing for them as well. If you're traveling with a potty-training youngster, remember to bring extra undergarments. Within Disneyland,

 Helpful Hint

Never fear, your loyal Baby Care Center is here! Baby Care Centers are on Main Street next to the Plaza Inn at Disneyland and behind the Mission Tortilla Factory at California Adventure. If you happen to run out of diapers or wipes or are in need of a pacifier, formula, or baby food, the Baby Care Center is ready to help. All these items can be purchased there, as well as teething gel and diaper cream. In addition, baby food and bottles can be warmed in the Baby Care Center kitchen.

there are a few locations that have toddler toilets: the Baby Care Centers and Mickey's Toontown. Forewarn your little ones that some of these toilets are "magical" and flush automatically when the child stands up. A pacifier, binki, nukki, plug—whatever you might call it—can be vitally important on your trip, both to you as well as your little one. Pack extras, along with a pacifier holder. Many a lost pacifier has been seen lonesome and abandoned on one side of the park while an inconsolable infant is screaming on the other.

CHAPTER

4

Touring the
Disneyland
Resort

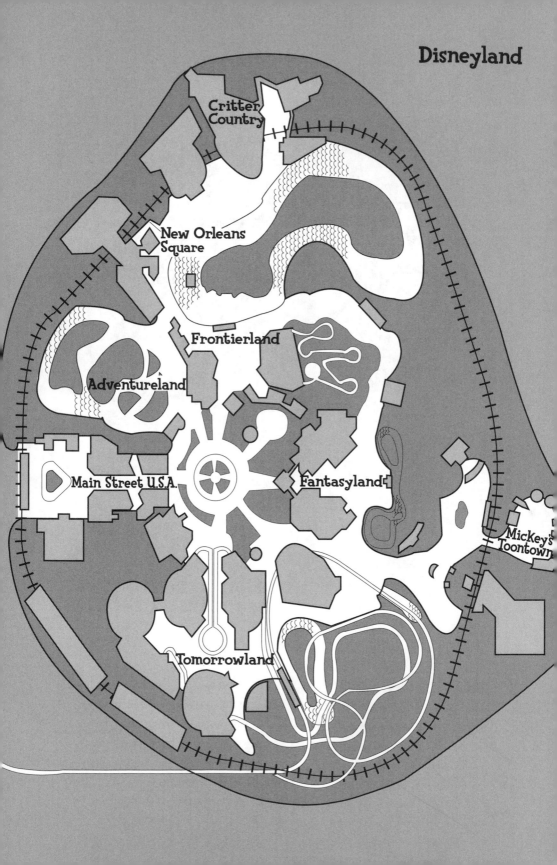

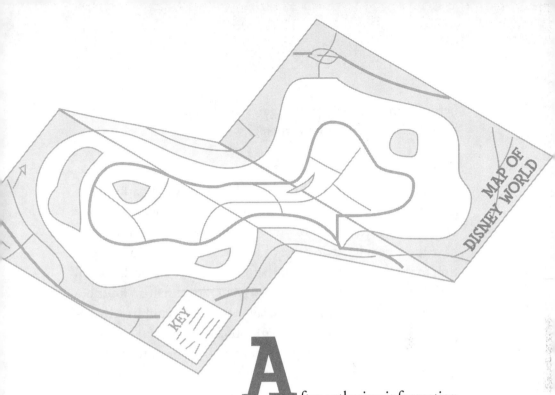

MAP OF DISNEY WORLD

After gathering information from many different families and Disney cast members, as well as from our own family's experiences at the Disneyland Resort, we've come up with hints, tips, and suggestions that will help make your family's vacation to the Happiest Place on Earth the best it can be.

Plan Your Day

Although most people are good at planning their daily schedule at work or at home, they often fall short during vacations. They plan their destination and find a place to stay, but they often leave the rest to chance. We have found that a little bit of additional planning can go a long way. Disneyland is a large place with lots of exciting things to do and see. While talking to different families, we were surprised that some hadn't seen everything they wanted to even after spending two or three days at the park. In each case, the family didn't take the time to plan or even find out what Disneyland had to offer.

Although you don't need to plan each and every hour at Disneyland, there are a few basic things you should consider before stepping through the gates at the main entrance or at least during your first hour there.

Before Entering the Parks

One of the first things you need to find out is the parks' operating hours. You can find this on the Disneyland Web site or by asking at the front desk of your hotel. The Disneyland hotels have the schedule, as do most of the nearby hotels. Plan on getting to the front gates an hour before opening. Disneyland will usually begin letting guests in onto Main Street half an hour before the park opens. The monorail into Disneyland usually begins operating as soon as the park officially opens. However, it may also run earlier during early entry days for hotel guests— or even later depending on the season or events taking place.

If you need to board a pet in the kennel for the day, you should get to the kennel 15 to 20 minutes before it opens, to avoid the lines. The kennel opens 30 minutes before the park officially opens.

Helpful Hint

As a security measure, Disneyland and Disney's California Adventure now search your backpacks and bags as you enter the park. To save time in line, have your bags open and ready for inspection before reaching the cast member.

If you want to watch the *Fantasmic!* show from premium viewing areas, you will have to make reservations in advance at Guest Relations, to the right of the front gates. Since these spots are limited, it's best to phone in your reservations up to 30 days in advance by calling 714/781–4400. The premium viewing seats a limited number of people, so make your reservations as early as possible. We suggest calling first thing in the morning exactly 30 days in advance to secure these reservations. The charge is a steep $59 per adult and $49 per child, but it includes a beverage and a dessert sampler in a keepsake box or a child's dessert in a Mickey Mouse souvenir cup. If you can afford it, and don't want to wait an hour for seats to see *Fantasmic!*, this is a good way to see the show.

What to Eat

Everyone has to eat sometime. If children get hungry, they will not have a good time—and neither will you. The first step to planning is to determine what types of meals your family will have for the day. Will you eat breakfast at the hotel, at a fast-food restaurant, or in the park? What about lunch and dinner? Will you have a big lunch with a light dinner or a light lunch with a big dinner? If you wait

Time-Saving Tip

As we have mentioned before, remember that it's important to purchase your tickets in advance. Most packages include tickets. They can also be purchased at some hotels, at Disney stores, from AAA, and through some employee organizations. The last thing you want to do is stand in line at the ticket booths in front of Disneyland. Sometimes your wait in line can be more than an hour on busy days! And then you still have to get into the park.

until you're hungry, then it's too late. Planning your meals in advance saves time and money. That way, your family is not spending time trying to figure out where to eat after everyone has already become hungry, and it's easier to budget the cost if you know what to expect.

We recommend eating a good breakfast. You want to hit a lot of popular rides in the morning before they get too busy, so don't spend time eating then. As for lunch, you should try to eat this meal in the early part of the afternoon, between 1 and 3 PM when the attractions are usually at their busiest and the restaurants and eateries have shorter lines. Then have a light dinner later in the evening. The meals on the lunch menus are often less expensive than the same items on the dinner menus. You may also decide to eat some meals outside of the park, either during the middle of the day or after the park closes. Although you can choose specific places to eat in advance, you can also decide later while waiting in line for attractions. Just knowing the types of meals and when you will eat them saves a lot of time and lets you schedule snacks and breaks throughout the remainder of the day.

Money-Saving Tip

Because snack foods and drinks can be expensive inside the park, it's a good idea to take some water bottles and snacks with you, such as granola bars, individual packages of nuts, or other snacks that will easily fit in a pocket, fanny pack, or backpack and that won't melt.

If you're spending several days at Disneyland, you may want to determine when you would like to eat at certain places. For example, you may decide to try the Blue Bayou restaurant for lunch on your second day. That means you'll need to make reservations early that same day or call and make reservations up to two months in advance. The same goes for a number of restaurants at California Adventure that offer reservations, such as Ariel's Grotto. For a guide to what is available at the Disneyland Resort, *see* Chapter 8, "Disney Dining." Use this guide before you even leave on your vacation to decide on some of the special places to eat.

Guided Tours

Both Disneyland and Disney's California Adventure offer guided tours. These can be fun whether it's your first visit or your fiftieth. Tours can be arranged at the Tour office near City Hall in Disneyland. You can also make reservations for a tour up to 30 days in advance by calling 714/781–4400. If planning a vacation during the busy season, reserve your tours in advance to make sure you can get the one you want when you want to do it. The Welcome to Disneyland Tour takes you through both parks and provides basic information. You also get priority seating to a stage show or parade. This two-and-a-half-hour tour runs $25 per person. For a behind-the-scenes look at Disneyland, try "A Walk in Walt's Footsteps." This tour offers a lot of trivia as well as information on how Disneyland was planned and built. It also includes a private lunch on Main Street, USA, and even a peek at the exclusive members-only restaurant, Club 33. This tour runs $59 per person and lasts about three and a half hours. Although the first two tours are designed more for adults, the Discover the Magic tour focuses on children ages 5–9 as well as their families. This is more of an adventure than a tour: you work with Disney characters to look for clues, search for treasure, and even outwit villains. Including a frozen treat and a souvenir gift, this two-and-a-half-hour tour runs $59 for the first two people, and $49 for each additional person. Finally, for a unique tour, try Cruzin' Disney's California Adventure Park. For this tour you'll learn how to ride a Segway Personal Transporter and then cruise on it through the park. These tours take place before the park opens, and is only for those 16 years and older. The price is $99 per person for a three-hour tour. Not all tours are available year-round, and new ones may be added. Be sure to check the Disneyland Web site for the latest information. Although the prices of the tours can be steep, annual pass holders get a 20% discount as do AAA members or those with a Disney VISA card.

What to Do First

Even before you pass through the main gate at either of the parks, you should have an idea of which attractions you want to do first. Once you're inside the park, you can walk quickly to that attraction before the lines get long. Since you can quickly get on many attractions first thing in the morning, don't waste your time deciding what to do next. As a general rule, prior to entering the park you should plan the first three or four attractions you want to visit. Chapters 5 and 6 provide suggestions for each park based on the ages of your children.

When to Get There—Early!

Disneyland allows you to enter the park about 30 minutes before it officially opens. You're held on Main Street or in the Central Plaza until opening time. However, you can shop and visit the eateries for a quick breakfast. At the official opening time, you're then allowed to enter the rest of Disneyland. If you want to hit Main Street early so you can line up near the Central Plaza prior to opening, get to the main gate about an hour before the official opening time. Another good way to get into the park is by monorail. The station is in Downtown Disney and is the best way for guests of the Disney hotels to avoid the rush at the main gate. It's a good idea to get in line at the station at least 30 minutes before Disneyland opens. At times they may actually begin boarding the monorail prior to opening so

Time-Saving Tip

Remember to purchase your tickets in advance. If for some reason you cannot, then get in line at the ticket booths an hour before the parks open or even earlier. The ticket lines can get quite long, and after you purchase your tickets, you still have another line to get into the park.

that it's ready to roll as soon as the park opens. Taking the monorail puts you right into Tomorrowland, so you're close to some of the popular rides and can get to them before most of the people coming from the main gate.

California Adventure does not allow you in early, so you need to arrive at the main gate only 30 minutes in advance. If you're a guest of one of the Disney hotels, use the private entrance at Disney's Grand Californian Hotel. It puts you in the park near Grizzly River Run.

Many visitors don't arrive until the parks open or even later, making the lines to get into the parks grow longer throughout the morning—especially during the busy season. Therefore, be sure to get in line early.

The FASTPASS System

The FASTPASS system was designed so that guests at Disneyland would not feel they were spending most of their day waiting in long lines. For those willing to make an "appointment" to do an attraction, there's a much shorter line with a wait time of usually no longer than 10 to 15 minutes. Sound good? Here's how it works.

At a ride that has the FASTPASS system, near the entrance will be a number of small machines that look like they might make change. Instead, these issue FASTPASS tickets. Insert your ticket as directed by the instructions on the machine, and it will issue you a FASTPASS for the attraction. On the ticket will be two times, one hour apart. This is your time window when you can return to the attraction and enter it using the much faster FASTPASS entrance. At the entrance to the FASTPASS machines is a sign that lists current FASTPASS time windows the machines are issuing tickets for, as well as the length of the stand-by wait for those without a FASTPASS. The return window of time can vary from half an hour later to three or more hours later, depending on how many guests are using the system. While your FASTPASS is reserving you a place in line, you can go visit other attractions, shop, or have a meal.

The FASTPASS system has some ground rules. First, you can only get one FASTPASS at a time per ticket (*see* "Strategies for Using the FASTPASS System" below for exceptions to this rule). Also, every person in your party who is old enough to need a ticket for entrance into the park must have his or her own FASTPASS. At this writing, Disneyland is currently offering the FASTPASS system on the following attractions:

- Autopia
- Big Thunder Mountain Railroad
- Buzz Lightyear Astro Blasters
- Indiana Jones Adventure
- Roger Rabbit's Car Toon Spin
- Space Mountain
- Splash Mountain

During November and December, the holiday version of "it's a small world" gets temporary FASTPASS status.

California Adventure also uses the FASTPASS system. Because this park has fewer attractions, guests tend to group more at the few popular ones. Therefore, using the FASTPASS system becomes even more important for saving time. The following California Adventure attractions currently use the FASTPASS system:

- California Screamin'
- Grizzly River Run
- Mulholland Madness
- Soarin' Over California
- The Twilight Zone Tower of Terror

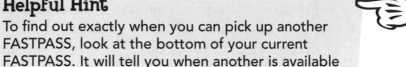

Helpful Hint

To find out exactly when you can pick up another FASTPASS, look at the bottom of your current FASTPASS. It will tell you when another is available for you.

Strategies for Using the FASTPASS System

From talking to other families and Disneyland cast members and from personal experience, we have found how best to use the FASTPASS system to save time during your vacation.

- Although everyone in your party needs a FASTPASS to board an attraction, not everyone has to wait in line to get his or her own FASTPASS. Instead, one person can take everyone's tickets and get FASTPASSes for them all while they're waiting in line for another attraction, meeting characters, or at a story time.

- Most of the FASTPASS attractions are rides for older children and adults. Because the FASTPASS tickets are not assigned to a specific person, families with children unable to go on these attractions can still use the children's tickets to get FASTPASSes for adults or older children. Therefore, you could get two FASTPASSes for the same attraction or different attractions at the same time.

- The FASTPASS system is set up so you only get one FASTPASS at a time per ticket, but at a certain point, you can get another. After you get a FASTPASS, you can get another after the hour-long window of the first ticket has begun. You then have an hour to use that FASTPASS and, during that time, you can get a second FASTPASS. That way, while you're on the first attraction, you're also waiting for the window of the second. For example, you have a FASTPASS for Space Mountain with a window of 1 to

2 PM. After 1 PM, you could first get a FASTPASS for Autopia, then go on Space Mountain. Your current FASTPASS ticket also states the time you can get another FASTPASS.

@ As a general rule, always get another FASTPASS before using the one you have.

@ For attractions where the window is more than two hours away, you can get a second FASTPASS two hours after you have received your first one. If you can't remember when you picked it up, the time is on the bottom right corner of your FASTPASS.

@ There's no penalty for not using a FASTPASS. If you miss your window or decide to skip an attraction, you can get another FASTPASS using the above guidelines. Therefore, you should always try to have a FASTPASS in your possession, even if you're unsure whether you'll be able to use it.

@ Except for Main Street, New Orleans Square, and Fantasyland, every land has at least one attraction using the FASTPASS system. If you pass by one and think you might want to ride it, get a FASTPASS.

@ Some attractions, especially Splash Mountain and Indiana Jones Adventure, can have very long waits for a return window, or will run out of FASTPASSes by early afternoon. Therefore, if you want to get a FASTPASS for these

Helpful Hint

When you have two lines to choose from, whether for an attraction, a shop, or a dining venue, choose the line on the left. Studies show that people tend to choose the line on the right, so the left line is often shorter.

two rides, it's usually best to get them in the morning. If you have to wait more than two hours to return, be sure to look at the bottom of your FASTPASS for the time you can get another FASTPASS.

@ If you're going to eat a meal, get a FASTPASS first so you can be waiting while you're eating.

Although the FASTPASS system is the best way to do the most popular attractions, it may not always fit your schedule, and at times the stand-by wait may be quite short. Even if you don't use the FASTPASS system on an attraction, the fact that it's there often reduces the wait in the stand-by line because many guests are willing to come back later.

Height Requirements *page 120-125*

Some of the rides at Disneyland and Disney's California Adventure require riders to be at least a certain height. (To view height requirements for each attraction, *see* chapters 5 and 6.) Disney cast members are strict on height requirements. It's a good idea to measure your children in the shoes they will be wearing at the park before you leave home. Then you can determine which rides they can go on and those they can't before they get to the parks.

Parent Swap

To accommodate families with small children who are unable to go on attractions that have height requirements or that might be too scary for them, Disneyland and California Adventure offer rider swaps. This allows part of a family to go on a ride while a parent or another adult waits with the younger children. Let the cast member at the entrance to the attraction know you want to do a parent swap, and he or she will give the waiting adult or group a pass. After the first group has waited in line and done the attraction, the waiting group can then go in through the exit or other designated area and give a cast member the pass. The group will then be allowed to board with little or no wait. Some attractions let you do a parent swap together with a FASTPASS. Ask the cast member at the entrance of the attraction for more information about parent swaps.

The Baby Care Centers

If you have infants or young children, the Baby Care Centers may become some of your favorite spots in the theme parks. They're great for changing diapers and taking care of other needs, and the cast members here are especially helpful.

Insider's Secret
If any of your little ones are potty training, be sure to bring them to the Changing Room, where there are two small toilets that are just their size. There's even a short sink where they can wash up.

The Baby Care Center in Disneyland is at the end of Main Street, by the photo shop and near the Plaza Inn. Disney's California Adventure also features a Baby Care Center. It's near the Mission Tortilla Factory in the Pacific Wharf District. When you first enter, a cast member will welcome and direct you where to go based on your need. The Changing Room is nice and contains four padded changing tables. Each has high sides and Velcro belts to help keep your child safe. In addition, there's a dunking toilet for rinsing out cloth diapers and a sink for washing up. Although most restrooms around the park have small changing stations, it's worth the walk to visit the Baby Care Center unless you're in a hurry. Both moms and dads can take a child into the Changing Room.

The Baby Care Center also has a Feeding Area with several high chairs. A cast member can warm up baby food or a bottle for you if needed. Some children have trouble eating in loud areas with lots of action going on, and that describes most of Disneyland's restaurants. The Feeding Room is nice and quiet, giving both the child and the parent a chance to rest and relax for a bit. The Nursing Area has several comfortable chairs for mothers to nurse a child. You can use this area for bottle feeding as well. Unlike in the other areas, fathers are not allowed here.

The Baby Care Center has some rules that must be followed. Each adult can take only one child in at a time, and only one adult can go in per child. This can be difficult for families with more than two small children or single parents with more than one small child. However, if it's a slow day and the Baby Care Center is not busy, these rules may be relaxed a bit.

Helpful Hint

Two words about Disneyland Resort bathrooms: magic toilets. Many of the restrooms at the Disneyland Resort have an automatic flush feature. Although this is convenient and sanitary, some children may be frightened when the toilet flushes by itself. These toilets can be identified by their little red sensor. Warn your children in advance that these toilets flush on their own, so they will think the toilets are cool rather than scary.

The Baby Care Center also sells a number of commonly needed items. These include diapers, baby wipes, powder, diaper rash ointment, formula, bottles, baby food, pacifiers, and even children's acetaminophen (Tylenol). You will pay more for these things here than at a regular store, but if you need them, they're available.

First Aid

Each park has its own first-aid station. In Disneyland, it's by the Plaza Inn. California Adventure's first-aid station is next to the Mission Tortilla Factory. In addition to taking care of minor injuries, each first-aid station has a variety of medicines for allergies, coughs, diarrhea, and pain. These are provided one dose at a time. The first-aid station will also record when you took the dose and let you know when you can come back for another dose if necessary.

Helpful Hint
It's always a good idea to carry basic first-aid supplies (such as bandages and cleansing wipes) in your backpack. This allows you to take care of small cuts, scratches, and blisters without having to go to the first-aid station.

Expectant Mothers

Disneyland and California Adventure both have several attractions that could be dangerous for expectant mothers. Each is noted in the guides for the parks as well as at the entrances to the rides themselves. Heed these warnings! They are not there just for legal reasons. Even if you have been on the ride before and don't think it's too rough, still refrain. These rides may have sudden stops or jolts during the course of operation, possibly causing injury or complications.

Although most people would not think this ride rough, there are warning signs even on the Autopia at Disneyland. The ride may seem tame, but the driver behind you may not stop in time and may hit your car, causing a sudden bump. Also, the drops in Pirates of the Caribbean can be uncomfortable for some expectant mothers. Check with your doctor before going on vacation, and ask what types of attractions you should avoid.

Although there are some things expectant mothers cannot do at the Disney Resort, there are even more things they can do. Most rides are fine, and of course there are also lots of shows and other nonride attractions.

Stroller Rentals

You can rent strollers at a number of places within the Disney parks. At Disneyland and California Adventure, the rental place is on the right, just inside the main gate. Strollers are $12 for the day. Be sure to keep your receipt. If your stroller is lost, or if you leave the park and come back later, you can take the receipt to a stroller rental location, and the attendant will be happy to provide another for you.

Money-Saving Tip

If you have a Disney VISA card, you can rent two strollers per day at Disneyland and Disney's California Adventure for free. Even if you are taking your own stroller with you, getting an additional stroller in the evening can let a tired, older child take a ride, allowing you a few extra hours at the parks.

We suggest bringing your own stroller if at all possible. Not only does this save you money each day, but you also have the stroller for transporting tired children back to the car or hotel after a long day at the park. It's also a good idea if you plan on visiting Downtown Disney or the hotel shops and restaurants.

It's important to mark your stroller in some way. No matter where you got your stroller, chances are, there is at least one just like it at the park. We have found that brightly colored luggage tags work quite well. Attach the tag to the handle, or right

Insider's Secret

At the Tomorrowland monorail station, there's an elevator for handicapped guests. However, cast members also let families with sleeping children in a stroller use the elevator. You still have to take them out before boarding the monorail, but you can hold off until the train actually arrives. The Downtown Disney station's elevator has no restrictions.

If you'll be doing several attractions close to one another, such as in Fantasyland, park your stroller in a central location and leave it while you do all the attractions. This saves the time of loading, moving the stroller to the next stop, and then unloading again.

next to it, so other people will see right away that the stroller is not theirs. Be sure you have your name printed on the tag. Balloons also work well for distinguishing your stroller from someone else's. During the day, you will have to park and leave your stroller several times while going on attractions. Try to park the stroller close to the attraction's exit so you can quickly load up and head on to the next attraction. Also, be sure to take any

Lockers

Both parks offer lockers for storing items while visiting. These are great for holding coats or sweatshirts during the day so you don't have to carry them around. Then get them when it gets cold. At Disneyland, the lockers are on Main Street near the cone shop, by the Fantasyland Theatre, and outside of the main gate. The lockers in California Adventure are inside and to the west of the main gate. Locker rentals run from $7 to $15 a day depending on the size, and are available in five different sizes.

valuables with you. If your stroller is missing when you come back, don't panic. At times, cast members move strollers to a parking area to clear an area for a parade or another event. Just look around or ask a cast member for help.

When riding the monorail or a tram, you'll have to fold up your stroller to take it aboard. A cast member is usually around to help out if needed.

Rain and Bad Weather

During your vacation at the Disneyland Resort, you may get some rainy weather. This is less likely during the summer, but it can happen at any time of the year. Often short showers drop a bit of rain and then move on, leaving the remainder of the day nice and sunny. However, at times you may have nonstop rain all day long. Although many of the attractions are actually indoors, a few are not. However, even the outdoor attractions still operate in the rain. If the rain continues, parades, character greetings, and outdoor shows will probably be canceled.

Helpful Hint
One of the biggest fears for a parent is a child who gets separated from the family. Before you enter the parks, let your younger children know what they should do if they can't find the rest of their family. Tell them to ask a cast member for help and be sure to show them a cast member's name tag as an example. The cast member will take the child to the Baby Care Center at the end of Main Street, USA, in Disneyland or next to the Mission Tortilla Factory in Disney's California Adventure. Lost children in Downtown Disney will be taken to the Baby Care Center in Disneyland.

If you expect rain, bring a raincoat or poncho. You can also purchase ponchos inside the parks: children's are $5, and adults' are $6. Not only do they keep you dry, but they also make great souvenirs. An adult poncho easily covers most strollers and keeps the occupants dry.

Although rainy days may seem like a bad time for Disneyland or California Adventure, attendance then is usually down and lines are quite short. When we visited the parks on rainy days, we could walk onto just about every attraction without a wait. The Jungle Cruise was a lot of fun, and the rain made the attraction all the more realistic.

Child Safety

Disneyland is a large place with lots of people, especially small children. A child can easily slip away from your group, causing instant panic for mom and dad. Here are a few tips to keep your child safe and easily identifiable.

- For each day you're at the resort, pick a bright color, such as yellow, orange, or blue, for all family members to wear. This will help you easily spot your children in a crowd and also make it easier for your children to see you.

- Carry a photo ID card or a photo with vital information on the back for each child touring with you. Then if they get separated, you have a photo to show to cast members and you can tell them he or she is wearing the same color that you are.

- In your child's pocket or shoe, place a card with your child's name, your name, your cell phone number or other number where you can be reached, the name of your hotel, and at least one emergency contact.

- Choose a location as a family where you can meet if someone gets separated. Depending on where you'll be during

Lost & Found

If you lose something at the Disneyland Resort, be sure to check the Lost and Found outside the main entrance of Disney's California Adventure. Everything found will be brought to this location. If you don't realize you're missing something until you get home, you can call 714/817–2166 during normal park hours to check on the item. It can then be sent to you at home.

the day, pick locations your children can easily find such as in front of Sleeping Beauty's Castle, or by a favorite ride.

@ Do not dress your child in Christmas colors if you're traveling during the holiday season. Just about every small child will be wearing red or green during this time.

@ If you have a child who is always running away or wandering off, try using a child safety leash. These are available at most children's stores and can prevent a lot of parental stress because you won't have to chase your child down Main Street. Some children even feel more secure while wearing a safety leash. If your child does not want to wear it, try explaining that you're using it so mommy or daddy will not get lost.

CHAPTER

5

Disneyland— The Magic Kingdom®

Disneyland Attractions

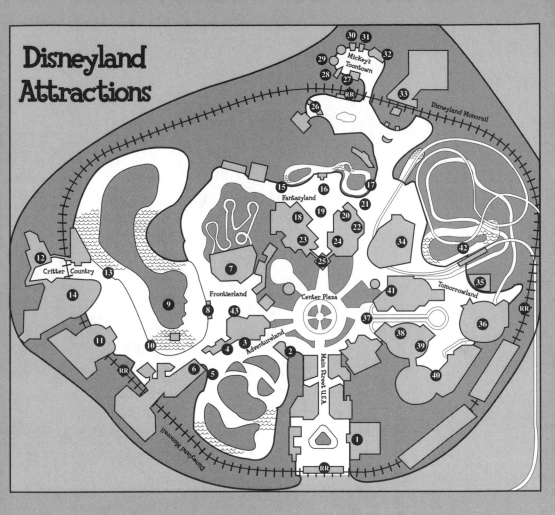

Disneyland first opened on July 17, 1955. Since that time, millions of families have enjoyed this wonderland and created memories that will last a lifetime. This chapter has everything your family needs to know about making magic at the happiest place on earth.

Plan Your Day

Chapter 4 emphasized the importance of planning your day at the Disneyland Resort. In addition to getting your tickets in advance and deciding on the types of meals you want to eat in the park, you should also have an idea of what attractions are available, where they're located, and when you want to do them. Following are some hints and suggestions to help you see and do as much as possible during your visit.

What to Do First?

By the time you walk through the front gates of Disneyland, you should know what attraction you're going to hit first. When the park first opens, and for about the first hour or two, lines for most attractions are quite short. Try to hit the most popular rides first. If you have young children, this is simple—go to Fantasyland. This land gets really busy and congested by midmorning and will usually remain that way until evening. If you want to ride the Buzz Lightyear Astro Blasters or the Tomorrowland Autopia afterward, make a detour and pick up some FAST-PASSes for one of them on your way to Fantasyland.

Helpful Hint

The newest attractions often are the busiest. At Disneyland, the Finding Nemo Submarine Voyage is one of the hottest tickets, and has one of the longest lines (there is no FASTPASS). On busy days, such as in summer, the line can be up to three hours long! Be sure to get to this ride first since the lines will only get longer later on. If you have an early entry one day of your vacation, that's a good time for this ride.

For families with older children, head toward Splash Mountain, the Indiana Jones Adventure, and Big Thunder Mountain. Or you can do Space Mountain, the Matterhorn, and Autopia. You want to spend most of your time riding during the first hour or two, so try to keep walking to a minimum. If you'll be visiting Disneyland for two or more days, choose one side of the park to start on one morning and then hit the other side the next morning.

Although the morning may seem a rush, you don't have to keep up this pace all day. In fact, once the queues start to get long, you can take a break and begin seeing the shows or more restful attractions.

Time-Saving Tip

If you need a stroller, you can rent one just inside the front gate on the right side. However, to save both time and money, it's often advisable to just bring along your own stroller. If size and weight are a concern, small umbrella strollers are light and fold up quite nicely.

Shows and Parades

Along with meals, you should also plan which shows and parades your family would like to see. These take place only at certain times (and only on certain days) during the off-season. At Disneyland's Web site, you can see the days and times for the major shows and parades. They're also listed in the *Disneyland Today* guide, which you can pick up at the entrance. During your time waiting in line, figure out which shows you want

Insider's Secret

Disneyland's fireworks show features a choreographed display of fireworks and music with a special appearance by Tinker Bell, who flies down from the Matterhorn and over Sleeping Beauty's Castle—then back and forth between the two. A lot of guests line up in front of Sleeping Beauty's Castle, which is lighted up during the show, and some fireworks actually launch from the castle itself. Since this area can get crowded, try to find a place to sit or stand at least an hour before the fireworks start. You can also watch from Fantasyland or near the entrance to "it's a small world." Just be sure you can see the top of the Matterhorn as well as the castle.

to see and when. As a general rule, the early showings are usually less crowded.

Disney's fireworks display is one of the most elaborate shows ever done at Disneyland—and it happens almost every night. This show features not only special fireworks (look for the Mickey heads) but also music, flames shooting from the castle, and projections on the castle, the Matterhorn, and even "it's a small world." If you'll be at Disneyland for more than one day, be sure to see this show more than once. Try a different location each time, since it's hard to see everything from one spot.

Insider's Secret

Disneyland's parades change every year or two. They always feature lots of Disney characters, music, and fun; some have stops where a mini-show is put on. Try to see the parade at least once during your visit. If you're going to see it a second time, pick a different location so you can catch a different mini-show during the stops.

Disneyland parades are filled with music, dancing, and lots of Disney characters. Check the *Disneyland Today* guide for the days and times it runs. As a general rule, you want to find a seat close to where the parade begins. If there's only one parade during the day, it will begin by "it's a small world" and end at Main Street. This is the same route the parade takes for the first showing when it runs twice a day. For the first showing, you want to find a place to sit near "it's a small world." That way, once the parade has passed, you can get back to the attractions. The second showing of the parade takes the same route but in reverse, beginning on Main Street. Therefore, try to find a seat near the Central Plaza. Main Street is often crowded, so try to avoid it. The other big show you should see is *Fantasmic!* See the Frontierland shows section of this chapter.

Time-Saving Tip

Even if you don't plan on watching a parade or a big show like *Fantasmic!* check out when these start. During the parade, it can be difficult, if not impossible, to get from Tomorrowland to the rest of the park. Also, these events attract a lot of guests, meaning shorter lines at the popular rides. Take advantage of this.

Character Greetings and Locations

This section applies primarily to families with younger children. When you receive a copy of the *Disneyland Today* guide, check it for the times and locations of character greetings. You can also find the times for the character storytelling, which is great for the little ones. Because the characters are usually at the park for most of the day, you don't have to rush around to catch them. However, if you'll be in an area nearby, you might as well stop and see them. Most characters head back to their homes later in the afternoon or early in the evening, so don't put off meeting them until late or you may miss them.

Before You Leave the Park

If you plan on leaving the park during the day and returning later, be sure to have your hand stamped and hold on to your tickets. You'll need both to get back in. Also, if you rented a stroller, return it and hold on to the receipt and you can get another stroller when you come back to the park later that day. The same goes for your parking ticket. Save it and you will not have to pay a parking fee again for the day.

If the park closes early and the wait isn't too long, take the monorail to Downtown Disney and spend time at these shops and restaurants, some of which stay open as late as 2 AM when Disneyland stays open until midnight. Check the Disneyland

Insider's Secret

No matter what time the park closes, there's always a mad rush to the front gate around closing time. Rather than wait in another line, stay and enjoy Disneyland some more. Although the lines close, the attractions often remain open until everyone in line has been through. Therefore, get in a line right before closing for one last thrill. Also, most of the shops—especially those on Main Street, USA—will stay open for an extra hour after closing. You can do your shopping before you leave and not have to worry about carrying around your purchases during the day.

Web site for show times if you plan to see a movie or take in some of the live entertainment at one of the restaurants. This is a good idea when the park closes at 6 PM and you have to drive. Not only do you want to avoid the rush out of the parking lots or garage, but you also want to miss the rush-hour traffic on the freeways of Southern California.

Touring Plans

It's always a good idea to have a Disneyland touring plan. That way you do not waste time deciding every little thing while you're at the park and you're sure not to forget anything. In this section, we have put together some tips for making your own touring plan and have provided some sample plans of our own. Because every family is different, use our samples as a guide, and then customize one to fit your family.

The key to a good plan is to be prepared. First, a week or two before you leave on your vacation, get a map of the park to acquaint yourself with where everything is located. You can find a map on the Disneyland Web site or request one by calling 714/ 781–4560. Second, read about each attraction in the following section of this chapter. Depending on your family, not all attractions will appeal to you. Third, once you're familiar with the attractions available, have a family meeting where everyone gets to provide input as to what he or she wants to do at Disneyland.

Fourth, divide each day into morning, afternoon, and evening. In the morning, hit the popular attractions, which get busy later in the day. The afternoon is good for meals and restful attractions. If you're staying for several days with younger children and the park is open late, you might even consider returning to the hotel so they can take a nap before returning in the evening. In the evening, you can watch the parade, the fireworks, and *Fantasmic!* and also hit some more attractions.

While organizing all the attractions into your schedule, use the map so you're not running back and forth from one side of the park to the next. Not only would that waste time, but it would also wear out your family. We're not recommending you see everything in one area before moving to the next; that would be just as bad. Instead, think of your plan as making laps around the park. During the morning make one lap, hitting the popular rides. In the afternoon make a second lap, covering shows and attractions with shorter queues as well as the popular rides with FASTPASSes. A final evening lap lets you hit the attractions you missed earlier or want to do again.

The following lists divide the attractions according to the best times to do them. Throughout this book, we refer to younger and older children. Where the cutoff is depends on your child. Younger children are the ones who will not care for the roller coaster and fast rides or are not tall enough to meet the minimum height requirements. These children are usually 5 or 6 years of age or younger. Older children love the fast and wild rides and want to avoid the kiddie rides. They're 7 years or older. If you have children in both categories, then you will have to make compromises to keep everyone happy. Now let's take a look at what to do when.

Popular Attractions for the Morning Lap

Here's a touring plan for first thing in the morning:

Younger Children (6 and Under)

The Fantasyland rides (Dumbo and the dark rides: Peter Pan, Mr. Toad, Snow White, Pinocchio, and Alice)

Toontown—best seen in the morning because it gets busy in the afternoon and closes early

Finding Nemo Submarine Voyage

Buzz Lightyear Astro Blasters

Autopia

Astro Orbitor

Older Children (7 and Up)

Indiana Jones Adventure

Splash Mountain

Big Thunder Mountain Railroad

The Matterhorn Bobsleds

Space Mountain

Finding Nemo Submarine Voyage

Popular Attractions for the Afternoon Lap

Now that you've been in the park all morning, here's a plan for the afternoon:

Younger Children (6 and Under)

Disney Princess Fantasy Faire or Star Wars Jedi Training Academy.

"it's a small world"

Enchanted Tiki Room

Jungle Cruise

Tarzan's Treehouse

Pirates of the Caribbean

The Many Adventures of Winnie the Pooh

Canoes and Riverboat

Pirate's Lair on Tom Sawyer Island

Disneyland Railroad

Innoventions

Character Greetings

Afternoon Parade

Main Street Cinema

Older Children (7 and Up)

Pirates of the Caribbean

Haunted Mansion

Jungle Cruise

Pirates Lair on Tom Sawyer Island

Canoes and Riverboats

Innoventions

Star Tours

Mad Tea Party

Popular rides with FASTPASSes

Popular Attractions for the Evening Lap

To finish up your day at Disneyland, here's a touring plan to please all ages:

Honey, I Shrunk the Audience

Fantasmic!

Fireworks

Anything you missed earlier or want to do again

These are just basic lists to give you a good idea of when to do the various types of attractions. You may have noticed that we did not list every attraction. However, you can get the general idea from those included.

Next we put together some sample plans. The first two are for those families with only a single day at the park, with separate plans for younger and older children. The final two are two-day plans for younger and older children, respectively. For all plans, arrive at Disney an hour before opening so that you can enter Main Street early and be near the end of Main Street when the rope drops and you're able to enter. Alternatively, if you're staying at one of the Disney hotels, get in line for the monorail early so you can take the first train into the park. (*Note:* You may not have time to do everything on these sample plans. They're designed for a typical day. On days when it's busy, you will have to cut some of the attractions.)

Sample One-Day Touring Plan (Children 6 and Under)

Morning

Right at the start, head straight to Sleeping Beauty's Castle. Pass through the castle and ride the Dumbos.

Ride all the dark rides you care to (Peter Pan's Flight, Mr. Toad's Wild Ride, and so on), as well as the Casey Jr. Circus Train. Walk toward the Matterhorn and then turn left and continue past "it's a small world" to Mickey's Toontown. Ride Roger Rabbit's Car Toon Spin and Gadget's Go Coaster. Have a snack while you wait in line for Mickey's House.

Go to Minnie's House.

Helpful Hint

While it's usually a good idea to get in line for the Finding Nemo Submarine Voyage, young children are not going to want to wait around as soon as they get inside Disneyland. Therefore, let them go on some Fantasyland rides first, then get a snack to eat while you wait in line.

Afternoon

Have a late lunch somewhere other than Toontown or Fantasyland. If you eat in Tomorrowland, get a FAST-PASS for Buzz Lightyear Astro Blasters or the Autopia first. Elsewhere, get a FASTPASS for Splash Mountain first.

In Tomorrowland, ride Buzz Lightyear Astro Blaster and the Autopia, and then go to Splash Mountain for a FAST-PASS; otherwise, take in the following attractions after lunch until your FASTPASS time for Splash Mountain.

Ride Pirates of the Caribbean.

Ride the Jungle Cruise.

Visit Tarzan's Treehouse.

Go to the Disney Princess Fantasy Faire or Star Wars Jedi Training Academy.

Evening

If the park is open late, have dinner. (If it closes early, eat afterward.)

Ride "it's a small world."

Watch the parade.

Ride anything you missed earlier or want to do again.

See the fireworks.

See *Fantasmic!*

Sample One-Day Touring Plan (Children 7 and Up)

Morning

Right at the start, head left to Adventureland and ride the Indiana Jones Adventure.

Take a left at the exit and head toward Splash Mountain. Ride it.

Backtrack to Tomorrowland and pick up a FASTPASS for Space Mountain.

Ride the Finding Nemo Submarine Voyage.

Ride Buzz Lightyear Astro Blasters.

Ride Space Mountain.

Afternoon

Go to New Orleans Square and get a FASTPASS for the Big Thunder Mountain Railroad.

Eat lunch in Frontierland or New Orleans Square.

Ride the Jungle Cruise.

Pick up a FASTPASS for Indiana Jones Adventure or Splash Mountain (whichever you would like to do again).

Ride Big Thunder Mountain Railroad.

Ride Pirates of the Caribbean.

Ride the Haunted Mansion.

Visit the Enchanted Tiki Room or the Many Adventures of Winnie the Pooh.

Use the FASTPASS you picked up earlier.

Evening

Get a FASTPASS for the Autopia.

If the park is open late, have dinner. (If it closes early, eat afterward.)

Ride Star Tours.

Ride the Autopia.

Watch the parade.

Ride anything you missed earlier or want to do again.

See fireworks.

See *Fantasmic!*

Sample Two-Day Touring Plan (Children 6 and Under)

With a couple of days, you can see more attractions and slow down the pace a bit.

Day 1—Morning

Right at the start, head to Fantasyland. Ride the Dumbos.

Try out the other rides in Fantasyland.

Go to the Disney Princess Fantasy Faire.

Day 1—Afternoon

Have lunch away from Fantasyland and then head back to the hotel. Or head back to the hotel and eat nearby. (*Note:* If the park closes at 6 PM, stay at the park and skip ahead to the evening activities.)

Rest by the pool or take a nap.

Return to the park and pick up a FASTPASS for Buzz Lightyear Astro Blasters.

See the Star War Jedi Training Academy.

Day 1—Evening

Get a FASTPASS for the Autopia.

Ride Buzz Lightyear Astro Blasters.

See Innoventions or have dinner.

Ride the Autopia.

Ride "it's a small world."

Watch the parade.

Ride the Astro Orbitor.

As the children get tired, the adults can choose some rides, using the parent swap if necessary.

Watch the fireworks.

Head back to the hotel and rest up for Day 2.

Day 2—Morning

Eat at one of the character breakfasts before the park opens.

On entering the park, head to the Finding Nemo Submarine Voyage and ride it.

Go to Mickey's Toontown.

Ride Roger Rabbit's Car Toon Spin.

Ride Gadget's Go Coaster.

Line up at Mickey's House and get a family picture.

Visit Minnie's House.

Day 2—Afternoon

Ride the Disneyland Railroad.

Eat lunch in Frontierland or Critter Country.

Ride the canoes and/or riverboats.

Ride the Many Adventures of Winnie the Pooh.

If the children are old enough, take the rafts over to Pirate's Lair on Tom Sawyer Island.

Ride the Jungle Cruise.

Day 2—Evening

Have dinner in New Orleans Square.

Ride Pirates of the Caribbean.

Go on any other rides you missed or want to try again.

See *Fantasmic!*

Sample Two-Day Touring Plan (Children 7 and Up)

Day 1—Morning

At the start, head to the Indiana Jones Adventure and pick up a FASTPASS.

Then go to Café Orleans or the Blue Bayou restaurant and make reservations for around 2 PM if you did not call ahead for reservations.

Continue on to ride Splash Mountain.

If it's time for the Indiana Jones Adventure, pick up a FASTPASS for Big Thunder Mountain Railroad and then return to Adventureland.

Ride the Indiana Jones Adventure.

Ride Pirates of the Caribbean.

Ride Big Thunder Mountain Railroad.

Ride the Haunted Mansion.

Day 1—Afternoon

Pick up a FASTPASS for one of the rides you want to do again.

Have lunch at Cafe Orleans or the Blue Bayou Restaurant.

Ride the Jungle Cruise.

Ride the FASTPASS attraction you selected before lunch.

Ride canoes or riverboat.

Take rafts to Pirate's Lair on Tom Sawyer Island.

Day 1—Evening

Pick up a FASTPASS for Big Thunder Mountain Railroad.

Have dinner in Frontierland.

Ride Big Thunder Mountain Railroad.

Watch the parade.

Watch the fireworks.

Hit some of the popular rides or Fantasyland as people begin to leave.

Day 2—Morning

At the start, head for Space Mountain and pick up a FASTPASS.

Continue on to ride the Finding Nemo Submarine Voyage.

Ride the Matterhorn bobsleds.

Get a FASTPASS for Autopia.

Ride Space Mountain.

Ride Star Tours.

Ride Autopia.

Day 2—Afternoon

Have lunch in Tomorrowland.

Ride the Astro Orbitor.

Pick up a FASTPASS for Buzz Lightyear Astro Blaster.

See Innoventions.

Ride Buzz Lightyear Astro Blaster.

Day 2—Evening

See attractions you missed earlier or want to do again.

Have a light dinner.

See *Fantasmic!*

Ride the Matterhorn and other popular rides before the park closes.

Depending on how busy Disneyland is when you visit, you may have to either delete some of the attractions from the plan or add more to fill in time.

Three Days or More at Disneyland

If you have time for three or more days at Disneyland, use the two-day touring plan and then fill it in with more attractions. From talking to different families, as well as from personal experience, we have found that spending three days or more at Disneyland lets you take a more leisurely pace and makes your family's vacation less stressful. You have time to go back to the hotel and take a nap or go for a swim without feeling as if you'll miss something. Also, you have more time to spend at Disneyland for shows as well as the attractions that you can see at your leisure, such as Innoventions or Pirate's Lair on Tom Sawyer Island.

During the mornings, still try to hit as many of the popular attractions as possible; then relax during the afternoon, picking up the pace a bit in the evening. Families that purchase a four- or five-day Park Hopper ticket may want to spend a day at other attractions in Southern California and then come back to Disneyland in the evening. No matter how you choose to spend your time, we suggest spending the last day of your vacation at Disneyland as "favorites" day, going back to the attractions you liked best for one last time.

Because you have more time at Disneyland, you can also spend some of it shopping as well as experiencing the number of great restaurants. In addition to those inside, there are now

Insider's Secret

The Disney cast members are very knowledgeable and always happy to help. Feel free to ask them questions about attractions, shows, characters, dining, and so forth. They are a great source of information if it is your first visit, and we still learn a lot by talking to cast members. (Some may even provide hints for spotting Hidden Mickeys.)

a number of great shops and dining establishments just outside the park, at Downtown Disney.

Disneyland FASTPASS Rides

At this writing Disneyland is currently offering the FASTPASS system on the following attractions:

- Autopia
- Big Thunder Mountain Railroad
- Buzz Lightyear's Astro Blaster
- Indiana Jones Adventure
- Roger Rabbit's Car Toon Spin
- Space Mountain
- Splash Mountain

Time-Saving Tip

Both Splash Mountain and Indiana Jones Adventure offer single-rider service. If only one person in your group wants to ride (or you don't mind being split up), cast members will select guests from this much shorter line to fill in empty seats. Speak to the cast member at the entrance to get a single rider pass, and he or she will direct you where to go.

As a general rule, you should always try to have a FASTPASS for some attraction in your possession. You might as well be waiting for a FASTPASS time while waiting in line for another attraction, watching a show, or having a meal.

For more information on using the FASTPASS system, *see* Chapter 4.

The FASTPASS system may later be added to other attractions. During November and December, a temporary FASTPASS system is added to the holiday version of "it's a small world."

The Lands of the Magic Kingdom

Disneyland is divided into eight different lands—Main Street, Fantasyland, Tomorrowland, Mickey's Toontown, Frontierland, Adventureland, New Orleans Square, and Critter Country. Each has its own unique theme, and the cast members dress differently depending on where they're working. The remainder of the chapter is organized by land. Each section contains information on the attractions in that land, shows you can see there, where to meet characters, basic tips for saving time in the land, and brief descriptions of the dining and shopping in the land.

The Scare Factor

In the following Quick Guide, as well as others covering attractions and rides, there's a column listing the scare factor for attractions. This provides a general guide for how frightening

Time-Saving Tip
Don't forget to use the parent swap if you have small children who are unable to go on a ride. This allows part of a group to go on a ride while the rest stay with the younger children. When the first group is through, the waiting group can then go on without having to wait in the line again. This works great if you're waiting for a ride with height or age restrictions or if you have a baby sleeping in the stroller. *See* Chapter 4 for more information on this service.

the ride may be for young children. The causes for this range from a ride in the dark to a wild, breathtaking roller coaster or even an attraction where things pop out at you. To find out just what makes a ride scary, read the description of the ride within the chapter. Here's a key for the scare factor for this and other chapters in this book:

0 Not scary at all.

! Might be somewhat frightening for some children. Usually either dark or a mild roller coaster.

!! Most young children will find this scary.

!!! This attraction may frighten some adults. This is usually reserved for high-speed roller coasters and other thrill rides.

Main Street, USA

After entering the Magic Kingdom at the main gates and passing through one of the two tunnels under the railroad, you'll find yourself on Main Street, USA. It's designed to represent a typical American town around 1900. Although Main Street consists mostly of shops, there are a few attractions here as well. As you stroll down the street, you may hear ragtime music, a barbershop quartet, or similar entertainment from this era. The streets are lined with gaslights that once lighted the city of Baltimore, and the two cannons in the Town Square are French-made guns from the Franco-Prussian War.

Although most guests rush down Main Street to get to the rest of the Magic Kingdom, there's a lot to see here. If you have the time, check out the buildings that line the streets and the fake shops on the second and third floors—the names of the proprietors are actual people who had a part in building Disneyland or were corporate executives. You may notice that the ground level seems a bit shorter than usual. This is espe-

Hidden Mickeys

In recent years, more and more of the general public has started playing the game of spotting Hidden Mickeys—those outlines of the Mouse that are placed in just about everything built by or for Disney, including their hotels, restaurants, and stores as well as their theme-park attractions. With all the excitement over finding Hidden Mickeys, people are finding them everywhere—even where there are none. Therefore, there must be a standard. The following list gives the most commonly agreed-on ground rules we have been able to find.

1. The Mickey must consist of three circles—two smaller circles of the same approximate size attached to a larger circle to make the famous head and ears.

2. The Mickey must be intentionally placed, not an accidental arrangement.

3. The Mickey must be hidden. A Mickey pattern in carpet or wallpaper or other repeated use of the image does not count as a Hidden Mickey.

Now that the basic rules are in place, you're ready to begin your hunt. There are more than enough Hidden Mickeys at Disneyland to write a complete book about. We mention a few in the descriptions of the rides and attractions; however, this represents only a small fraction of those out there. Check out www.hiddenmickeys.org for more locations. While visiting Disneyland, politely ask cast members about Hidden Mickeys on the various attractions. Although most will not tell you specifically where one is, some may offer hints on where to look. Looking for Hidden Mickeys can add a new excitement to Disneyland for those on their first visit as well as veterans. Have fun, and good luck on your hunt!

Quick Guide to

Attraction	Location	Height or Age Requirement
Alice in Wonderland	Fantasyland	None
Astro Orbitor	Tomorrowland	None
Autopia	Tomorrowland	54 inches to drive, 32 inches to ride
Big Thunder Mountain Railroad	Frontierland	40 inches
Buzz Lightyear Astro Blasters	Tomorrowland	None
Casey Jr. Circus Train	Fantasyland	None
Davy Crockett's Explorer Canoes	Critter Country	None
Disneyland Monorail	Tomorrowland	None
Disneyland Railroad	Main Street	None
The Disneyland Story	Main Street, USA	None
Dumbo the Flying Elephant	Fantasyland	None (7 years to ride alone)
Enchanted Tiki Room	Adventureland	None
Fantasmic!	Frontierland	None
Finding Nemo Submarine Voyage	Tomorrowland	None
Frontierland Shootin' Exposition	Frontierland	None
Gadget's Go Coaster	Toontown	35 inches
Golden Horseshoe Stage	Frontierland	None

0 Not scary at all.
! Might be somewhat frightening for some children. Usually either dark or a mild roller coaster.
!! Most young children will find this scary.
!!! This attraction may frighten some adults. This is usually reserved for high-speed roller coasters and other thrill rides.

Disneyland Attractions

Duration	Scare Factor	Age Range
4 minutes	0	All
1½ minutes	0	3 and up
Approx. 4 minutes	0	All
2 minutes	0	All
15 minutes	0	All
3 minutes	0	All
Approx. 10 minutes	0	5 and up
N/A	0	All
N/A	0	All
Approx. 25 minutes	0	All
2 minutes	0	All
Approx. 15 minutes	0	All
Approx. 25 minutes	!	All
14 minutes	!	4 and up
N/A	0	7 and up
1 minute	0	3 and up
Approx. 15 minutes	0	All

(continues)

Quick Guide to

Attraction	Location	Height or Age Requirement
Goofy's Playhouse	Toontown	None
Haunted Mansion	New Orleans Square	None
Honey, I Shrunk the Audience	Tomorrowland	None
Indiana Jones Adventure	Adventureland	46 inches
Innoventions	Tomorrowland	None
"it's a small world"	Fantasyland	None
Jungle Cruise	Adventureland	None
King Arthur Carousel	Fantasyland	None
Mad Tea Party	Fantasyland	None
The Many Adventures of Winnie the Pooh	Critter Country	None
Mark Twain Riverboat	Frontierland	None
Matterhorn Bobsleds	Fantasyland	35 inches
Mickey's House	Toontown	None
Minnie's House	Toontown	None
Mr. Toad's Wild Ride	Fantasyland	None
Peter Pan's Flight	Fantasyland	None
Pinocchio's Daring Journey	Fantasyland	None

0 Not scary at all.
! Might be somewhat frightening for some children. Usually either dark or a mild roller coaster.
!! Most young children will find this scary.
!!! This attraction may frighten some adults. This is usually reserved for high-speed roller coasters and other thrill rides.

Disneyland Attractions

Duration	Scare Factor	Age Range
N/A	0	3 to 7
Approx. 7 minutes	!!	5 and up
Approx. 25 minutes	!	4 and up
3 minutes	!!!	7 and up
N/A	0	All
Approx. 12 minutes	0	All
8 minutes	0	All
2 minutes	0	All
1½ minutes	0	3 and up
2½ minutes	0	All
14 minutes	0	All
Approx. 2 minutes	!	4 and up
N/A	0	All
N/A	0	All
2 minutes	!	4 and up
2 minutes	0	All
3 minutes	!	4 and up

(continues)

Quick Guide to

Attraction	Location	Height or Age Requirement
Pirate's Lair on Tom Sawyer Island	Frontierland	None
Pirates of the Caribbean	New Orleans Square	None
Roger Rabbit's Car Toon Spin	Toontown	None
Sailing Ship *Columbia*	Frontierland	None
Snow White's Scary Adventures	Fantasyland	None
Space Mountain	Tomorrowland	40 inches
Splash Mountain	Critter Country	40 inches
Star Tours	Tomorrowland	40 inches
Storybook Land Canal Boats	Fantasyland	None
Tarzan's Treehouse	Adventureland	None

0 Not scary at all.
 ! Might be somewhat frightening for some children. Usually either dark or a mild roller coaster.
!! Most young children will find this scary.
!!! This attraction may frighten some adults. This is usually reserved for high-speed roller coasters and other thrill rides.

Disneyland Attractions

Duration	Scare Factor	Age Range
N/A	0	5 and up
Approx. 14 minutes	!	4 and up
3 minutes	0	5 and up
14 minutes	0	All
2 minutes	!	4 and up
Approx. 3 minutes	!!!	7 and up
Approx. 10 minutes	!	5 and up
7 minutes	!!	5 and up
10 minutes	0	All
Approx. 10 minutes	0	All

cially apparent at the porch with a bench on it. The ground level is really ⅞ scale, whereas the second floor is ⅝ scale, and the third floor is ½ scale. The buildings were designed this way to give the impression that they are actually taller than in reality, using the technique of forced perspective.

Main Street, USA, is also the business part of the Magic Kingdom. City Hall is the information center, where you can inquire about shows and guides for guests with disabilities, as well as pick up lost children. This is also the place to find out where and when specific characters will appear throughout the park.

AAA has a Touring and Travel Services Center, where all guests can purchase traveler's checks or AAA memberships. AAA members can pick up maps and tour guides and take advantage of several other services, such as hotel reservations and complimentary towing. The Baby Care Center has facilities for preparing formula and baby food, nursing, and changing diapers. It also sells various baby sundries.

 Helpful Hint
You can fold up your stroller and take it on the train with you. Otherwise, you'll have to go back to the station where you boarded to pick up your stroller instead of getting off at a different station during your ride.

Disneyland Railroad
The main station for the Disneyland Railroad is at the south end of Main Street and is the first thing guests see as they enter the park. Here you can board one of five steam-powered trains that circumnavigate the Magic Kingdom. (The number of trains running depends on the day and the expected crowd.) The train also makes stops at New Orleans Square, Mickey's Toontown, and Tomorrowland. In between the Tomorrowland and Main Street stations, the train passes through a large diorama depict-

Insider's Secret

If it's a slow day and the railroad is not very busy, ask one of the conductors if you can ride in the steam engine. Each has either one or two jumpseats, which are for adults only. The conductor will ask the engineer if it's all right. Main Street Station is the only place where you can board and disembark from the engine. Be warned that the engineer's compartment is oily.

ing the Grand Canyon. After passing by the various wildlife of this area, the train continues into the Primeval World, which has 46 animated dinosaurs. Although most young children love this part and want to see it again, it may be scary for some. You can either get off at Tomorrowland before the diorama or just tell them to close their eyes. Usually the dark tunnel preceding the diorama is scarier than the animatronic dinosaurs. The train takes around 20 minutes to circle the park.

The Disneyland Story, featuring "Great Moments with Mr. Lincoln"

Housed in the Disneyland Opera House, this attraction has two parts. First, there's a museum-type exhibit with artifacts from Disneyland's history. You can see original tickets for the park, original design sketches, and a scale model of Disneyland

Insider's Secret

This attraction is a good place to visit in the afternoon. It's usually not crowded and offers a chance to sit down and rest for a while. Unlike with other attractions, you can stay as long as you want, and on hot days, the air-conditioning makes it nice for cooling down.

Insider's Secret

If you have any problems or issues with rides, FAST-PASSes, cast members, or other guests, head to guest services at City Hall. They will try to make it up to you in some way. This is also the place to go to leave praise or compliments for cast members. If the skipper on the Jungle Cruise was extremely hilarious or a cast member offered great service, stop in and leave a comment.

as it appeared in 1955. The second part of the attraction features a slide show of the Civil War narrated by an actor portraying Matthew Brady, the famous photographer of this conflict. When it is over, a seated audio-animatronic Abraham Lincoln rises and begins speaking. His dialogue is taken from various speeches the president made.

This is a good attraction for the entire family. Young children like to look at the model of Disneyland, and older children will like the exhibit as well as the Civil War portion. Mr. Lincoln's speech is very stirring and patriotic, and children who have studied the president will be impressed. Younger children may

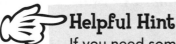

Helpful Hint

If you need some cash, ATMs are at the main entrance, at the Bank of Main Street, and in Frontierland, Fantasyland, and Tomorrowland.

not care for the Civil War portion. However, you can leave after viewing the Disneyland exhibit and before entering the theater.

Main Street Cinema

This small theater continuously plays old Mickey Mouse cartoons. Since the theater is air-conditioned, it makes a good place to take a break. Children also usually like to see the older

Insider's Secret

If you're at Disneyland on a family member's birthday, be sure to tell a cast member at City Hall. He or she will give you a personalized sticker to wear. People wearing these stickers will be wished happy birthday by cast members throughout the day, and characters will give them special attention.

cartoons, which are rarely shown outside this theater. If your family is waiting on Main Street for a parade, part of your group can go watch some of the cartoons while the rest hold the spot. Then you all can swap so everyone has a chance to enjoy the entertainment.

Main Street Vehicles

Four different vehicles travel along Main Street, carrying passengers from Town Square to Central Plaza. You can choose to ride a horse-drawn streetcar, a fire engine, a horseless carriage, or an omnibus. Each has its own stop at either end of Main Street, and the ride is one-way only. They stop operating in the afternoon or an hour or more before the parades begin. Although young children may enjoy the ride, older children will want to get on to the rides in other areas of the park.

Central Plaza

At the opposite end of Main Street from the train station, Central Plaza is the hub of the Magic Kingdom. The Partners

Fun Fact

Walt Disney used to stay in an apartment over the Fire Station. As a memorial to Disneyland's founder, a light in the window remains lighted at all times. During the holidays, the light is replaced by a small Christmas tree.

statue, featuring Walt and Mickey, stands in the middle and makes a great place for a family photo. If you look at the ring on Walt's finger, you will see a Hidden Mickey.

Shows

Although Main Street does not have any shows per se, you can find live performers here throughout the day. There's usually a pianist at the Refreshment Corner. Keep an eye out for the Dapper Dans. This quartet sings while pedaling down Main Street on a four-person bicycle. Just after the park officially opens, the Disneyland Marching Band parades from Town Square, down Main Street, through Sleeping Beauty's Castle, and into Fantasyland. At times they'll board the King Arthur Carrousel and treat guests to a rousing performance that may include the "William Tell Overture" (the theme from the *Lone Ranger*). At sunset each day you can watch a short ceremony as the flag at Town Square is lowered.

Fun Fact

The Main Street Station contains a display of a model train that was hand-built by Walt Disney himself.

Helpful Hint

In the Central Plaza, near the entrance to Adventureland, is an information center. The cast member here can provide information on show times and most other types of questions. In addition, there's an information board showing which attractions are closed for the day and approximate wait times for the more popular attractions. Because this is in the center of Disneyland, pass by here after you leave one area to help plan where you should go next.

Character Greetings

Children can meet several different characters near Town Square and by the Fire Station. These characters are usually here from park opening until later in the afternoon.

Main Street Tips

Although Main Street is the first area you enter at Disneyland, just walk right down to the end and head to one of the other areas containing popular rides. It's better to come back to Main Street later and use the attractions here as a break or rest for the children.

Main Street opens 30 minutes before the rest of the park. If you arrive that early, while you're waiting you might want to pick up a cinnamon roll and some orange juice or a hot drink, or browse through the many shops.

People begin lining up along Main Street 30 minutes to an hour before a parade. If you want to view the parade here, get your place early. Otherwise, make sure you stay clear of the area until after the parade has passed. The crowds can be difficult to get through, especially with a stroller.

Dining on Main Street

Main Street is a great place to have a snack or lunch because most guests are in other parts of the park and eating there. The Plaza Inn serves a character-breakfast buffet in the morning and buffeteria-style dining for lunch and dinner. Carnation Café, the only table-service restaurant on Main Street, serves salads, sandwiches, and other meals. At Refreshment Corner you can find foot-long hot dogs and Mickey Mouse pretzels. The Blue Ribbon Bakery serves great cinnamon rolls and other baked goodies. For ice cream or frozen yogurt, try the Gibson Girl Ice Cream Parlor or the Main Street Cone Shop for just ice cream. Seasonally, there are two carts near the Plaza Inn. One sells corn dogs—the only ones in the park—and the other sells turkey legs and chimichangas. There's also a fruit stand that sells a variety of seasonal fruit. For more details on these restaurants, including pricing and sample menus, *see* Chapter 8.

Main Street Shopping

You can do almost all of your shopping on Main Street. The Emporium stocks just about every Disneyland souvenir imaginable. There are also several other specialty shops that line Main Street. Disneyana sells Disney collectibles, including figurines and animation cels, along with other types of limited-edition art. At the 20th Century Music Company you can find all types of Disney music, including sheet music to play yourself. The Candy Palace sells yummy treats, some of which are made in a kitchen with a large window facing Main Street. During the Christmas season, be sure to ask one of the cast members in the shop when they'll be making candy canes. It's fun to watch; if you want to buy some, stay close because they sell as fast as they're packaged. Adjacent to this shop is the Penny Arcade, where you can find penny-type candy as well as old-time arcade games to play. The China Closet carries snow globes and figurines, and Crystal Arts sells glass and crystal creations. Be careful taking small children into these two shops. Disney Clothiers, Ltd. sells fashionable clothing (not souvenir-

Helpful Hint

No matter what your budget, you can find something on Main Street to remind you of your visit to Disneyland. The inexpensive Mickey and Minnie antenna balls are very popular. DVDs and CDs are also great ways to relive your vacation long after you have returned home. Note that most of the merchandise you find at Disneyland is available nowhere else—not even at the Disney Stores in many shopping malls. However, if you forget something you just have to have, you can call the Disneyland order line: 800/362–4533.

type T-shirts) and accessories that feature Disney characters in some way. The Disney Showcase is the place for other types of Disney character clothing.

The Main Street Magic Shop stocks not only magic tricks but also gags and books on the subject. Need some mouse ears? The Mad Hatter Shop can help cover you with a variety of headwear. The Main Street Photo Supply Company sells cameras and film and will even help you with your camera if it develops problems. If you have souvenir photos taken by a cast member somewhere in the park, this is where you go to view and purchase them. You can also find some nice frames for displaying your family's photo. The Market House has gourmet food, kitchen accessories, and treats. New Century Jewelry offers Disney-inspired pieces, and Fortuosity is the place for watches and clocks as well as unique accessories, apparel, and gift items. Finally, at the Silhouette Studio, you can buy portraits made of a cut-out paper outline. At this store, watching your souvenir being created is not only interesting but also half the fun.

Fantasyland

Fantasyland is where many of Disney's animated features come to life. The area has a medieval European village theme, with Sleeping Beauty's Castle as the focal point. There are several attractions here, and because this is where many of the kiddie rides are located, Fantasyland can become quite congested, even

Time-Saving Tip

If your family is using a stroller, park it in one location while in Fantasyland. All of the attractions are fairly close to one another, so it's easier to just carry a small child from one ride to the next rather than loading and unloading the stroller at each place.

on a day with a moderate number of guests. Families with younger children are likely to spend quite a bit of time here, probably going on some of the rides a number of times.

Fun Fact

Sleeping Beauty's Castle is adorned by a number of 22-karat gold-plated spires. However, you may notice that one spire is not gold plated. Walt Disney did this as a reminder of his quote that Disneyland would never be completed as long as there was imagination left in the world. The shield over the drawbridge displays the Disney family crest.

Sleeping Beauty Castle Walkthrough

This attraction takes you up into the castle, where you'll walk past three-dimensional scenes telling the tale of Princess Aurora. The attraction also includes special effects. The exhibit requires climbing up and down several flights of stairs. For those guests who have trouble with stairs, a ground-floor chamber features a "virtual experience" which includes all of the scenes from the walkthrough projected onto a single screen.

King Arthur Carrousel

It was during weekend visits riding the carousel at Griffith Park with his young daughters that Walt Disney first began thinking of creating Disneyland. Therefore, it's no surprise that he wanted his carousel as the center of Fantasyland. The ride contains 72 unique horses that were carved more than 100 years ago in Germany. This ride is a favorite for children of all ages, and there's rarely a long line because it can accommodate so many guests at a time. The carousel plays Disney music as it goes around and is a sight at night when all lighted up.

Helpful Hint

For a great place to watch the fireworks display, sit on the planters that surround the carousel, on the side toward Mr. Toad's Wild Ride. Not only can you sit down, but you're also in perfect position to view Tinker Bell as she flies right over you.

Peter Pan's Flight

One of the five dark rides in Fantasyland, Peter Pan's Flight carries guests in hanging pirate ships out through the nursery window, over London, and on a journey to Never Land. The ride does an excellent job following the story line of the movie, and most children of all ages will enjoy it. Some children may not like the darkness of the ride. However, we have found that if you point out different things to look at, they'll soon forget that the ride is dark and want to go on it again. There are several Hidden Mickeys in this ride—look for one on the moon while flying over London.

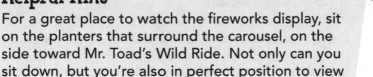

Fun Fact

As you go through the nursery, notice the picture of Mickey Mouse and the blocks on the floor that spell *Peter, Pan,* and *Disney.* (The *s* in *Disney* is an upside-down 5.)

Mr. Toad's Wild Ride

One of the more popular rides in Fantasyland, Mr. Toad's Wild Ride usually has the longest lines of the five dark rides. It takes guests on little motor cars through various scenes from the movie *The Adventures of Ichabod and Mr. Toad.* After crashing through

The Scare Factor

Although small children often want to ride this attraction because they can turn the steering wheel on the car and pretend they are really driving, many get scared during the ride, especially during the inferno at the end.

Fun Fact

Above the entrance to the attraction, a shield bears the motto *Toadi Acceleratio Semper Absurda*. Translated from the Latin, this means "Speeding with Toad is always absurd."

a fireplace, the cars take you through a number of close calls due to Toad's crazy driving, before ending in a fiery inferno with heat added for realism.

Snow White's Scary Adventures

Just as its name suggests, this ride can be scary for little children. Guests board mine cars and ride along through scenes from the movie, including the house of the Seven Dwarfs, the mine where they work, a dungeon, and a scary forest. The evil queen even offers you a poisoned apple (it's a hologram). Even during the scary parts, you can point out things that aren't so scary to divert kids' attention. In the room where Snow White is going up the stairs, look at the shell of the turtle to find a Hidden Mickey.

The Scare Factor

Some children may be frightened by Snow White's Scary Adventures, but others really like it. Use their reactions to scary parts of the movie as a way to judge what their reactions might be.

Insider's Secret

Watch the windows above the entrance to this ride. Every so often, the evil queen looks out from behind a curtain. Also, when you're at the entrance to the ride, be sure to touch the golden apple. It will cause thunder to sound and the evil queen to give a wicked laugh. Also look for the hidden Mickey created in red gem stones on the right side as you go through the mine.

Pinocchio's Daring Journey

Similar to the other dark rides, this one takes you through various scenes from the movie. It tends to be a bit scary in several places, such as when Monstro the Whale jumps up at you, Stromboli tries to cage you, or the bad guys on Pleasure Island try to crate you up and ship you off to the salt mines. However, the scary parts pass quickly.

The Scare Factor

The darkness of Pinocchio's Daring Journey is usually what frightens young children the most. See how they do on Peter Pan's Flight first, and if the darkness is no problem, they'll probably be fine on this one as long as a parent or older sibling is sitting next to them.

Insider's Secret

At the end of the ride, be sure to point out the Blue Fairy to kids. She appears only for a moment, and if you're looking somewhere else, you'll miss her. It's a neat effect. Also, look for Jiminy Cricket with his new badge. If you are looking for a hidden Mickey in this ride, look down at the popcorn painted on the ground in the Pleasure Island section.

Alice in Wonderland

On this ride, you travel in caterpillars following the White Rabbit through Wonderland. Although this is listed as a dark ride, Alice in Wonderland is actually quite bright. There are several special effects and lots of things to look at. In fact, be sure to look in all directions, even behind you, as some characters are difficult to see until you pass them by. After meeting the Queen of Hearts and then escaping from her deck of card retainers, the ride continues on to the Mad Tea Party, with an exploding "unbirthday" cake as the finale.

The Scare Factor

Young children should have no trouble on this ride because there's so much to look at and none of it is scary.

Insider's Secret

If you look down at the pathway outside this attraction, you'll see the footprints of the White Rabbit. Also look for a Hidden Mickey in the scene where the cards are painting the roses red. On a rock on the left side, you'll see three paint drops that make the classic design.

Fun Fact

While going through the five dark rides, you may notice that the main character in each rarely appears. For example, Alice and Snow White appear only once in their respective rides. The reason is that in each ride, you're supposed to be experiencing the story as the main character.

Dumbo the Flying Elephant

This has to be one of the most popular rides for younger children. There's almost always a long wait here, even on slow to moderate days. On busy days, waits can be up to an hour long. Part of the attraction is your ability to make the little elephants go up and down as they fly around in a circle. All the while, a circus-type organ belts out Disney tunes. Children 7 years and up can ride alone (this is a rite of passage in our family).

Usually the busiest time on this ride is late morning through the afternoon. Get to this ride early and do it a few times before the queue lengthens. In the evening, the lines shorten as families with young children begin to leave the park.

Insider's Secret

You can do a parent swap on this ride if you have a baby that is asleep or you just don't want to take your baby on the Dumbos. Just have the parent in the queue tell one of the cast members that you want to do a parent swap and explain why. They'll then let the other parent in after the first parent and child are finished. If you have only one child in addition to the baby, that child can go on the ride twice in a row without having to wait.

Casey Jr. Circus Train

Based on the train that carried Dumbo and his circus around the country, this attraction takes you on a ride around Storybook Land. You can ride in one of two gondola cars or the caboose. However, most children want to ride in either the Wild Animal or Monkey Cage

Fun Fact

The Casey Jr. Circus Train was originally planned as Disneyland's first roller coaster ride.

cars. Although these are a bit cramped for adults, children love to look out through the bars. This ride is fun for all ages, and the lines can move pretty quickly because two trains often run at a time. On slower days, only one train runs, making the wait a bit longer. However, the line is usually shorter to begin with.

Mad Tea Party

For this ride, you sit in oversize teacups reminiscent of the tea party in Disney's animated classic *Alice in Wonderland* and spin them by turning a wheel in the center. Because you control the speed of rotation, you can make it as mild or as wild as you want. The queue for the Mad Tea Party can vary without regard to time of day. One moment you can walk right on; 10 minutes later you may have to wait. This is one ride for which it's a good idea to check the queue as you walk by. If it's not busy, go for it. Otherwise, check back later.

Insider's Secret

The plain lavender cup seems to be the fastest in our opinion, though other families claim different cups have more speed. However, there are a few things you can do to make any of the cups go fast. First, spread out your weight as evenly as possible. Adults should sit across from each other rather than together. Second, take turns spinning the wheel. If more than two people are turning the wheel, their hands will usually get in each other's way. Even two people need to synchronize their moves. Finally, all riders should lean toward the center as much as possible without getting in the way of the person turning the wheel. Sometimes, when things are slow, the cast member operating the ride may serve as a judge and announce which teacup is spinning the fastest.

Storybook Land Canal Boats

The canal boats take guests into the mouth of Monstro the Whale and then on through miniature villages and buildings based on classic Disney movies. All the plants here are real. The towering 12-inch pines and other trees are really bonsai trees shaped to look like larger trees. There's no animation on this ride, and often boys do not care for it much. Girls seem to like it better: the small buildings are a lot like dollhouses. The canal boats travel past Cinderella's Castle, the houses of the Three Little Pigs, the castle of Agrabah from *Aladdin,* the home of the Seven Dwarfs, Prince Eric's castle and ship from *The Little Mermaid,* and much more. This ride closes before and during parades. Right after the parade passes, it will start up again, so if you're close by, get in line and the wait will be short.

Helpful Hint

To make the ride more enjoyable for the whole family, make a game out of seeing who can find unique details throughout Storybook Land. Can you find the White Rabbit's mailbox, Cinderella's coach, or the mine of the Seven Dwarfs? Also, try riding this at night. All of the little buildings are lighted up and it's a different experience than during the day.

"it's a small world"

This ride will fascinate young children, and even older children will like going through it once. Don't be surprised if your little ones begin singing along or even dancing to the music. The tune is infectious and will stay in your mind for the rest of the day. The queue for this ride is usually not too long, and even if it is, it moves quickly. This ride is a great way to take a 12-minute break, and in summer the air-conditioning inside can be quite welcome. It also provides an opportunity for mothers

Insider's Secret

Recently several new dolls dressed as characters from Disney films have been added. Look for Peter Pan, Alice, Cinderella, Pinocchio, Mulan, Jasmine and Aladdin, Timon and Pumba, Ariel, Lilo and Stitch, and Woody and Jessie.

to nurse babies while keeping the other children entertained at the same time. Outside on the quarter hour, the clock chimes and numerous wooden children parade around the clock. Throughout the fireworks show, this attraction may be closed.

During the winter holiday season, beginning in mid-November and lasting through December, the ride is transformed into a holiday version. "Jingle Bells" is interspersed with the standard tune. The mermaids have their own version of the holiday classic—"Jingle Shells."

Helpful Hint

The best place to sit in these boats is the front row. If you're assigned a different row, just ask the cast member if you can wait for the next boat and sit up front. Not only do you have a better view because no one is in front blocking your children, but also this row has more space for stowing backpacks and other carry-on items.

Matterhorn Bobsleds

Disneyland's first roller coaster, the Matterhorn Bobsleds, was actually the first tubular steel roller coaster in the world—designed to give a smooth ride similar to an actual bobsled. Riders board sleds that can seat up to eight people (two per seat) and are then pulled up a dark climb. At the top of the climb, the sleds begin their downward journey to the bottom, passing through tunnels inside the mountain as well as around the outside. You pass by the growling abominable snowman a few times during your descent. The ride ends with a splashdown in an alpine lake. The ride is a bit wilder than Big Thunder Mountain, mainly because

Insider's Secret

There are two different tracks on the Matterhorn, and each gives a bit of a different ride. The right queue, next to Alice in Wonderland, is the slower side. The turns are a bit wider, and there are no sudden drops. This side also has a more scenic ride because it's on the outside track. The left queue, toward Tomorrowland, is the faster track. The turns are tighter, and there's one quick drop as your sled dives beneath the other track. The ride on the right, slower track is about 30 seconds longer than the one on the left, faster track. No matter which track you ride, to maximize your thrills ask the cast member seating guests the best place to sit. The cast member is usually happy to strategically place your party. The main key is to put the heavier people in back.

the cars are smaller and whip around tighter turns. The minimum height requirement for this ride is 35 inches. Although a few 4-year-olds are fine on the ride, most children should wait until they are 5 or 6 years old. The dark climb and the abominable snowman (rather than the motion of the sleds) seem to be the scariest part of the ride for young children. Our daughter Beth rode it when she was 3. She just closed her eyes during the climb and when the snowman went by. The snowman is rather small, and your bobsled rushes by him quickly.

Pixie Hollow
Near the walkway from Main Street to the Matterhorn, this garden features Tinker Bell and her fairy friends. Follow the

winding path leading past an enchanted pond, and you'll feel like you've shrunken down to fairy size yourself as you're surrounded by giant plants and flower. At night, the gardens are lighted and are quite beautiful.

Snow White's Grotto

This quiet little spot is to the east of the moat around Sleeping Beauty's Castle. There are statues of Snow White and the Seven Dwarfs here next to a waterfall fountain. You can hear Snow White singing "I'm Wishing" here. Although the Snow White statue appears larger than those of the dwarfs, it's actually about the same size. Disneyland again used forced perspective to make her look larger by putting her up higher.

Shows

Though there are currently no shows playing at the Fantasyland Theatre, the area does host the Disney Princess Fantasy Faire. In addition to meeting Disney Princesses, you can also watch the Royal Coronation Ceremony, which takes place several times each day. Young children will become princesses and knights during this short show. In addition, there are a number of craft stations open throughout the day. Be sure to check the times for the show as well as the hours the faire is open. In summer you can stop by from 10 AM to 6 PM. The faire can be closed on some days during the off season.

The Sword in the Stone ceremony takes place near the King Arthur Carrousel, daily in summer and on weekends the rest of the time. Merlin chooses a child to pull Excalibur from the stone. If you have little children, be sure to see this.

Character Greetings

All of the characters in Fantasyland can be found in two specific locations. Tinker Bell and her fairy friends are in Pixie Hollow, while various Disney princesses are happy to meet guests at the Disney Princess Fantasy Faire.

Fantasyland Tips

If you plan on visiting Fantasyland, do it first thing in the day. As the morning progresses, this area just gets busier. Even if you want to hit some of the more popular rides throughout the park, take your young children on the Dumbos and a few of the dark rides before heading for the Indiana Jones Adventure or another popular ride. After the park has been open for a couple of hours, Fantasyland is usually quite busy. Things die down in the evening hours as families with young children begin to leave. So come back after 7 PM and try the rides you missed earlier, or do them all again.

If you want to go from Tomorrowland or Toontown to Frontierland, don't think you can save time by cutting through Fantasyland. The area is usually congested, and it's faster just to go through the Central Plaza.

Fantasyland offers some great places to take a family picture. The main spot is in front of Sleeping Beauty's Castle. However, you can also get some great shots elsewhere, such as at the Mad Tea Party, on the stationary Dumbo next to the ride, or even a shot of the children peering through the bars of the Wild Animal Cage on the Casey Jr. Circus Train.

When you first enter the park, check the *Disneyland Today* schedule for the times for the Sword and the Stone Ceremony and to find out when character greetings are taking place.

Dining in Fantasyland

Fantasyland has only two places for meals. The Village Haus Restaurant is across from the Casey Jr. Circus Train along the pathway to Frontierland. Here you can find individual-size pizzas and hamburgers, as well as a limited selection of sandwiches and salads. Enchanted Cottage, Sweets and Treats is near the entrance to the Fantasyland Theatre and is usually open only on the days the Disney Princess Fantasy Faire is available. You can get Bavarian sausages, pretzels, and desserts here. For more de-

Insider's Secret

Fantasyland restaurants do not offer anything exclusive or special. Because this area is often busy, especially during lunchtime and most of the afternoon, it's usually a good idea to eat elsewhere to avoid the crowds.

tails on these restaurants, including pricing and sample menus, *see* Chapter 8.

Fantasyland Shopping

Fantasyland has several quaint little shops where you can purchase souvenirs as well as gifts. The Mad Hatter Shop sells mouse ears and other types of Disney headwear. Even if you don't want to buy anything here, take the children in to see the mirror hung up near the ceiling. Every so often, the Cheshire Cat appears within the mirror and then disappears. Castle Heraldry sells histories of family names as well as a number of items emblazoned with your family crest. The Tinker Bell Toy Shoppe carries all types of Disney toys, including dolls and plush characters. After riding "it's a small world," you exit through "it's a small world" Toy Shop, which sells many types of Mattel toys as well as other popular items. If you're just looking for some quick souvenirs, you can find these at Fantasy Faire Gifts, Le Petit Chalet Gifts, or Stromboli's Wagon.

The Bibbidi Bobbidi Boutique, located in Sleeping Beauty Castle, is a salon where little girls are transformed into Disney princesses. These makeovers can include hair styling, make-up, nail polish, accessories, a princess gown, shoes, wand, and even a photo package. Prices vary depending on the options you select and range from $45 to $200. It is a good idea to make reservations in advance by calling 714/781–7895. Children must be at least 3 years old.

Tomorrowland

When Tomorrowland first opened in 1955, it was designed to show how the future might be in far-off 1987. Since that time, Tomorrowland has undergone a number of makeovers to keep pushing the ever approaching future farther away. In addition to enjoying the attractions, it's fun just to look around this land. The planters are all filled with fruit trees and edible plants. Many children, and even adults, are amazed at what their favorite fruits and vegetables look like on the tree or in the ground.

Astro Orbitor

At the entrance to Tomorrowland, this ride is the centerpiece of the redesigned area. Guests ride in two- or three-passenger rockets as they fly around a constellation of spinning planets. Riders use a control stick to make the rockets go up and down. Basically, this is a Dumbo-type ride that appeals to older children and adults because it goes higher and faster. Although there are no height restrictions, children must be at least 1 year of age and small children must ride with an adult. The queue for this ride is usually shorter than the one for Dumbo, and the Astro Orbitor is fun to ride at night when Tomorrowland is all lighted up.

Fun Fact *Trivia*

When you look at the tail fins of the 12 rockets, notice that each has a different sign of the zodiac.

Finding Nemo Submarine Voyage

Disneyland's newest attraction opened in summer 2007. The destination of your submarine voyage is to an undersea volcano. Along the way, the captain turns on the hydrophones so you can hear the fishes talk—and you get more than you expect. You get to hear the cast from *Finding Nemo* talk to each other. From that point on, the ride tells a story where Marlin is looking for his

Fun Fact

The original submarine ride was the first "E" ticket attraction and opened in 1959. The subs were painted navy gray and named for each of the nuclear submarines in the U.S. Navy fleet at that time—Nautilus, Triton, Sea Wolf, Skate, Skipjack, George Washington, Patrick Henry, and Ethan Allen. These original subs have been painted yellow and blue and renamed for the Finding Nemo Submarine Voyage—Explorer, Scout, Voyager, Mariner, Seafarer, Nautilus, Neptune, and Argonaut.

son Nemo. As you sail on, the characters continue to look for the little guy, and so can you. What is amazing about this attraction is that you're moving through a three-dimensional area, but the Nemo characters appear as two-dimensional animations just like in the movie. This new technology was created just for the attraction. There are two sides of the submarine, but it doesn't matter which side you sit on. You'll see the same things, though not at the same times. Also, the show can vary a bit depending on whether you sit toward the front or the back. You may find Nemo in different places, but you'll see him the same number of times regardless of seating. There are no bad seats.

The submarine will sail through different areas such as a graveyard of sunken ships, along the Eastern Australian Cur-

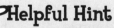

Helpful Hint

Since guests must climb down narrow stairs to get into the submarines, those in wheelchairs who can't navigate the steps can still experience the attraction at the "Observation Outpost." There they can see the same thing guests aboard the subs see, but on a high-definition porthole cam.

Scare Factor!

While most children will want to go on the submarines and see Nemo, there's one scary moment during the voyage. While traveling through an old World War II minefield, some of the mines "explode." As a result the entire submarine shakes, red lights go on inside the sub and a collision siren sounds. This can be frightening to some younger children. However, you can prepare them in advance by watching the movie and explaining during a similar scene that something like that will happen on the submarines at Disneyland, but that everything is safe.

rent, and even meet up with some hungry sharks. Of course, they seem to like canned food and they happen to be looking right at you. But don't worry about the sharks. They won't eat you. However, watch out for whales that tend to swallow submarines whole.

The subs are electric and use a new electrical–magnetic technology known as Inductive Power Transfer, remodeled from the original submarines (used for the Submarine Voyage ride that closed in 1998) that ran on diesel. Another innovation is the way the lagoon is painted. Since sunlight and chlorine fade colors, Disney Imagineers used more than 30 tons of recycled glass that was applied to the lagoon for vibrant colors that won't fade. In fact, the Imagineers even developed more than 40 unique colors just for the lagoon so it would appear like the colorful coral reef in the movie.

Buzz Lightyear Astro Blasters—A FASTPASS Attraction

This attraction takes you to "infinity and beyond." Prospective space rangers board Star Cruisers armed with two laser blasters. As the vehicles rotate 360 degrees, you use the Astro Blasters to shoot at targets and help defeat the Evil Emperor Zurg. This

Fun Fact

At the end of the ride, you can send a photo of your-self on the ride to your home e-mail address. Kiosks are set up for this free souvenir. This is the only at-traction where you can get a free photo. In addition, people at home can play a Buzz Lightyear game on their computers. They're teamed up with guests in a Star Cruiser and work together. As the players at home hit certain objects, targets in the ride light up. If you hit these targets, you can score extra points and provide bonus targets for the players at home.

ride is an interactive experience as you rack up points for each target you hit. Your scores are displayed on the console of the Star Cruiser. Although the ride is in the dark, the targets and characters inside are well lighted; most children don't even re-alize it's dark. Kids love this ride because it's like a giant video game. The competitive nature of the scoring will keep older

Insider's Secret

Throughout the attraction, there are four different types of targets. Each shape is worth a different num-ber of points. Circles are worth 100 points, squares are worth 1,000 points, diamonds are worth 5,000 points, and triangles are worth 10,000 or more points. If these targets are lighted up, they're worth even more. There are also a few secret targets worth a lot of points. Look in between the blocks in the first area as well as between Zurg's chest plates in the two places he appears. Also, as you go through the short, dark tunnel, look for targets that appear as lights along the walls and ceiling. In order to maximize your score, concentrate on the high-value targets and forget about the circles.

children and adults coming back for more as they try to beat their highest score and achieve a higher ranking as a space ranger. If you have time, you'll want to do this more than once.

Star Tours

Did you ever want to enter one of the *Star Wars* movies and take a ride through hyperspace? Star Tours gives you that chance. You board Starspeeders for a flight to Endor, home of the Ewoks. These aircraft are the same type of flight simulators used to train military and commercial pilots. Your Starspeeder is piloted by a robot named Rex. If his voice sounds familiar, that's because it's the voice of Paul Reubens, who played Pee-Wee Herman. Rex makes one mistake after another. Although you never make it to Endor, you do get to go crashing through a comet, get caught in a tractor beam, and then follow a flight

Fun Fact

There are lots of inside jokes and secrets throughout Star Tours, especially in the queue area. Be sure to look at everything. Listen to the announcements and pages, too! You may hear an Egroeg Sacul paged to the booth. That is George Lucas spelled backward. Also, for you *Star Wars* diehards— notice that after the destruction of the Death Star as the X-Wings go into hyperspace, they do not retract their S-foils but leave them extended in the X configuration.

of Rebellion X-Wings during a bombing run on the Death Star. During this flight, you're bumped and jostled around, making you feel as if you're really flying in outer space. Star Tours has a 40-inch height requirement. The combination of motion in synchronization with the movie makes your brain think you're doing a lot more moving. If it gets to be too much for you or your children, just shut your eyes and you'll notice the ride tones down. It's a bit rough for children under 5. Although this attraction has been around for nearly 16 years, Star Tours is still impressive to both children and adults.

Insider's Secret

The intensity of the ride depends on where you sit. If there isn't much of a crowd, you can usually pick your seat. When it's busier, you can usually ask the cast member giving seating assignments if you could wait for the next speeder and choose your row. The mildest ride is toward the front and center of the speeder. Try sitting in the back row in one of the corners for the most motion.

Space Mountain—A FASTPASS Attraction

What would it be like to ride a roller coaster in the dark so that you could not see the track ahead? If you have ever asked yourself that question, you'll find your answer on Space Mountain. Although the ride is pretty mild as roller coasters go, consisting primarily of fast turns and a few quick drops, the fact that it's difficult to anticipate the next turn multiplies the thrill. Space Mountain reopened in 2005 after a two-year refurbishment. During this time, the ride itself was completely redone and new special effects along with a new sound track were added. The minimum height requirement for this ride is 40 inches. Even if a young child likes Thunder Mountain, if he or she doesn't like the dark, then Space Mountain will be just too much. Most children between 7 and 8 years of age and older seem to handle it fine.

Fun Fact

Space Mountain is sunk into the ground nearly 20 feet so that it does not dwarf Sleeping Beauty's Castle.

Insider's Secret

Although a lot of people like to ride roller coasters with their hands up in the air, follow the directions to keep your hands in the car. The clearances are quite low, and you could seriously injure your fingers or hands if they're up.

Honey, I Shrunk the Audience

This 3-D film carries on the continuing story that began in the Disney movie *Honey, I Shrunk the Kids*. Reprising his role, Rick Moranis plays the inventor of a shrinking ray and accidentally shrinks the audience. This film combines 3-D illusions with special effects, including a shaking floor and several things that jump out at you, such as a snake and a cat—both giant-size because you're shrunk down. Because most of the effects that could be scary are visual, young children can close their eyes to avoid them. Although it's fine for children 4 and up, you're the best judge for your younger children.

Helpful Hint

All the exits are on the second floor. To get out you must go up. An elevator is in the center hub. There's a small emergency bathroom upstairs; however, don't rely on using this. Instead, use the one outside behind the Hatmosphere shop.

Innoventions

The latest attraction housed in the building that was home to Carousel of Progress and America Sings, Innoventions allows you to learn about and explore how innovation and invention will affect your life in the near future. The robot Tom Morrow hosts the attraction. The bottom floor contains five different pods covering various aspects of our lives: entertainment, sports, transportation, work, and, of course, the home. At each pod, a cast member gives a brief presentation illustrating new types of products that will make our lives easier. In the hub of the first floor are a number of computer terminals and exhibits displaying a variety of software, from the educational to the purely entertaining. All these games are free to play, so you won't need any quarters. You can also visit the Dream Home, which showcases the newest technology of today and tomorrow Up the stairs are a number of interactive exhibits and games sponsored by various companies. Be sure to see the ASIMO show as this humanoid robot shows off its remarkable abilities. Innoventions is a great place to take a break during the day, and the air-conditioning makes it good for cooling down on hot days. All ages will find something to do here.

Fun Fact
You may recognize the voice of Tom Morrow. It's the actor Nathan Lane, who did the voice for Timon in *The Lion King*. Also, if you can't read the note in his pocket, it says "Buy 10 W 30." If you have the time, watch the robot after he gives his spiel and the other guests have moved on. He'll move and act like a person who is bored and waiting for his next group of guests.

Autopia—A FASTPASS Attraction
In 2000 the completely new and redone Tomorrowland Autopia opened. Combining both the old Fantasyland and old Tomorrowland Autopias, the new attraction features four lanes of traffic and travels through an entertaining course with lots of things for you to look at. Part of the course even goes "off road." This attraction is popular, so you may often have a long

wait in the queue. Children of all ages love this ride because they get to drive a car. Children must be at least 54 inches tall to drive alone, and passengers must be at least 32 inches tall.

Fun Fact

The Tomorrowland Autopia features three types of cars. Suzy is the little coupe. Dusty is the off-road vehicle. Spark is the classy sports car.

You're given a complimentary driver's license and can buy a photo to put on the license at the kiosk near the exit.

Insider's Secret

There are a lot of cool things to watch for during your drive. There's a stand selling "hot nuts" (the nut-and-bolt type) and a mouse crossing complete with mouse holes in the curb. Also, water shoots up as you drive through a puddle off road.

Disneyland Monorail

One of Disneyland's hallmark attractions, the monorail first opened in 1959 and carries passengers from Tomorrowland to Downtown Disney and back. (It used to stop at the Disneyland Hotel.) The track is 2½ miles long and leads across the front of Disneyland, then circles around Tomorrowland. After stopping at the station, the monorail continues outside Disneyland and toward Disney's California Adventure, where it crosses the Golden Gate Bridge over the entrance to this theme park and on through the Grand Californian Hotel. Although the monorail is a great way to get from the hotels and Downtown Disney to the Magic Kingdom and back, many guests just take the round-trip ride to see the sights.

Starcade

Starcade is a two-story video game arcade with all types of games. Prices range from a quarter to $4 per game. Because many children lose track of time in an arcade, it's best to avoid this area altogether, especially if you're on a tight schedule or a short vacation. Otherwise, give the kids either a time limit or a budget, and use this as a break for yourself and younger children in the afternoon.

Shows

Throughout the day, Star Wars Jedi Training Academy takes place on the Tomorrowland Terrace stage. A Jedi Master picks younglings in the audience who are strong in Force. They're brought up, dressed in Jedi robes, and given a practice lightsaber. The Jedi Master and his or her assistants train the younglings on basic lightsaber skills. Then, as a test of what they learned, the younglings face off against either Darth Vader or Darth Maul. The show will take about 20 young volunteers. However, if your children want to take part, you may need to go to more than one show so they get picked. During most evenings, you can listen to various types of live music at the stage. Check the *Disneyland Today* schedule for show times.

Character Greetings

Although there are no scheduled character greetings, you can sometimes find Mickey Mouse or one of his friends in Tomorrowland, usually in between Innoventions and Redd Rockett's. Also look for Buzz Lightyear walking around the area.

Tomorrowland Tips

Tomorrowland contains some popular rides. Luckily, three of them have FASTPASSes. For younger children, the Autopia can get quite busy in the morning and stay that way for most of the day. So get there early, or get FASTPASSes for the ride and then hit other attractions while you're waiting.

Buzz Lightyear Astro Blasters, even though it has a FAST-PASS system, usually does not have a long wait except on busy days. So get a FASTPASS for Space Mountain or another ride and then hit Buzz Lightyear Astro Blasters while you wait. *Honey, I Shrunk the Audience,* the Astro Orbitor, and Innovations are other great things to do while waiting for FASTPASS times.

It's best to hit Tomorrowland in the morning or evening. At night, it's all lighted up.

For younger children, Finding Nemo Submarine Voyage, Buzz Lightyear Astro Blasters, and the Autopia are the main attractions in this area. Other than Fantasyland attractions, this may be an area you want to head for first. In fact, get a FAST-PASS for one of the latter two rides before getting in line for the Finding Nemo Submarine Voyage, and when you get off, it will almost be time to use your FASTPASS.

Dining in Tomorrowland

Tomorrowland has two restaurants as well as a drink stand. Redd Rockett's Pizza Port offers pizza (whole or by the slice), pasta, and salads. The Tomorrowland Terrace features breakfast meals in the morning, then burgers, chicken sandwiches, wraps, fried chicken, and Caesar salads. At the Spirit of Refreshment, underneath the Moonliner rocket, you can order soft drinks, which are launched into the hands of the cast member serving you.

Fun Fact

Trivia

The Moonliner rocket outside of Redd Rockett's Pizza Port is one of the few things reminiscent of Disneyland in 1955. This rocket is actually a ⅔-size replica of the rocket that stood outside the Rocket to the Moon attraction, located where the restaurant now stands.

Fun Fact
The burger conveyor-belt grill was first used at the
Tomorrowland Terrace. You can see this type of grill
at a number of fast-food restaurants.

For more details on these restaurants, including pricing
and sample menus, *see* Chapter 8.

Tomorrowland Shopping

Star Traders carries a large selection of Disneyland souvenirs,
from T-shirts to plush characters, with mugs and key chains as
well. In addition, one part of the shop is dedicated to *Star Wars,*
with all types of toys, clothing, and other items based on the
movie series. You can even build your own lightsaber here for
around $19. Star Tours exits through this shop as well. Little
Green Men Store Command stocks Tomorrowland and Buzz
Lightyear items as well as pins for trading. Finally, at the Hatmosphere, you can find all types of Disney headwear, including
mouse ears.

Mickey's Toontown

Disneyland's newest land, Mickey's Toontown, which opened
in 1993, allows you to see how your favorite cartoon stars live
and work. Although there are several attractions in Toontown,
there are also lots of other things to see and do. The curvy architecture almost begs you to find a straight line. In the downtown area, there are all types of interactive gags. Take your
children around and have them lift lids, push buttons, pull on
doorknobs, listen to phones, and so on. Just about everything
does something. For example, pushing the plunger by the Fireworks Factory sets off a series of explosions. These interactive
gags not only are a lot of fun but also make great photo opportunities. Although Toontown is designed for children, the jokes
and gags make it a lot of fun for adults.

Roger Rabbit's Car Toon Spin—A FASTPASS Attraction
In this attraction, Benny the Cab takes you for a ride. As you drive around trying to find and save Jessica Rabbit, the weasels try to get you with the Dip. If the car begins to spin, turn the wheel to straighten it out. Or you can spin it to better see things along the ride. The cabs are similar to the teacups at the Mad Tea Party in that riders can spin them around as much or as little as they like. The ride contains many sight gags as well as cartoon clichés.

The Scare Factor
Even though Roger Rabbit's Car Toon Spin is in Toontown, it's dark inside and contains a lot of loud sounds and strobe lights, making it scary for young children. We recommend children under 5 skip this one.

Gadget's Go Coaster
The inventing mouse from *Chip-n-Dale's Rescue Rangers* has created a kiddie coaster from things she found lying around. Gadget's Go Coaster seats riders in a train of acorn shells, carries them up one climb, and takes them twisting and turning back down to the loading platform. Riders must be at least 35 inches tall. Most children will like the ride, but the entire course is visible before entering the queue, so let children make their own decision on whether they want to ride.

Mickey's House
Mickey's House is a fun walk-through attraction. There are a lot of things to look at and great photo opportunities. You walk through the house, out into the backyard, and on to the Movie Barn. Here you find a queue for getting your picture taken with Mickey. While you're waiting, Goofy and Donald will show you scenes from some of Mickey's movies. You'll then be es-

corted in small groups for photos with Mickey on one of four sets from his movies *Steamboat Willie, Through the Mirror, The Band Concert,* and *The Sorcerer's Apprentice.* On busier days, all four sets will be used. Although the cast members will not admit there's more than one Mickey, if you request a certain set, they may tell you to wait for the next group. The photographer will take a photo for you to buy on Main Street if you wish. The cast member in the studio will also be happy to take a shot with your own camera.

Fun Fact

When you enter Mickey's House, the first room contains a passport with stamps from everywhere a Disneyland is located.

Minnie's House

Like Mickey's House, Minnie's House is full of things to look at and do. Press buttons on her oven and dishwasher to see them work. In her dressing room, children can design new fashions for Minnie on her computer. Minnie can be found at her house during most hours of the day for photos.

Chip-n-Dale Treehouse

This attraction is pretty simple. It's essentially a tree with stairs inside; children can climb to the top and look around. Although you might take some photos here, usually it's best just to skip this one.

Donald's Boat

Docked on Toon Lake, the *Miss Daisy* is Donald's houseboat. Children climb a spiral staircase or a rope ladder to get to the top. From there they can steer the wheel and toot the horn.

Goofy's Playhouse

Goofy's Playhouse is designed for younger children and is a great place to burn some energy. In this house, children can climb on all the furniture and even slide down objects. Outside is a small play area. Parents can watch from the benches and admire all the strange plants in the garden.

Character Greetings

Mickey and Minnie can be found at their houses during most of the Toontown open hours. Goofy, Donald, Pluto, and other characters are also around at various times throughout the day for autographs and photos.

Mickey's Toontown Tips

Toontown can get quite busy, so you should try to hit it early—usually right after you do the popular rides at Fantasyland.

If there's a long line for Roger Rabbit's Car Toon Spin, get a FASTPASS and then browse around Toontown looking at the gags, get a snack, or see "it's a small world."

Don't wait in a long line for Gadget's Go Coaster. The ride is only 45 seconds long. Instead, come back later.

Toontown closes earlier than the park because the fireworks are launched right over it. Be sure to find out when it closes, and try to get there about an hour before, when lines are shorter and the area is less crowded.

Dining in Mickey's Toontown

Mickey's Toontown has only fast food and snacks available. Daisy's Diner serves individual-size pizzas. Pluto's Dog House is where you can find hot dogs. Goofy's Free-Z Time sells slushy drinks. Clarabelle's is where you can find sandwiches, salads, and frozen treats. There aren't a lot of places to sit down for a meal in Toontown, so we recommend eating elsewhere or just getting snacks while in Toontown rather than meals. For more details on these restaurants, including pricing and sample menus, *see* Chapter 8.

Mickey's Toontown Shopping

The only shops are the Gag Factory and the Toontown Five and Dime, which are essentially the same store, just different entrances. Here you can find all types of Toontown souvenirs with some of the town's most famous residents emblazoned on them.

Frontierland

As you walk through the doors of the wooden fort, you're instantly carried back to the days of the Old West. Welcome to Frontierland!

The Scare Factor

Although some 4-year-olds really like Big Thunder Mountain Railroad, some of the dark parts in the caves are a bit scary. We recommend it for those 5 years and older.

Big Thunder Mountain Railroad—A FASTPASS Attraction
This is the only big attraction in Frontierland. Big Thunder is a roller coaster with a runaway mine train theme. Guests ride in ore cars pulled along by a small engine that takes them up and down hills, in a cave of bats, past assorted wildlife, and even through a cave-in. As far as roller coasters go, this one is fairly tame and has only short drops and several fast turns. The hard bench seats can be a bit shaky, and children sitting together or an adult alone may slide right and left in the seat as the coaster goes around the turns. The height requirement is 40 inches.

Insider's Secret

For the best ride on Big Thunder Mountain Railroad, ask the cast member giving seat assignments if you can sit in the very back. Because the drops are not all that high and the train is quite long, those in the front are almost to the bottom before the last car is over the hump and the train begins to pick up speed.

Pirate's Lair on Tom Sawyer Island

In the middle of the Rivers of America, pirates have taken over Tom Sawyer Island, which is accessible only by pirate manned rafts. Once across the river, children will have a great time as they explore the island's many features. Captain Jack Sparrow often visits the island and battles villainous pirates throughout the day. This show is quite entertaining. While walking around the island, be on the lookout for treasure. You can work a bilge pump to remove the water from a submerged boat, or turn a capstan to raise up a chest of treasure—as well as the skeleton guarding it. There's a tree house complete with spyglasses, several rock formations that create castles to climb around in, as well as a teeter-tottering rock and one that spins around. The pontoon bridge is fun to cross, as is the suspension bridge. For those who don't mind the dark, explore Dead Man's Grotto. Be sure to get a family photo in the bone cage. There's a lot to do and see here, and this gives children a chance to run around and burn off some excess energy. Plan on spending at least an hour here, and come late in the morning or early in the afternoon. The island closes at dusk, so be sure to note when the last rafts will be leaving.

Fun Fact

Tom Sawyer Island was officially annexed and recognized by the Missouri state legislature in 1956.

Mark Twain *Riverboat*

This steam-powered riverboat was one of the original attractions when Disneyland first opened in 1955. The steamboat sails around Tom Sawyer Island, and Mark Twain gives a spiel over the speakers. The ride is fairly slow and takes about 15 minutes. You may wait for 10 minutes just for passengers to board before you even get moving. If you're on a tight schedule, you should usually skip this attraction. However, it's a good break during the middle of the day and gives you a chance to rest. Although there are only a few seats, many guests just sit on the deck, and we have seen several small children fall asleep for a quick nap.

Fun Fact
Walt Disney used to love to pilot the *Mark Twain* around the river. On one of his first times, he blew the whistle over and over again. A cast member told him to lay off or the boat would run out of steam. Sure enough, the steam pressure got too low and the boat was stuck until the pressure could build up again.

Sailing Ship Columbia
The other ship that sails around the Rivers of America is the *Columbia.* This is a full-scale replica of the original ship built in 1787, which was the first American ship to circumnavigate the globe. It runs only occasionally, and you board it at the same dock as the *Mark Twain.* Below deck is a small maritime museum that shows how sailors of the time lived. It's amazing how men could live on such a small boat for such a long time. The around-the-world cruise took three years.

Insider's Secret
If you would like to ride in the pilot house on top of the boat, ask one of the cast members as you're boarding. This is limited to adults and possibly older children. The cast member will let you know if you can on that day and will give you instructions on what to do. Once you're up there, the captain will let you turn the wheel (don't worry, the boat is really on a track) and tell you when to ring the bell and blow the whistle.

Big Thunder Ranch

Located along the trail behind Big Thunder Mountain Railroad leading toward Fantasyland, this area features several goats that guests can pet. A cow, mule, and other animals complete the ranch. Sometimes you can even see the official turkey pardoned at Thanksgiving by the President of the United States. This is a good place to stop by during the day when you need a break from the crowds, and children who love animals may want to stay for longer than expected.

Frontierland Shootin' Exposition

This shooting gallery uses infrared rifles that cause targets to react when a hit is registered. This is fun for children and a good break. Unlike most attractions, this one costs extra: 50¢ for 20 shots.

Shows

Frontierland offers one of the best shows in Disneyland. The Golden Horseshoe Stage hosts *Billy Hill and the Hillbillies,* a funny show with great music and comedy. Billy and his broth-

Helpful Hint

You should find a spot about an hour (or more) before *Fantasmic!* starts and camp out. However, not everyone has to stay at the spot. One or two can hold it for the rest, using jackets, backpacks, or a stroller to reserve the area. Meanwhile, the rest of the family can go on some of the nearby rides and other attractions. Or you can get a meal or snack and eat while you're waiting. The best view is right along the riverfront between Pirates of the Caribbean and the rafts to Tom Sawyer's Island. Other good locations are the bridge over the entrance to Pirates of the Caribbean, the outside dining area for the Riverbelle Terrace, and the patio area near the French Market restaurant.

ers, all named Billy, perform a variety of music, from Elvis tunes to classic bluegrass. Walt Disney loved to watch shows here and had a private box in the upper level to the left of the stage. As you're walking through Frontierland, you may witness a show by the Golden Horseshoe, featuring a sheriff trying to apprehend an outlaw or two. There are no stunts, just good laughs.

One of the biggest shows ever at Disneyland is *Fantasmic!* Running twice nightly in summer and on weekends and holidays throughout the remainder of the year, this show combines lasers, animation, pyrotechnics, and live action. The 22-minute show is incredible, and if you haven't seen it before, you must. People begin to pick seating and wait more than an hour before it starts. Because the show is on Tom Sawyer Island in the Rivers of America, it can be seen from just about anywhere along the Frontierland and New Orleans Square riverfront. Although the show does have some scary parts, there are also a lot of parts that younger children will like. Those 6 and older will like the whole show, but younger ones may need to hide their eyes or hold on to a parent at times.

Insider's Secret

For the ultimate *Fantasmic!* experience, you can watch from premium viewing areas. Space is limited, and you must make reservations by calling 714/781–4400 up to 30 days in advance or by trying to find an opening first thing the morning of the performance. Visit the Guest Relations window at the park entrance. The cost is $59 for adults and $49 for children and includes a dessert, drinks, and more. These spots sell out quickly, so it's best to call exactly 30 days before to ensure you reserve a place for the day you want.

Character Greetings

The western characters from the *Toy Story* movies often stroll around Frontierland. Check your *Disneyland Today* schedule for times and locations.

Frontierland Tips

Big Thunder Mountain Railroad is the only major attraction in this area. Although you can get there early, you'll usually want to spend the morning hours elsewhere. Instead, do Big Thunder later or even in the evening. It's fun to ride at night.

While waiting for a FASTPASS time for Big Thunder, go over to Pirate's Lair on Tom Sawyer Island or hit nearby attractions in New Orleans Square or Adventureland.

If you're going to see a show at the Golden Horseshoe, pick up a FASTPASS for Big Thunder or other nearby attractions so you can do your waiting while being entertained. Get to the Golden Horseshoe at least 10 to 15 minutes early. That way you can get a good seat and still have time to pick up something to eat or drink at the eatery inside.

Pirate's Lair on Tom Sawyer Island and the boats on the river all stop operating at dusk. If you plan on doing them, be sure to fit them in while the sun is still shining. The *Mark Twain* may run on evenings that *Fantasmic!* is not showing.

Dining in Frontierland

Frontierland has some great places to eat. Rancho del Zocalo features Mexican cuisine. This is a great place for dinner because it offers a variety of items; just about everyone in a family can find something he or she likes. The River Belle Terrace serves breakfast in the morning and hot sandwiches for lunch and dinner. The Stage Door Café serves finger foods such as chicken strips, fish-and-chips, and mozzarella sticks. At the Golden Horseshoe you can purchase cheese sticks, chicken strips, chili cheese fries, and desserts.

For more details on these restaurants, including pricing and sample menus, *see* Chapter 8.

Frontierland Shopping

There are several nice shops in Frontierland. Bonanza Outfitters carries Western-style clothing and gift items. Pioneer Mercantile is a great place to find Western-inspired toys, books, videos, and even children's costumes. Remember the coonskin cap Davy Crockett wore? You can pick one up here—and they come in adult sizes, too. To help calm a sweet tooth, the Westward Ho Trading Company sells a variety of goodies.

Adventureland

As you leave Central Plaza and pass through the bamboo gateway, you're taken back in time as well as transported across the world to a land of adventure. This area has the look and feel of a jungle outpost in the 1930s. Although Adventureland has only four attractions, they're ones you don't want to miss.

Enchanted Tiki Room

This attraction was the first at Disneyland to incorporate audio-animatronics. You sit in a Polynesian-style building around a central fountain. When the doors close, the birds come to life, as do the plants and wooden tikis. The air fills with music as the various characters sing a number of songs. The special effects are dated, but the Enchanted Tiki Room is a good place for a rest in the afternoon. Small children usually enjoy the show and sing along with the birds. The only part that might be scary is the thunderstorm; however, the characters just keep singing right through it. Many older children would rather do something more exciting than watch this show.

Indiana Jones Adventure—A FASTPASS Attraction

One of Disneyland's wildest rides is the Indiana Jones Adventure. Based on the popular movie character, this attraction is incredible. You enter through ancient ruins and make your way to the boarding area. Toward the end of the queue, you come to a room showing a movie hosted by Indy's trusty sidekick, Sallah. He explains the story line of the ride. You're in the temple of Mara, an Indian deity who can grant eternal youth, earthly riches, or knowledge of the future. However, don't gaze directly into the eyes of Mara or bad things will happen.

The Scare Factor

The Indiana Jones Adventure ride is very intense and rough. The 46-inch height requirement is a good gauge of who will like this ride.

Helpful Hint

The queue for the ride is fun in itself as you make your way past booby traps that have already been sprung or are blocked for your protection. However, throw caution to the wind and touch or move things near the signs that warn you not to. In the spike room, shake the pole vigorously—it will seem as if the roof is about to cave in.

With that warning given, you're ready to board 12-person vehicles that will take you farther into the temple. These vehicles are very special in that they use hydraulics for all the motion during the ride. The road is perfectly flat and level. Computers control the bumps and rocking of the vehicles and

Fun Fact

The Indiana Jones Adventure contains lots of props from the original movies. The truck near the entrance is the actual one used in *Raiders of the Lost Ark,* in which Indy falls off the hood and is dragged below it. Look for other props in his office in the queue area.

allow for more than 160,000 randomly generated combinations. Therefore, you'll never get the same ride twice. Of course, someone in your vehicle has to look at Mara, so all of you are doomed. Luckily Indiana Jones is in the temple and helps you get through a variety of dangers, including a shaky suspension bridge over lava, a giant snake, mummies and skeletons, bugs, flying darts, and, of course, a giant rolling boulder. The queue on this ride can be up to two or three hours on busy days. Your best bet is to get there early and use the FASTPASS station so you can bypass the long wait. If you don't mind having your party split up, the single rider line can be much shorter

Jungle Cruise

This is one great ride that everyone we talk to enjoys. There are lots of things to see along your cruise, and the boat skipper's spiel makes it funny and entertaining. You board boats patterned after the *African Queen* and sail through jungles filled with lions, tigers, snakes, elephants, hippos, piranhas, and even headhunters. The cruise, which takes about eight minutes, is fun for the entire family.

Helpful Hint

If it rains while you're at Disneyland, try riding the Jungle Cruise. The boats are covered, and the rain really adds to the feeling of being in a jungle.

Tarzan's Treehouse

Although veteran Disneyland guests may remember this as the Swiss Family Robinson Treehouse, it has been refurbished as the home of Tarzan. At the base of the tree is a camp area where children can explore and play with a variety of items, most of which create noise or other effects. You climb stairs up the tree and cross a suspension bridge to small huts built in the tree. As you go from hut to hut, the story of Tarzan unfolds. This attraction is primarily designed for children, though parents will

Fun Fact

The scientific name of the tree that houses Tarzan's Treehouse is *Disneyodendron semperflorens grandis,* which means "large ever-blooming Disney tree."

Trivia

have to help younger ones climb the stairs or even carry them. Older children will usually be bored unless they're taking their younger siblings through.

Shows

There are no regularly scheduled shows in Adventureland. However, various shows appear seasonally, usually as part of a promotion or theme. The Trinidad Tropical Steel Drum Band plays near the entrance to the Jungle Cruise on select days throughout the year. Check the *Disneyland Today* schedule for times.

Character Greetings

Aladdin and Jasmine are available for photos and autographs at various times throughout the day near Aladdin's Oasis.

Adventureland Tips

Head over to the Indiana Jones Adventure when the park first opens and the lines are short. On busy days, waits can be quite long—you may have to wait from two to three hours to come back with your FASTPASS.

Because of the popularity of the Indiana Jones Adventure, Adventureland can be quite congested. It's usually quicker to move through Frontierland when traveling between Central Plaza and New Orleans Square.

The Jungle Cruise and the Enchanted Tiki Room are good places to spend time while waiting for an Indiana Jones Adventure FASTPASS slot.

Dining in Adventureland

Dining is somewhat limited in Adventureland. Bengal Barbecue serves grilled meat and vegetables on skewers with delicious sauces, along with breadsticks and pretzels. The Tiki Juice Bar, by the Enchanted Tiki Room, carries refreshing pineapple spears, pineapple juice, and a whipped pineapple sorbet. Indy's Fruit Cart is where you can purchase fresh fruit as well as bottled drinks. For more details on these restaurants, including pricing and sample menus, *see* Chapter 8.

Adventureland Shopping

Adventureland has some interesting shops that carry items appropriate for this area. The Adventureland Bazaar carries some of the jungle's best items, including plush animals and other jungle dwellers such as rubber snakes and spiders. At the Indiana Jones Adventure Outpost you can find fedoras like Indy's, clothing fit for an expedition, and even artifacts for your home museum. South Seas Traders carries more casual wear such as Hawaiian-style shirts and other comfortable items. Tropical Imports, next to the Jungle Cruise, sells rubber snakes, skulls, and insects as well as other fun items kids love.

New Orleans Square

New Orleans Square is a unique area with a couple of Disneyland's most beloved attractions. As you stroll through this land, the air filled with the scent of Cajun cooking and the music of a Dixieland band, you can almost imagine yourself on Bourbon Street in the Big Easy. In fact, Disney released two feature films based on New Orleans Square attractions in 2003: *The Haunted Mansion* and *Pirates of the Caribbean*.

Pirates of the Caribbean

This attraction is a guest favorite and fun for the entire family. You board boats and begin your cruise through a nighttime bayou of fireflies, croaking frogs, and even an alligator. Just as everyone is relaxing, a talking skull and crossbones warns of trouble ahead. The boat then drops down a couple of chutes, and you find yourself in a cavern filled with pirate treasure and

Helpful Hint

When you get to the front of the queue, ask the cast member if you can sit in the front row. He or she will usually ask you to wait for the next boat and then let you sit in front. Small children can see better in front, and there's also more room for legs and carry-ons such as backpacks.

the skeletons of its owners. After you view the cursed treasure, your boat is transported back a few centuries to a pirate raid on a Caribbean port town. It begins with broadsides by a pirate ship and return fire from the town's fort, with your boat sailing right in between the two and cannonball splashes all around. The cruise continues through the town as you watch the pirates plunder, pillage, and then burn the town down. Although this may seem violent and brutal, Disney has turned this raid into a musical, and the pirates themselves are more humorous than bloodthirsty. If you're not careful, you may even find yourself singing along to the song "Yo-Ho, Yo-Ho, A Pirate's Life for Me." At the end of the ride, your boat is carried up a ramp to the loading dock. Don't worry—there's not a large drop like on Splash Mountain; you're just being carried back up to ground level. Although this ride is somewhat dark and the drops can be a bit wild, it's fine for children of all ages. Except when you're cruising through a tunnel to the raid scenes, there's always something to look at, and once the singing starts any fears are

Fun Fact

The name of the pirate ship is the *Wicked Wench*. While sailing through the scene where the ship is firing cannons at the fort, look for a cluster of three holes made by cannonballs on the side of the fort. They make up a Hidden Mickey.

cast overboard. In 2006, just prior to the Disneyland movie premier of *Pirates of the Caribbean: Dead Man's Chest* the attraction was updated with characters from the movies. Jack Sparrow appears three different times, Captain Barbossa is on the ship in the battle scene, and Davy Jones appears in a waterfall effect right after you glimpse the cursed treasure.

Haunted Mansion

Another favorite, the Haunted Mansion is more humorous than frightening and is intended as a family attraction rather than one for only teens and adults. You enter through the front door of the mansion and are escorted into a portrait chamber. The doors close, and the room appears to get taller. A hidden door then opens, and you walk through a gallery of spooky paintings to the Doom Buggies. These carry you around the remainder of the mansion.

During your journey, you will see the 999 inhabitants throughout the many rooms of the mansion as well as the graveyard outside. Near the end of the ride, you're warned against picking up hitchhiking ghosts. Before you know it, you look into a mirror and there's a ghost riding with you! There's a lot to see and great detail in this attraction. Therefore, if you have time, ride it two or three times, preferably close together, to try to see most of it. Although the ride was designed with children in mind, the part most children find scary is the darkness. Most of the ghosts themselves are actually funny looking.

The Scare Factor

Children 5 and up who have no problem with the dark will be fine on the Haunted Mansion ride; 7 and up is more appropriate for other children.

Trivia Fun Fact

The organ in the hall with the party is the one from *20,000 Leagues Under the Sea.*

As you go through the ride, you may notice several ravens. In the original plans for the attraction, the ravens would tell the story of the mansion. However, Disney decided to make it a musical so guests could enjoy it over and over again without getting tired of hearing the same old story. There were actually several story lines proposed for the ride, and in the end the developers combined them all to create the different scenes.

Beginning in October, the Haunted Mansion takes on a holiday theme. From October through New Year's, the attraction features Jack Skellington and other characters from the Tim Burton movie *The Nightmare Before Christmas*. The interior is modified for the new story line and features an all-new soundtrack as Halloween and Christmas come together in one ghostly holiday extravaganza. During this time, the attraction is a little less scary than the original program, so younger children are not as likely to be frightened. If you plan on visiting during this time period, be sure to have your family view the movie in advance so you know the background of the story. The attraction is usually closed in September, during its transformation, as well as in January, when it's changed back.

Shows
There's almost always some type of live performance taking place in New Orleans Square. You can find various types of bands, singing groups, and mimes throughout the area.

New Orleans Square Tips
Although both the Haunted Mansion and Pirates of the Caribbean are popular attractions and are usually busy, they can both handle a lot of guests. So even if the lines are long, they move fairly quickly.

If you're not going to watch *Fantasmic!*, go to the Haunted Mansion and Pirates of the Caribbean during the show. You can usually walk right into each attraction; if there's a line, it's a very short wait.

There's no need to hit New Orleans Square first thing in the morning. Instead, do the rides that get the long lines (Splash Mountain, Indiana Jones Adventure, Big Thunder Mountain Railroad, etc.), and then come here later in the day.

Dining in New Orleans Square

Some of the best dining at Disneyland is in New Orleans Square. The famous and distinctive Blue Bayou restaurant looks out at the bayou area of the Pirates of the Caribbean. The menu features a variety of meals, including seafood, prime rib, and the Monte Cristo sandwich. Reservations are highly suggested, and if you plan on dining here, come early to make the reservations, which can be made for the same day only. The best time to come is during lunch, usually around 2 PM. Café Orleans serves a variety of French- and Creole-inspired dishes, including sandwiches, salads, and other tasty dishes. French Market is a good spot for dinner. Here you can find jambalaya, fried chicken, and pasta. The prices are quite reasonable. Royal Street Veranda serves gumbo and clam chowder in bread bowls. If you just want to sip a mint julep (nonalcoholic) or snack on some fritters, try the Mint Julep Bar. For more details on these restaurants, including pricing and sample menus, *see* Chapter 8.

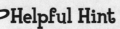

Helpful Hint

If you plan on eating at the Blue Bayou restaurant or Café Orleans, be sure to make reservations in advance. These can get busy at lunch and dinner times and on busy days, you won't be able to get in.

New Orleans Square Shopping

New Orleans Square contains some very interesting shops where you can find all types of gifts and souvenirs. Cristal D'Orleans carries a variety of crystal items. Jewel of Orleans sells antique jewelry, some dating back to 1850, as well as more modern pieces. For Christmas ornaments and other decorations year-round, visit L'Ornement Magique, which also features the work of artist Christopher Radko. La Mascarade de Orleans carries pin trading goods, while Le Bat en Rouge sells merchandise for the Haunted Mansion Holiday as well as gourmet food and Mardi Gras supplies. For the little cutthroats in your crew, Pieces of Eight carries all types of buccaneer supplies.

Critter Country

Formerly known as Bear Country, this land was renamed Critter Country when Splash Mountain opened. The area is rather small and can become quite congested by afternoon with all the guests wanting to ride Splash Mountain and the Many Adventures of Winnie the Pooh.

The Many Adventures of Winnie the Pooh

This attraction is a dark ride similar to those in Fantasyland. You climb aboard "hunny" pots, each with their own unique name, and take a journey through some of Pooh Bear's more popular stories. As the hunny pots bounce around through the ride, you follow Pooh for a blustery day, save the hunny pot from the floody place, and enter one of Pooh's dreams with Heffalumps and Woozles. This is a ride the entire family can enjoy, and most families can fit within a single hunny pot, since

Insider's Secret

Some of the characters from the Country Bear Jamboree, which used to be located where the Many Adventures of Winnie the Pooh is now, stayed behind. After exiting the scene with Heffalumps and Woozles, and as you enter the honey room, look straight up. You will see Buff, Max, and Melivin—the talking heads on the wall of the former attraction.

each seats four to five people. Pick up a FASTPASS for Splash Mountain, and then wait in line and ride through the Many Adventures of Winnie the Pooh while counting off the minutes for Splash Mountain.

Time-Saving Tip

Splash Mountain can get busy, and the queue can be two hours long or more on very busy days. There's a FASTPASS system for this attraction, but when it gets busy you may have to come back three or four hours later! Therefore, try to get there by midmorning, when the FASTPASS returns are only about an hour away. Then come back and get on in 10 to 15 minutes. Single rider service is also offered for this attraction. While your party is split up to fill in empty seats in the logs, the wait time is quite short.

Splash Mountain—A FASTPASS Attraction

Disneyland's one and only flume ride, Splash Mountain was inspired by the Disney movie *Song of the South* and features Brer Rabbit as well as his nemeses Brer Fox and Brer Bear. You board log boats and are carried into the water-filled mountain. Inside, the characters sing as you ride through swamps and bayous,

Helpful Hint

Believe the warnings around this ride—you will get wet. You really will. If you want to stay as dry as possible, ask the cast member at boarding to seat you at the back of the log. The people in front tend to get the wettest. Also, try to ride this attraction when the sun is shining and it's warm outside. You don't want to have children going around in the cold with wet clothes.

watching Brer Fox and Brer Bear trying to catch Brer Rabbit. Finally, they do catch him and decide to throw him into the briar patch. At this point, your log races down a five-story drop into a pond below, surrounded by briars, and then heads back into the attraction for a musical finale. During the drop, your picture is taken, so try to smile. Many families even pose during this part and use it as a family picture. The photos can be purchased near the exit to the ride. Most of the ride is fun and upbeat, with only one dark area where you go down a little drop. However, the scariest part of the ride is the drop down the tall chute. Although the ride has a height requirement of 40 inches and children must be at least 3 years old to ride it, it's probably best to wait until children are at least 4 or 5.

Davy Crockett's Explorer Canoes

One of the best ways to travel the Rivers of America is in these canoes. Each canoe has two guides that help keep the craft on track while you have the opportunity to paddle nearly half a mile on your cruise around Tom Sawyer Island. Most children enjoy this ride because they get to help with the paddling. Although there's no height requirement, children under 6 must wear life jackets. This attraction closes at dusk and does not operate every day. Check the sign at the entrance to the attraction for operating hours.

Fun Fact

When the canoes were first introduced to Disneyland in 1956, they were called the Indian War Canoes.

Trivia

Character Greetings

Throughout most of the day, you can find Winnie the Pooh and some of his friends at the Thotful Spot near the Country Bear Playhouse. A cast photographer is on hand to take pictures that you can purchase on Main Street. Cast members will also be happy to take a photo for you with your own camera.

Critter Country Tips

Because Critter Country can become congested in the afternoon due to the crowds waiting for Splash Mountain, it's best to come here in the morning, if only to get a FASTPASS for later.

A good strategy for covering this land is to get here about an hour or two after the park officially opens. Get a FASTPASS for Splash Mountain and then ride the Many Adventures of Winnie the Pooh while waiting. If you have time, also try the canoes or browse around in the shops.

Dining in Critter Country

The Hungry Bear restaurant is a nice, quiet place to have lunch because most of the tables overlook the Rivers of America rather than the crowds. It serves hamburgers, sandwiches, and onion rings. Harbour Galley offers soup, chowder and chili in bread bowls as well as salads.

For more details on these restaurants, including pricing and sample menus, *see* Chapter 8.

Critter Country Shopping

If you're looking for Pooh-inspired items, Pooh Corner has it all, from clothing to toys to all types of household items with the cuddly little bear or his friends on them as well as fresh-made candy and treats. The Briar Patch sells hats and other Disney merchandise.

CHAPTER

6

Disney's California Adventure™

Disney's California Adventure

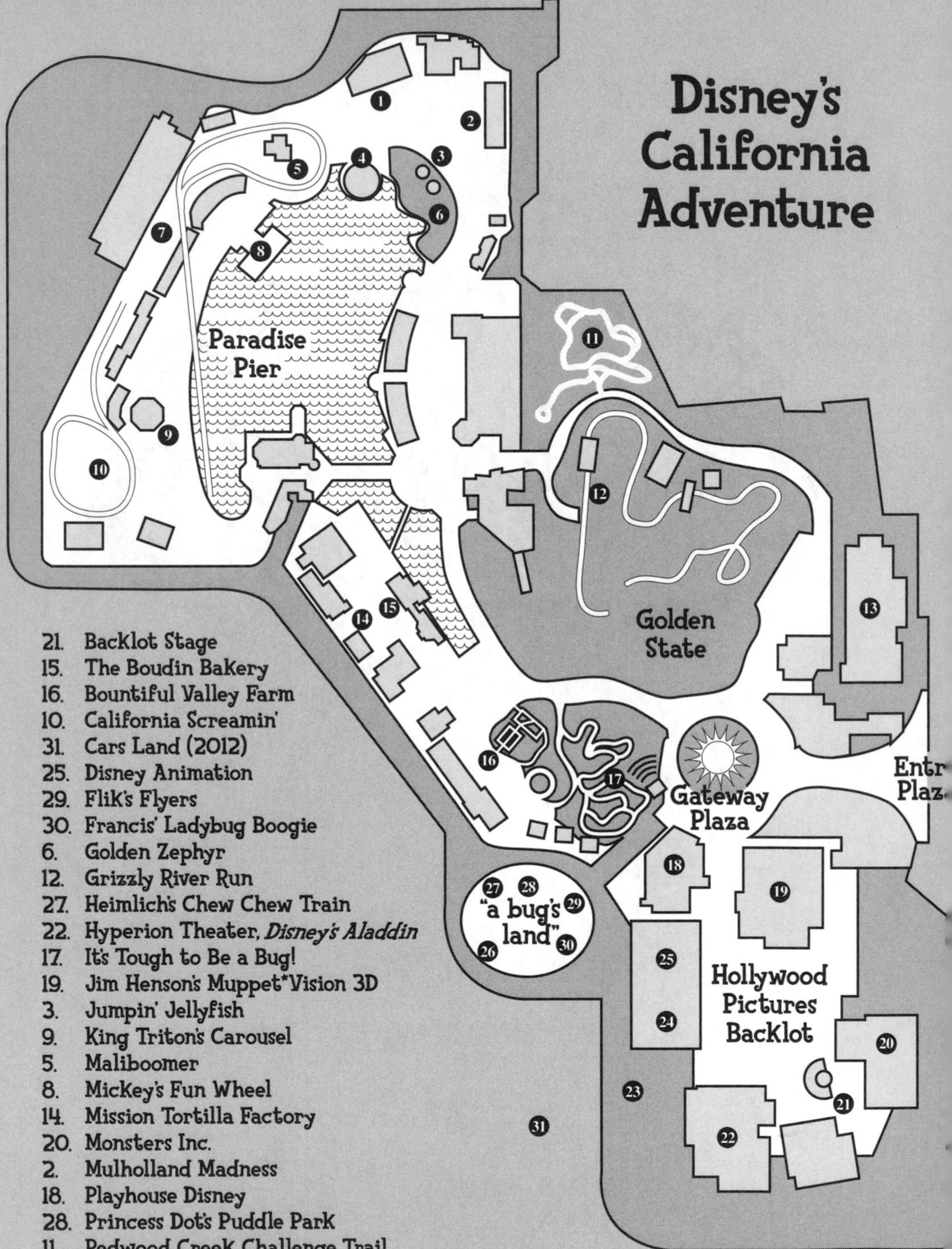

Paradise Pier
Golden State
Gateway Plaza
Entr
Plaz
"a bug's land"
Hollywood Pictures Backlot
N

21. Backlot Stage
15. The Boudin Bakery
16. Bountiful Valley Farm
10. California Screamin'
31. Cars Land (2012)
25. Disney Animation
29. Flik's Flyers
30. Francis' Ladybug Boogie
6. Golden Zephyr
12. Grizzly River Run
27. Heimlich's Chew Chew Train
22. Hyperion Theater, *Disney's Aladdin*
17. It's Tough to Be a Bug!
19. Jim Henson's Muppet*Vision 3D
3. Jumpin' Jellyfish
9. King Triton's Carousel
5. Maliboomer
8. Mickey's Fun Wheel
14. Mission Tortilla Factory
20. Monsters Inc.
2. Mulholland Madness
18. Playhouse Disney
28. Princess Dot's Puddle Park
11. Redwood Creek Challenge Trail
4. Silly Symphony Swings
13. Soarin' Over California
1. S.S. *Rustworthy*
7. Toy Story Mania
26. Tuck and Roll's Drive 'Em Buggies
24. Turtle Talk with Crush
23. Twilight Zone Tower of Terror

Disney's California Adventure, which opened on February 8, 2001, is the newest Disney theme park in the United States. The main gate is directly across from Disneyland's main gate, behind giant letters that spell out CALIFORNIA. If you're staying at one of the Disneyland hotels, there's a private entrance so you don't have to wait in line.

To Go or Not to Go—That Is the Question

One of the major decisions families with young children must make is whether they should spend a day at California Adventure or spend the time at Disneyland or another area theme park, given that California Adventure is designed primarily for adults and older children. However, in the years since California Adventure opened, Disney has added several new attractions targeted at younger children, making the park a much better experience for families with children of all ages.

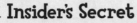

Insider's Secret

As you tour California Adventure, be sure to note the names of the shops and restaurants as well as of the attractions. Many of the names are puns based on California cities, locations, or terms—for example, Maliboomer (Malibu), Baker's Field Bakery (Bakersfield), Bur-r-r Bank Ice Cream (Burbank), and so forth.

If you'll be at the Disneyland Resort for only one day, you should know that standard single-day tickets allow entrance into either Disneyland *or* California Adventure—but not both. However, Park Hopper tickets for two or more days allow you to come and go as much as you like between the two parks. You can also purchase a single-day Park Hopper ticket for an additional charge. In our opinion, and that of several families we have talked to, if your family consists of only young children, you can probably spend half a day in California Adventure and see everything you want. If all your children are older (around 6 years and up), then California Adventure should not be missed, and you will want a full day there. The tough decision comes for families with children in both age groups. If your young child is just a baby and would not do much at Disneyland anyway, go for California Adventure. Otherwise, try spending half a day at California Adventure with the older kids, which will still allow some time for the younger children at Disneyland. If the parks stay open late, hit California Adventure in the evening, when the younger kids are tired and sleeping in the stroller. With Park Hopper tickets, there's no reason not to try California Adventure. If your family is not having a great time, then head next door to Disneyland for the rest of the day.

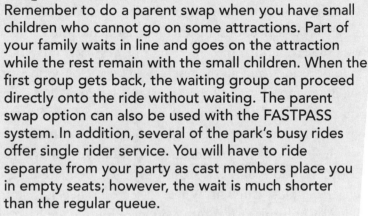

Helpful Hint

Remember to do a parent swap when you have small children who cannot go on some attractions. Part of your family waits in line and goes on the attraction while the rest remain with the small children. When the first group gets back, the waiting group can proceed directly onto the ride without waiting. The parent swap option can also be used with the FASTPASS system. In addition, several of the park's busy rides offer single rider service. You will have to ride separate from your party as cast members place you in empty seats; however, the wait is much shorter than the regular queue.

Plan Your Day

Before you arrive at California Adventure, it's important that you take time to acquaint yourself with the park and plan your visit so you're not walking all over looking for specific attractions. For most families, plan an entire day at the park. You may want to add to or decrease that time depending on how busy the park is as well as the ages of your children.

Touring Plans

To save time, as well as to see and do as much as possible, your family should have a general plan for the day.

The key to a good plan is to be prepared. A week or two before you leave on your vacation, you should get a map of the park to acquaint yourself with where everything is located. You can find a map on the Disneyland Web site at www.disneyland. com or request one by calling 714/781–4560. You can also use the map included in this book. Second, read about each attraction in the following section of this chapter. Once you're familiar with all the attractions and their locations, have the family create a plan.

California Adventure is smaller than Disneyland, and there are fewer attractions, making it easier to navigate. You can divide the attractions into three main categories: busy rides, FASTPASS rides, and all the rest. Try to hit the busy rides first thing in the morning until their queues begin to get long, then again toward late afternoon and evening. FASTPASS attractions are great any time of day, as are the rest of the attractions.

The following lists divide the attractions according to the best times to do them. Throughout this chapter, we refer to younger and older children. Where the cutoff is depends on the child. At California Adventure, younger children are basically those not tall enough for the minimum height requirements. These children are usually 5 or 6 years of age or younger. Older children will make most if not all the height requirements and will enjoy the fast and wild rides while wanting to avoid the kiddie rides. They're 7 years or older. If you have children in both categories, then you'll have to make compromises to keep everyone happy. Luckily, this is easier here than at Disneyland because the attractions for younger children are usually near the ones for the older children. Now let's take a look at what to do when.

Popular Attractions for the Morning Lap

@ Younger Children (6 and Under)

Playhouse Disney—Live on Stage!

Mickey's Fun Wheel

King Triton's Carousel

Jumpin' Jellyfish

Golden Zephyr

"a bug's land" rides

ⓔ **Older Children (7 and Up)**

Soarin' Over California

Toy Story Mania

Maliboomer

California Screamin'

Mulholland Madness

The Twilight Zone Tower of Terror

Popular Attractions for the Afternoon Lap

ⓔ **Younger Children (6 and Under)**

Monsters, Inc. Mike & Sulley to the Rescue!

Muppet*Vision 3D

Disney's Aladdin—A Musical Spectacular

Turtle Talk with Crush

Redwood Creek Challenge Trail

ⓔ **Older Children (7 and Up)**

Grizzly River Run

Silly Symphony Swings

It's Tough to Be a Bug!

Monsters, Inc. Mike & Sulley to the Rescue!

Muppet*Vision 3D

Disney's Aladdin—A Musical Spectacular

Redwood Creek Challenge Trail

Disney Animation

Popular Attractions for the Evening Lap

Parade

Paradise Pier rides

Anything you missed earlier or want to do again

These general lists are intended to give you an idea of when to do each of the attractions. Following are some sample plans we have put together. Both are for a single-day visit, with the first designed for families with younger children and the second for those with older children. (*Note:* You may not have time to do everything on the plan. It is designed for a typical day. However, for days when it's busy, you'll have to cut some of the attractions.)

Sample Touring Plan (Children 6 and Under)

Morning

See *Playhouse Disney—Live on Stage!*

Head to "a bug's land" and ride the attractions there.

Head toward Paradise Pier.

Ride Mickey's Fun Wheel.

Ride the other kiddie rides in the Paradise Pier area.

Pick up lunch at Taste Pilot's Grill or have a snack.

Afternoon

Return to the Hollywood Pictures Backlot.

See *Disney's Aladdin—A Musical Spectacular*.

Ride Monsters, Inc. Mike & Sulley to the Rescue!

See Turtle Talk with Crush.

See *Muppet*Vision 3D*.

Head over and do Redwood Creek Challenge Trail.

Evening

Watch the parade.

Have dinner.

Ride the Paradise Pier attractions while they're all lighted up.

Ride anything you missed earlier or want to do again.

Sample Touring Plan (Children 7 and Up)

Morning

Right at the start, head to Soarin' Over California.

Ride the Twilight Zone Tower of Terror.

Continue to Paradise Pier and pick up a FASTPASS for California Screamin'.

Ride Toy Story Mania

Ride Maliboomer.

Ride Mickey's Fun Wheel.

Ride California Screamin'

Ride Mulholland Madness.

Head to Grizzly River Run and pick up a FASTPASS.

Afternoon

Have lunch at the Pacific Wharf food court area.

Ride Grizzly River Run.

Tour Mission Tortilla Factory and the Boudin Bakery.

See *It's Tough to Be a Bug*!

Head to the Hollywood Pictures Backlot.

See *Disney's Aladdin—A Musical Spectacular*.

Ride Monsters, Inc. Mike & Sulley to the Rescue!

See *Muppet*Vision 3D*.

Evening

Watch the parade.

Have dinner.

Visit Disney Animation.

Do any attractions you missed earlier or want to ride again.

Check out Paradise Pier at night.

More Than One Day at California Adventure

California Adventure can pretty much be visited in a single day. If it's really busy, you'll have to use the FASTPASS system to shorten waits on the popular attractions. Even then, you may have to forgo a few of the attractions. Plan ahead of time which attractions you really want to do and which you could skip if short on time.

When visiting for two days, or for a day and a half, see as much as you can the first day. Then see what you missed or want to do again on the next day. California Adventure has a lot of neat shops and good restaurants to visit, and a second day will let you spend more time at these.

California Adventure FASTPASS Rides

At this writing, California Adventure is currently offering the FASTPASS system on the following attractions:

- ℮ California Screamin'
- ℮ Grizzly River Run
- ℮ Mulholland Madness
- ℮ Soarin' Over California
- ℮ The Twilight Zone Tower of Terror

During the day, you should always have a FASTPASS for some attraction in your possession. That way you'll be waiting for a quick entry onto or into an attraction while seeing or doing others. Also, be sure to pick one up before eating a meal. One FASTPASS attraction is in the Hollywood Pictures Backlot, two are in the Golden State, and two are at Paradise Pier.

One strategy for using the FASTPASS system is to pick up one in the Golden State area on your way from Paradise Pier to a show in the Hollywood Pictures Backlot. After the show, pick up another FASTPASS in the Golden State on your way to the first FASTPASS you picked up before the show. After hitting both attractions in the Golden State, head on back to Paradise Pier.

Time-Saving Tip

Several rides offer single rider service. If only one member of your family wants to go on an attraction (or if you don't mind riding separately), you can save a lot of time. Six attractions have this option–California Screamin, Grizzly River Run, Maliboomer, Mulholland Madness, Soarin' Over California, and Toy Story Mania.

The Regions of California

Disney's California Adventure is divided into four main regions: the Hollywood Pictures Backlot, the Golden State, Paradise Pier, and "a bug's land." As you enter through the main gate to the Entry Plaza, the Hollywood Pictures Backlot is to your left, the Golden State is to your right, and Paradise Pier is on the other side of the Golden State. "A bug's land" is straight ahead and to your left.

Insider's Secret

Just past the Golden Gate Bridge is the Sunshine Plaza. From this spot, and this spot alone, you can see into three of the regions. However, once you enter a region, your attention will mostly be focused on just that region.

Entry Plaza

The Entry Plaza is right inside the California Adventure main gate. There are shops and places to eat, and the Sunshine Plaza is a central location where families can meet.

Shows

California Adventure features its own unique parades: the daytime parade and Disney's Electrical Parade. The daytime parade is a traveling show featuring characters from Disney Pixar movies that stops at three spots along the parade route. At each stop, the parade turns into a street show where you're encouraged to dance along and participate. Once the sun goes down, Disney's Electrical Parade lights up the parade route. This is pretty much the same parade that appeared at Disneyland as the Main Street Electrical Parade several years ago. Both parades begin at the Sunshine Plaza and make their way through the Golden State to Paradise Pier and exit near the Maliboomer. Sunshine Plaza is a great place to watch from because there are several places to sit. The amphitheater area across from Golden Dreams is another good spot for viewing.

Character Greetings

You can often find Mickey, Minnie, and other Disney characters dressed up for a California Adventure near the Sunshine Plaza or at other locations around the park. Flik and Princess Atta can be found in "a bug's land." Be sure to check out Disney Animation as well. Often you'll find Disney characters here that you'll not see at Disneyland or elsewhere in California Adventure. For the hours, check the *Disneyland Today* guide.

Entry Plaza Tips

If you plan on viewing the parade from the Sunshine Plaza area, get there at least a half hour early to stake out your spot. While part of the family or group holds the seats, the rest can visit the shops in the area or get a bite to eat and bring something back.

Dining at the Entry Plaza

There are only two snack stands at the Entry Plaza. Baker's Field Bakery offers a variety of baked treats and specialty coffees as well as salads and sandwiches. Bur-r-r Bank Ice Cream features ice-cream cones, waffle cones, and sundaes to help keep you cool in the California sun. Both of these are great places to hit for a bite while you are waiting for the parade.

For more details on these restaurants, including pricing and sample menus, *see* Chapter 8.

Entry Plaza Shopping

The Entry Plaza has two of the larger shops in California Adventure. Greetings from California is the main souvenir shop in the park. You can find everything here from shirts and other

Quick Guide to

Attraction	Location	Height Requirement
The Boudin Bakery	Golden State	None
Bountiful Valley Farm	"a bug's land"	None
California Screamin'	Paradise Pier	48 inches
Disney Animation	Hollywood Pictures Backlot	None
Disney's Aladdin— A Musical Spectacular	Hollywood Pictures Backlot	None
Flik's Flyers	"a bug's land"	None
Francis' Ladybug Boogie	"a bug's land"	None
Golden Zephyr	Paradise Pier	None
Grizzly River Run	Golden State	42 inches
Heimlich's Chew Chew Train	"a bug's land"	None
It's Tough to Be a Bug!	"a bug's land"	None
Jim Henson's *Muppet*Vision 3D*	Hollywood Pictures Backlot	None
Jumpin' Jellyfish	Paradise Pier	40 inches
King Triton's Carousel	Paradise Pier	None
Maliboomer	Paradise Pier	52 inches
Mickey's Fun Wheel	Paradise Pier	None
Mission Tortilla Factory	Golden State	None

0 Not scary at all.
 ! Might be somewhat frightening for some children. Usually either dark or a mild roller coaster.
 !! Most young children will find this scary.
 !!! This attraction may frighten some adults. This is usually reserved for high-speed roller coasters and other thrill rides.

California
Adventure Attractions

Duration of Ride	Scare Factor	Age Range
Approx. 8 minutes	0	All
N/A	0	All
3 minutes	!!!	7 and up
N/A	0	All
40 minutes	0	All
1 minute	0	All
1 minute	0	All
2 minutes	0	All
3 minutes	!!	6 and up
2 minutes	0	All
Approx. 10 minutes	!	4 and up
Approx. 15 minutes	0	All
1½ minutes	!	4 and up
2 minutes	0	All
1 minute	!!!	7 and up
Approx. 6 minutes	0	All
Approx. 6 minutes	0	All

Quick Guide to

Attraction	Location	Height Requirement
Monsters, Inc. Mike & Sulley to the Rescue!	Hollywood Pictures Backlot	None
Mulholland Madness	Paradise Pier	42 inches
Playhouse Disney— Live on Stage!	Hollywood Pictures Backlot	None
Princess Dot's Puddle Park	"a bug's land"	None
Redwood Creek Challenge	Golden State	None**
Silly Symphony Swings	Paradise Pier	48 inches
Soarin' Over California	Golden State	40 inches
S.S. *Rustworthy*	Paradise Pier	None
Toy Story Mania	Paradise Pier	None
Tuck and Roll's Drive 'Em Buggies	"a bug's land"	36 inches to ride, 48 inches to drive
Turtle Talk with Crush	Hollywood Pictures Backlot	None
The Twilight Zone Tower of Terror	Hollywood Pictures Backlot	40 inches

*** Some challenges have a 42-inch minimum height requirement.*
  0 Not scary at all.
  ! Might be somewhat frightening for some children. Usually either dark or a mild roller coaster.
 !! Most young children will find this scary.
!!! This attraction may frighten some adults. This is usually reserved for high-speed roller coasters and other thrill rides.

California Adventure Attractions

Duration of Ride	Scare Factor	Age Range
4 minutes	!	All
2 minutes	!!	4 and up
20 minutes	0	All
N/A	0	All
N/A	0	All
2 minutes	!	6 and up
Approx. 8 minutes	!	5 and up
8 minutes	0	All
8 minutes	0	All
2 minutes	0	All
15 minutes	0	All
2 minutes	!!!	8 and up

clothing to books and even snow globes and plush characters. Anything you can print a California Adventure logo on is here. Although there are other shops around the park, they usually sell items themed only to the region in which they're located. Engine-Ear Toys carries a number of items with a railroad theme, in addition to all types of other toys.

Helpful Hint

The best time to check these shops is while you're waiting for the parade or when you just want to take a break. Unlike the shops on Main Street at Disneyland, the shops in California Adventure do not always stay open after the park closes. This is particularly true on slow days or in the off-season.

Hollywood Pictures Backlot

You enter the Hollywood Pictures Backlot, located to the east of the Sunshine Plaza, through a grand entrance. This puts you on Hollywood Boulevard, complete with lines down the middle of the street and parking meters. Although it's only two short blocks long, the mural at the far end of the boulevard uses forced perspective to make it look as though it's much longer. By taking a left and heading north off Hollywood Boulevard, you'll enter the backlot area. Here you see that several of the fancy buildings on Hollywood Boulevard are nothing more than false fronts for a movie set.

Helpful Hint
While walking down Hollywood Boulevard, be sure to read the signs on the buildings. A Dr. Nippentuck runs a plastic surgery clinic called Gone with the Chin, and there's also an "epic" styling salon called Ben Hair.

The Twilight Zone Tower of Terror—A FASTPASS Attraction

At the far end of Hollywood Boulevard, and then to the right, is the Hollywood Tower Hotel, which truly towers over California Adventure. Cast members dressed as 1930s bellhops will help you check in. You make your way through the lobby and then into a study, where you watch a short episode of *The Twilight Zone* that provides the storyline to the ride. The queue area then continues through the boiler room, where you board an elevator.

Once passengers are seated and with seat belts secure, the lights go out and the elevator car rushes up, stopping at floors along the way to view ghostly scenes from the hotel's past. Eventually the elevator reaches the 13th floor, where the doors open and you're able to look out over California Adventure.

The Scare Factor
You must be at least 40 inches tall to ride the Twilight Zone Tower of Terror. The ride is mostly in the dark and features fast ascents as well as even faster drops. Most children under 10 will find this ride too scary. If you're not sure, ask a cast member at the entrance for a parent-swap pass if you have at least two adults in the group. Then an adult and older children can try it out to see if the younger children will like it.

However, that's just part of the ride. The elevator car then drops down the shaft at nearly twice the speed of gravity. It will then go back up and down again a few times before returning to the basement, where you exit and return to the normal world.

Insider's Secret

Although the ride is themed like an episode from the TV series *The Twilight Zone*, the story is a Disney original. The attraction debuted at the Disney MGM Studios at Walt Disney World. In 1997, Disney produced *Tower of Terror*, a TV movie starring Steve Guttenberg and Kirsten Dunst that expands on the story. You may want to watch the DVD before visiting the attraction so that your family has a better understanding of the storyline.

Monsters, Inc. Mike & Sulley to the Rescue!

Based on the Disney Pixar movie *Monsters, Inc.*, this ride takes you on a journey into Monstropolis. After boarding a cab, you're off. A small video screen on the left side of the cab tunes you in to the latest breaking news bulletins on the event that has the city in an uproar—a human child is on the loose! As the ride progresses, you'll follow the story of the two monster buddies, Mike and Sulley, as they try to get Boo back to her bedroom in the human world.

Although this is somewhat similar to the dark rides at Disneyland, this ride is updated and features some special effects. The ride is filled with sight gags from the moment you step into the queue area all the way to the end. Read the advertisements and the items available in the vending machine. As you go through the sushi restaurant, you can smell the pickled ginger. The abominable snowman's snow cones even smell like lemon. Keep your eyes open for Randall, the chameleonlike monster who wants to stop you from saving Boo. He disappears

The Scare Factor

This ride is dark in some areas, and you're surrounded by monsters that might be frightening to some children. However, none of the monsters are scary. Use the *Monsters, Inc.* movie as a way to judge whether your child will like the ride.

Insider's Secret

Look for a Hidden Mickey on Sully. There are several Sullys throughout the ride. However, this Hidden Mickey is on the last Sully when he's standing next to the pink door. Look on his upper left thigh to see a dark pattern of three connected spots.

during the ride and then changes color several times later on. At the end of the ride, Roz, who always bugs Mike about turning in his paperwork, will give you a personalized farewell.

Disney Animation

On Hollywood Boulevard, this attraction gives you a behind-the-scenes look at Disney animation. You first enter the Animation Courtyard, where the lobby is surrounded by a number of screens, on which various scenes and characters from Disney animated films are projected. From here you can continue into four separate areas, each taking a different look at the process of creating an animated feature.

In the Animation Screening Room, you can watch a short film about Walt Disney and animation projects.

At Drawn to Animation, a real-life Disney animator shows you how Disney characters are created and drawn. You can ask the animator questions as they watch the characters come to life.

The Sorcerer's Workshop contains three separate interactive areas where you can get involved in animation. In the first area, you can try drawing your own animation. In the second area, the Beast's Library, you sit at workstations where you can find out which Disney character you're the most like. A digital photo is taken of you; then you're asked a series of questions about your personality, such as, "Do you like to eat lunch with nice people, or do you like to eat nice people for lunch?" Your personality and face are then used to calculate which animated character you most resemble. Finally, in Ursula's Grotto, you provide the voice for a scene from a Disney movie. You can choose either to act or sing a part. Each family or group has its own workstation, so you need not worry about everyone else in the area watching your efforts.

Helpful Hint

You don't have to go into each of the four areas, especially if you're pressed for time. However, the Animation Screening Room movie is very good and only eight minutes long. Also, you should at least try the Beast's Library in the Sorcerer's Workshop. Kids and adults alike enjoy seeing which Disney characters they resemble.

The final area is the Art of Animation. This area is merely a display of artwork from Disney animated features, including preliminary sketches and storyboards.

Turtle Talk with Crush

Inside the Disney Animation building, this show features the surfer sea turtle from *Finding Nemo*. Using real-time animation, Crush will talk with members of the audience, tell jokes, and recognize guests. It's almost like being in an animated movie. In addition to telling the audience about the undersea world, Crush will also ask guests about the human world.

This show is aimed at younger children. However, older kids and adults will also enjoy it. Turtle Talk with Crush is a great break for the middle of the day. Since each show is different, if you have time, stop by for a second show.

Jim Henson's Muppet*Vision 3D

Remember *The Muppet Show*, which ran on TV from 1976 to 1981? Well, at *Muppet*Vision 3D,* you can experience the show firsthand and in three dimensions. While you're waiting to enter the theater, several Muppet characters provide a preshow on monitors throughout the lobby. Although most of the monitors are in the front of the lobby, there are a few in the back right corner that are a bit lower and easier for small children to watch.

Once you're inside the theater, the real show begins. Statler and Waldorf, the two complainers from the television show, sit in a balcony making comments throughout the production. The show contains several 3-D gags, with things reaching out toward you. However, there's nothing scary during the show. Dr. Bunsen Honeydew and his assistant, Beaker, create Waldo—the spirit of 3-D—who causes trouble throughout the show, culminating in the destruction of the theater.

Younger children will enjoy *Muppet*Vision 3D,* especially if they already know some of the characters. If you think they may not like the 3-D part of the show, they can take off their glasses or just close their eyes.

Shows

California Adventure's main shows are in the Hollywood Pictures Backlot. The Hyperion Theater puts on musical performances. At this writing, *Disney's Aladdin—A Musical Spectacular* is playing. This Broadway-caliber musical is fantastic and will be enjoyed by guests of all ages. During the 40-minute show, the story of Aladdin from the hit Disney movie is told on stage, using great special effects that include a flying carpet and, of course, the hilarious Genie. Unlike other shows where you just wait in line, *Aladdin* has tickets that you can pick up in advance from a booth in the Hollywood Pictures Backlot. You should still return to the Hyperion at least 30 minutes before the show begins so you can get a good seat, though there are really no bad seats in the theater.

Helpful Hint
During the day, especially with young children, you'll need some time to sit down and take a break. The shows are a great way to do this. They provide a chance for parents to sit down and little ones to take a nap.

Playhouse Disney—Live on Stage! is a new show designed for young children. It features the popular characters from the Disney Channel's *Playhouse Disney*. There are no seats in this theater, so plan to sit on the carpeted floor. Although this may seem odd at first, once the show gets started, the children can stand up to dance along with the characters. Expect to see favorites from Mickey Mouse Clubhouse, Handy Manny, Little Einsteins, and My Friends Tigger and Pooh. Since the lines for this show can get rather long, try to see it as early as possible. Check the show times on the Web site or in the pamphlet you receive as you enter. The first show is usually about 30 minutes after the park opens, so if you head there first, you should have no trouble getting in.

Character Greetings
Near Disney Animation, you can meet characters throughout the day from some of Disney's newest animated features. Often

this is the only spot at which you'll see these characters—they are usually not at Disneyland.

Hollywood Pictures Backlot Tips

If you want to ride the Twilight Zone Tower of Terror, go early in the morning or get a FASTPASS for later. Otherwise, the best time to visit here is in the late morning or afternoon. Use this as your downtime for the day before hitting the rides again in the evening. *Playhouse Disney—Live on Stage!* begins in the morning, but *Aladdin* does not begin until afternoon. Try to see the earliest showings for the shows. The later showings are often busier.

Dining in the Hollywood Pictures Backlot

The Hollywood Pictures Backlot has a few places to find a snack or light meal. Award Wieners offers several types of hot dogs and sausage sandwiches. Fairfax Market is a fruit stand that also sells vegetables, nuts, and other healthy snacks. Schmoozies is where you can find a variety of smoothies, juices, and specialty coffee drinks.

For more details on these restaurants, including pricing and sample menus, *see* Chapter 8.

Hollywood Pictures Backlot Shopping

Don't forget to check out the shops for your Hollywood paraphernalia. Gone Hollywood is a fun shop to browse even if you don't plan on buying anything. It carries dress-up clothing as well as trendy items celebrities would wear. Off the Page is at the exit to Disney Animation. Here you can find a variety of items featuring Disney's animated characters as well as collectible items such as animation cels and other artwork. If creatures are more your speed, check out the Studio Store, which features all types of Monsters, Inc. and Muppet-inspired items.

Golden State

The Golden State region is in the center of California Adventure; its districts represent the various parts that make up the state of California. Condor Flats represents the aerospace industry and is designed after a high-desert flight test area. The Grizzly Peak Recreation area represents California's outdoors with the look of Yosemite and the Sierra Nevada mountains. Pacific Wharf resembles a seaside town such as Monterey. The Bay Area is designed with the art and architecture of the San Francisco area in mind. Finally, the Golden Vine Winery represents the California wine country.

Soarin' Over California—A FASTPASS Attraction

This is the only attraction in Condor Flats. However, Soarin' Over California is all this district needs. We overheard visitors exiting the ride state that this was worth the cost of admission by itself. We agree. A large, hangarlike building houses the attraction. The queue area is filled with photos from California's aviation history. Riders are seated in 10-person rows, and once everybody is buckled in, the seats rise up into the air and posi-

Insider's Secret

The themes in the various districts are very well thought out. Heading along the walkway in front of Soarin' Over California, notice the flashing blue lights that make it look like a runway. The path leading to Grizzly River Run is designed to look like a scenic highway, complete with guard rails and cracks in the road. Check out the food and lodging sign by the entrance to the Grand Californian Hotel. Look at the cacti in this area: some have been trained to form a Hidden Mickey. Also be sure to read the signs in the windows of the Bay Area buildings.

The Scare Factor

Soarin' Over California has a minimum height requirement of 40 inches. Most children who are tall enough will enjoy the ride. There's nothing scary except that the seats are lifted up into the air and your feet hang down. Some children who are fearful of heights may not like this. However, their attention will usually be on the screen, and they quickly forget about how high they are in the air. Most children 5 and up will be fine.

tion the riders in front of a large movie screen. The screen curves around the riders so that it fills their vision. You're supposed to be hang-gliding over the state and are taken along a river, up onto snowy mountains with skiers, over the coast, across an aircraft carrier, and much more. It ends with a flight over Disneyland. Pay careful attention as you're flying over the golf course. A golf ball will come flying up at you. Don't blink or you'll miss a Hidden Mickey on the ball. Also look for the fireworks at the end of the ride that form the familiar Mickey head.

As you fly over California, the seats move in synchronization with the movie. Gusts of wind from different directions add to the realism. Even your sense of smell is used. You smell orange blossoms while flying over an orange grove and pine trees while flying over the mountains and rivers. With all the effects put together, you really feel as if you're flying.

Grizzly River Run—A FASTPASS Attraction

River rafting is a popular sport in California. With the Grizzly River Run, you can experience running the rapids with your family. Guests ride in circular rafts with everyone facing the center. The rafts are carried up a lift toward Grizzly Peak and then

The Scare Factor

Guests must be at least 42 inches tall to ride the Grizzly River Run, which is rougher and wetter than Splash Mountain at Disneyland. Some young children may find this ride too scary, especially if they do not like getting splashed with water. There are several places from which you can watch the ride. Let your children watch other people ride and then decide for themselves if they want to try it. Because of the roughness of the ride, children under 6 may find it too scary.

ride down the river flume through fast currents that buck the rafts up and down. The rafts spin around a bit, so everyone gets an opportunity to be in front, where you usually get the wettest.

Insider's Secret

With its drops and other effects, Grizzly River Run is the tallest and fastest raft ride in the world.

The turbulent river is filled with boulders that collide with the rafts. They descend two steep drops, one of which is a 22-foot waterfall.

Lockers are near the entrance for this ride, across from the shop. Use them to stow backpacks and other items you want to keep dry while you get wet on the river.

Helpful Hint

If you follow a pathway off to the left of the entrance, you'll come to a lookout point with an excellent view of the tall drop. This is a great place to take a picture of your family or group as they are rafting.

Redwood Creek Challenge Trail

Across from the Grizzly River Run, this outdoor activity center is great fun for active children. There are towers and rocks to climb, cargo nets, bridges to cross, and even cable slides. Several Park Rangers are on hand to help out where needed. Kids enjoy the opportunity to run around, since so many other attractions require sitting or standing in line. If you go inside the bear cave, look around for a Hidden Mickey created by an indentation on the roof.

Some of the challenges have a minimum height requirement of 42 inches. However, there's something here for children of all ages.

Mission Tortilla Factory

On this short factory tour, a cast member explains the history of making tortillas, and guests can watch video demonstrations of how tortillas used to be made at home during two different periods of time. The tour then leads to a modern factory setup. There you'll see two machines, one making flour tortillas and the other making corn tortillas. At the end of the tour, you're treated to a sample tortilla, which you just saw being made. The tour is fairly short, and children often like the free sample at the end.

The Boudin Bakery

Right across from the tortilla factory, the Boudin Bakery features a longer and more entertaining tour. Hosted by Rosie O'-Donnell and Colin Mochrie (from the television show *Whose Line Is It Anyway?*), this tour uses humor to explain how sourdough bread is made. During the tour, you move from one station to the next as your hosts describe what you're seeing through the large windows into the bakery. Even if making bread is not your thing, the tour is quite fun. Plus you usually get a free sample of sourdough bread at the beginning. If you want another taste of what you watched being baked, step into the Pacific Wharf Café next door for some fresh sourdough bread.

Shows

Inside the Redwood Creek Challenge Trail, you can watch a storytelling show. (This show usually runs during the busier seasons only.) Children from about 3 to 10 years of age will enjoy the show, and adults find it entertaining because the characters and cast members do a great job adding their own sound effects and joking around with the audience.

Character Greetings

At various times throughout the day, you can find Minnie dressed up as an aviator, as well as Mickey and the rest of the gang around the Golden State—usually dressed for the district in which they're located.

Golden State Tips

The Golden State region has a variety of attractions. There are six rides, an activity center, and two tours. Located between the Hollywood Pictures Backlot and Paradise Pier, the Golden State gets a lot of traffic. Two attractions use the FASTPASS system. Be sure to grab a FASTPASS for one of these when walking through the area. Or take the tours while waiting for a FASTPASS time. Try to hit Soarin' Over California and the Grizzly River Run in the morning before they get too busy. The afternoon or early evening is a good time to hit the rest of the attractions in this area; that's when the popular rides in the other areas are the busiest.

Time-Saving Tip
Tours are a good break between rides. However, if you're pressed for time, they should be cut.

Dining in the Golden State

The Golden State has some great places to eat. The Taste Pilot's Grill, right next to Soarin' Over California, serves gourmet burgers, ribs, and other tasty meals. At the Golden Vine Winery, the Wine Country Trattoria carries lasagna, baked pastas, and grilled sandwiches.

The Pacific Wharf area contains a great food court that is sure to offer something to please each person in your family. The seating is all centrally located between the eateries. At the Pacific Wharf Café, you can get soup or salad in fresh-baked bread bowls as well as tasty desserts. Cocina Cucamonga serves tacos and nachos. The Lucky Fortune Cookery offers Asian-style food. Rita's Baja Blenders is a great place for a cool, refreshing fruity drink. The Pacific Wharf Distribution Company offers beer.

For more details on these restaurants, including pricing and sample menus, *see* Chapter 8.

Golden State Shopping

The various districts in the Golden State have shops featuring area-theme merchandise. Fly 'n' Buy in Condor Flats carries a variety of aviation-theme items, including shirts, hats, posters, and much more. Rushin' River Outfitters, right next to the entrance to the Grizzly River Run, carries outdoor-theme items, including hiking and camping wear, and lots of items emblazoned with the Grizzly Peak icon.

"a bug's land"

Designed specifically for young children, "a bug's land" provides you with a bug's-eye view of the world. You enter through

Insider's Secret

"a bug's land" is shaded by 75 clovers. However, there's only one four-leaf clover in the mix. Can you find it?

Helpful Hint

"a bug's land" contains family bathrooms where a family, including all of the children, can go into a single, private room to take care of business. This is great for babies needing a diaper change and for families with small children.

a giant Cowboy Crunchies box and arrive in a land with benches made out of Popsicle sticks, lights made out of drinking straws and fireflies, and shade provided by giant clover. This area also features five attractions.

Heimlich's Chew Chew Train

This is a slow ride where you board a caterpillar train and "eat" your way through a garden. Heimlich provides a guided tour during which you can use all of your senses. For example, while traveling through a watermelon slice, you can smell the watermelon and get dripped on by "juice." This ride is best for children 6 and under. Older kids might be bored.

Flik's Fun Flyers

This is a flying ride where you climb into suspended gondolas that rise and fall as they spin. It's similar to the Dumbos at Disneyland except that riders here have no control over the height of the car. The gondolas are designed to look like boxes of apple juice, animal crackers, raisins, and Chinese food. They're suspended from "balloons" created by bugs from twigs and leaves. Most children will enjoy this ride.

Insider's Secret

The boxes you ride in rotate around a large tub of nondairy whipped topping. If you look at the nutrition label, you'll see that the topping contains no fat but 10 grams of fun per serving.

Francis' Ladybug Boogie

This is a fun spinning ride similar to the Mad Tea Party at Disneyland. You climb aboard ladybugs and then travel around in a figure-eight track. There's the added thrill of near misses at the intersection of the track as ladybugs almost crash into each other. This ride is good for children of all ages, since you can make the ride as thrilling or calm as you like.

Tuck and Roll's Drive 'Em Buggies

This attraction lets you drive around in pillbug-shape bumper cars. Each car seats two people and can be driven anywhere within the ring under the tent. If you want to drive off the track or bump into other cars on the Autopia, Tuck and Roll's Drive 'Em Buggies allows you to do so without breaking any safety rules. Riders must be at least 42 inches tall for this ride, and drivers must be at least 48 inches tall. This is a fun ride for both younger and older children, allowing them to ride together and bump into other cars. The ride is fairly gentle, so young children will not get bumped around roughly.

Princess Dot Puddle Park

This water-play area is for all ages, but it's targeted toward younger children. Water comes out of a fan sprayer at the end of a giant garden hose and also shoots randomly from little geysers in the ground. A great place to cool off on hot days, it also allows children to burn off some energy in the process. Adults will enjoy watching this attraction.

It's Tough to Be a Bug!

After you enter the theater through an ant hole, you're treated to a 3-D movie full of special effects. In the waiting area are several posters for movies with bug adaptations, such as *Antie* and *The Grass Menagerie*. On entering the theater, you sit on a bench and then don your bug eyeglasses. Flik, the ant from the movie, is your host. He introduces a number of bugs that show you how they live. There's the spider who shoots quills, the termite who spits acid (you just get hit with water), and even a stinkbug who demonstrates his ability.

Just as the show is becoming educational, Hopper arrives. He doesn't like humans because they kill bugs, so he sends swarms of hornets and black widow spiders to get you.

The Scare Factor
Young children may find *It's Tough to Be a Bug!* scary. In addition to the 3-D effects of things coming at the audience, the other special effects can be frightening, especially in the darkened theater.

If you're unsure if this movie is right for your kids, sit in the rear of the theater on the right side so you can exit during the show if needed. Our 2-year-old daughter was a bit scared, but she made it through fine by hiding her eyes and holding onto a parent. By the time children are 4 years old, they should not be afraid of the show.

Bountiful Valley Farm
California is an agricultural giant, and the Bountiful Valley Farm provides an interactive way to learn about it. There are gardens with all types of vegetables as well as groves of fruit trees. Children will enjoy playing in the water maze formed by sprinklers. Depending on the day, there are also demonstrations and exhibits on farming. The nice thing about this attraction is that you can spend as much or as little time here as you want. It's rarely crowded, and many children, as well as adults, enjoy seeing where their food comes from.

Character Greetings
At various times throughout the day, you can find Flik the ant and sometimes other characters from *It's Tough to Be a Bug!* around "a bug's land." If your children enjoy getting auto-

graphs, be sure to get these because they're not available at Disneyland.

"a bug's land" Tips

Other than *It's Tough to Be a Bug!*, most of the attractions in this area are for younger kids. There are no FASTPASSes here, but there are no major rides either. It's best to visit "a bug's land" either first thing in the morning or toward evening since the rides are less busy during these times.

Dining in "a bug's land"

There are some great places to eat in "a bug's land." At the Bountiful Valley Farmers Market, you can find sandwich wraps and salads as well as smoked turkey legs from nearby carts. Sam Andreas Shakes offers ice-cream shakes and cones.

For more details on these restaurants, including pricing and sample menus, *see* Chapter 8.

"a bug's land" Shopping

This area has limited shopping. The P. T. Flea Market sells candy and "a bug's life" products.

Paradise Pier

The fourth region of California Adventure is designed to resemble a classic boardwalk amusement park. As such, it contains a majority of the park's rides and tends to be one of the busier areas during the day. Everything here is intended to take you back to the glory days of the California surf scene. In ad-

Insider's Secret

Paradise Pier is built around Paradise Bay. If you take the time to look at the water, you'll notice this is no placid lake. Instead, Disney Imagineers have designed a wave machine into the bay so the water is always moving—just like the real ocean.

dition to the rides, the restaurants and shops resemble their sea-side counterparts and the air is filled with tunes from the Beach Boys and similar groups but played on a pipe organ. Paradise Pier is a lot of fun during the day, and as the sun sets the area comes alive with thousands and thousands of lights.

California Screamin'—A FASTPASS Attraction

Billed as the longest, fastest, and scariest ride at the Disneyland Resort, California Screamin' is a worthy addition to the resort's host of coasters. The ride is designed to resemble a classic wooden roller coaster. However, the experience is nothing like you would find on one of those rides. After riders board, their cars are halted on the tracks along the bay. The cars are then catapulted from 0 to 55 mph in only five seconds, giving the cars enough speed to climb the first hill. If you have ridden wooden roller coasters at other parks, you know how they shake the riders up. Don't expect this on California Screamin'. This is a steel tube coaster, so the ride is smooth—at least as far as the track is concerned. There are several hills with steep drops, fast turns, and a series of bumps that cause you to float above your seat for a moment. There's even a vertical loop—the first and only one at the Disneyland Resort. Most of the hills have scream tunnels. These are designed to amplify the intensity of the riders' excitement. So when you enter one of these tunnels, get ready to scream! You can purchase a photo of your family coming down one of the drops, at California Scream Cam, near the ride's exit.

Insider's Secret

At the start of the ride, electromagnets are used to accelerate the cars to 55 mph so they have enough speed to climb the first hill without chain assist.

The Scare Factor

California Screamin' has a minimum height requirement of 48 inches. The ride is more intense than any other at California Adventure or Disneyland. Be sure your children can handle all the other coaster-type rides before they try this one. If the kids liked Space Mountain, they'll probably be fine on California Screamin'. Ages 7 and up is a good suggestion.

Toy Story Mania

Toy Story Mania is an interactive ride similar to Disneyland's Buzz Lightyear Astro Blasters. Guests don 3-D classes and climb into ride vehicles with shooters mounted in front each seat. By pulling and releasing the firing mechanism on the shooter, you can launch projectiles at targets, and the ride keeps track of your score. At several points in the ride, your vehicle will stop and Toy Story characters will cheer you on as you fire darts as balloons, toss rings over Little Green Men, launch balls at plates being carried by army men, and even fire at targets in an old west game. Special effects include sprays of water spray gusts of air that are activated when you hit certain targets. Toy Story Mania is fun for all ages, and your family will probably want to go on this ride more than once.

Helpful Hint

Toy Story Mania is a popular attraction, but FAST-PASSes are not available. Try to ride earlier in the morning; you can expect to wait up to an hour at other times on busy days. Small children can ride on the laps of their parents, but be sure to hold onto them as the ride spins and make some quick turns.

Insider's Secret

In order to increase your score, fire as quickly as possible. The shooter "launches" a projectile when you release the cord—but if you hold onto it and just move your hand back and forth quickly, you can fire much more rapidly. Also, spend your time aiming for the higher value targets; though it may take awhile to hit a 1,000- or 2,000-point target, it will take less time than hitting 10 or 20 100-point targets.

Maliboomer

This ride resembles the midway hammer swinging game that test a person's strength. However, this time the riders are the object speeding up to ring the bell. The Maliboomer consists of three towers. Each tower has four rows of four seats. You're buckled into the seats and then shot 180 feet in the air. A bell rings at the top, and then you descend in a series of bounces. It's not a free-fall ride. Instead, the ascent is the thrill. Riders reach a maximum speed of approximately 55 mph.

Maliboomer has a minimum height requirement of 52 inches. The ride looks scarier than it really is. In fact, one adult we spoke with in the queue was about to chicken out. After-

Helpful Hint

The Maliboomer does not offer a FASTPASS system. However, there's another way to expedite your way through the queue: there's a line for single riders. If you don't mind riding apart from your group, or if a parent has to ride alone while the other parent watches the children, this line moves more quickly. The cast member at the boarding area uses the people in this line to fill out each row of seats.

ward, he said he really liked it and would do it again. The main sensation is that of being pressed down into your seat during the ascent. The way down is controlled, and you never feel as if you are floating. The worst part of the ride is the anticipation. The seats bounce up and down for a bit before launching skyward, keeping you guessing as to when you'll take off. Most children who meet the height requirement and like thrill rides will be fine on the Maliboomer. Ages 7 and up is a good guide.

Mulholland Madness—A FASTPASS Attraction

This minicoaster is designed to represent Mulholland Drive, the winding road that leads from Hollywood to Malibu. Riders board small cars, some decorated as highway patrol cruisers, which then climb to the top of the ride. After a series of fast turns that make you feel as if your car may leave the tracks, the ride takes you down a series of quick drops and climbs with more fast turns. From the outside, the ride appears fairly tame. However, when you're on it, you'll experience more of a thrill than you expected. As you're looking at the large map mural on the ride, look for a Hidden Mickey. There's a swimming pool in the classic shape. You can also find Hidden Mickeys on the Mulholland Madness Billboard license plate.

The Scare Factor

The minimum height requirement is 42 inches. The Matterhorn Bobsleds is a good comparison for this ride. If your children liked the Matterhorn, they'll have a good time on this ride as well.

Mickey's Fun Wheel

The main icon of California Adventure, Mickey's Fun Wheel is a sight to behold. Before you dismiss it as nothing more than a run-of-the-mill Ferris wheel, take a look at the gondolas on it.

Although the red gondolas (one out of three) are fixed to the outer edge of the wheel, the other two-thirds of the gondolas freely swing around on tracks built into the wheel. This provides an entirely new and thrilling experience to the ride. As the wheel rotates, these gondolas move around inside the wheel, taking some quick drops and then swinging wildly at the bottom.

Insider's Secret
Mickey's Fun Wheel provides a great view of California Adventure and the surrounding area. Try this ride during the day and then again at night when everything is lighted up.

There's no height requirement for this ride. Families with young children should opt for the stationary red gondolas. The queue for these is often shorter, as well. The swinging gondolas are a lot of fun for older children. However, if you're not sure whether they would like it, go in the red ones first, and watch what the other gondolas do during the ride.

Silly Symphony Swings
The Silly Symphony Swings attraction is similar to the swing rides found at most fairs and carnivals; but with a theme depicting "The Band Concert" from Walt Disney's *Silly Symphonies* cartoons. The swings not only go around but also up and down a bit. As the ride rises into the air, watch as the mural wrapped around the central tower begins to show an approaching storm.

The Scare Factor
Children who meet the height requirement and want to go on the ride should not be scared and will enjoy the ride. Children 5 and under may find it too scary.

The ride has a minimum height requirement of 48 inches, though smaller children can ride in two-seat swings with a taller rider.

Golden Zephyr

Based on another carnival-style ride, the Golden Zephyr consists of several rocket ships that swing around a central tower. As the ride picks up speed, the rockets swing out over the bay. This ride is similar to the Astro Orbitor at Disneyland, except that Golden Zephyr riders have no control over their rockets, which are suspended on cables rather than an arm. This is a fun ride for children of all ages, with no height or age requirements. Use the Astro Orbitor as a comparison to judge whether your young children will like it.

Jumpin' Jellyfish

This ride is a scaled-down version of the Maliboomer. You sit in pairs under jellyfish-like parachutes and are taken up to the top and then descend back down to the ground in a series of bounces.

The minimum height requirement for this ride is 40 inches. Most children who meet this requirement will enjoy Jumpin' Jellyfish. However, those who are afraid of heights or are uncomfortable with their feet hanging during a ride should skip this attraction.

King Triton's Carousel

What theme park would be complete without a carousel? Paradise Pier's own version differs from most. Instead of riding horses, you climb up on various creatures of the sea, including otters, whales, dolphins, fish, and even sea horses. This is a California Adventure favorite for young children.

S. S. Rustworthy

This water activity center is designed around a shipwrecked fireboat. Children can take part in a number of activities, in-

Helpful Hint

It's usually a good idea to have a dry change of clothes for your children after they play on this attraction, unless it's a warm day and they'll dry off quickly.

cluding squirting water cannons. This is a great place to cool down and burn off some energy.

Games of the Boardwalk

What boardwalk would be complete without some midway games? These games of skill and chance cost an additional fee, and winners receive prizes. To play, you'll need to purchase points that are loaded onto a plastic card. (This is done at electronic kiosks near the games; cash or credit/debit cards are accepted.) Once you've used all of your points, you can keep the card as a souvenir. If you have younger children, check out Goofy About Fishin', where everyone receives a prize.

Helpful Hint

To ensure that someone in your family wins a prize, play when no one else is there and only your family members are playing. Someone is sure to win. When you have a limited budget or are pressed for time, skip the boardwalk games.

Shows

In the spring of 2010, the waters of Paradise Bay will come alive at night with a new show called World of Color. The show combines Disney characters, music, lights, special effects, and 1,200 fountains that can shoot water over 200 feet into the air. Seating is provided in a new amphitheater along the northern shore of Paradise Bay. Since this show is new, try to find seats about an hour before it begins. While some of your family members hold your spots, the rest can go on rides or pick up dinner to eat while you are waiting.

Paradise Pier Tips

Paradise Pier is usually the busiest region in California Adventure, with the afternoon generally being the worst time. Try to hit Paradise Pier first thing in the morning, or wait until late afternoon. Be sure to visit this area at night and enjoy the lights. It's quite spectacular. Even when the area is busy, you can use the FASTPASS system on California Screamin' and Mulholland Madness. Pick up tickets before you have lunch or dinner or while you're watching a show; then come back and get right onto the rides after a short wait.

Dining on Paradise Pier

Just like the rest of California Adventure, Paradise Pier has some great places to eat. Ariel's Grotto is the main restaurant in the area. It serves three-course meals with a set price. You can choose your main course, and the family shares appetizers and desserts. If you're just looking for a quick meal, Pizza Oom Mow Mow is the place for pizzas on surfboard-shape crusts. Don Tomas offers turkey legs and chimichangas, or you can pick up a hot dog at the Hot Dog Hut. Corn Dog Castle is the home of large, meal-size corn dogs. Finally, for a refreshing snack, Catch a Flave offers soft-serve ice-cream cones with various flavors swirled in.

For more details on these restaurants, including pricing and sample menus, *see* Chapter 8.

Paradise Pier Shopping

Whether you need a T-shirt, candy, or some Paradise Pier souvenirs, the shops here will have what you're looking for. Man Hat 'n' Beach carries a variety of surfing-theme clothing and, of

Insider's Secret

Disney is spending a billion dollars to expand and improve California Adventure over the next few years. The changes begin in the spring of 2010, when Paradise Pier will premier a new night show called World of Color. The Little Mermaid–Ariel's Undersea Adventure is scheduled to open in the spring of 2011; this dark ride will take guests seated in seashells on a new adventure. Then, in 2012, Cars Land is expected to open behind "a bug's land" and the Hollywood Pictures Backlot. Themed after the Disney Pixar movie *Cars*, this new land will feature shops and dining venues as well as three new attractions. Guests will float around on tires at Luigi's Flying Tires and then have the chance to whip around turns as they make their way through Mater's Junkyard Jamboree. The E-ticket ride for this area will be called Radiator Springs Racers. Guests will take a tour of Radiator Springs before racing against other guests.

course, all types of headwear. At Pacific Ocean Photos, you can insert your family into one of several scenes from California Adventure. These make great family souvenirs. Point Mugu Tattoo sells temporary tattoos as well as souvenirs, while Sideshow Shirts has all types of T-shirts. For items themed after the classic boardwalks, check out Treasures in Paradise. Here you can find collectibles, toys, and California Screamin' merchandise as well as tasty treats.

CHAPTER

7

Downtown Disney

T his upscale shopping area of restaurants, shops, and entertainment venues is in between the main gates of Disneyland and California Adventure and the Disneyland Hotel. Most of the venues in Downtown Disney are geared toward older children and adults. However, there are a few places young children will enjoy. Downtown Disney stays open after the theme parks close—as late as 2 AM. It's an option for fun activities after a day at the park, especially during the off-season, when the parks close earlier.

Downtown Disney has a monorail station near the Rainforest Café. This used to be the Disneyland Hotel monorail station. From here, guests with valid tickets can ride to the Tomorrowland station in Disneyland and back.

This chapter takes a look at the various entertainment venues as well as the shops. For information on the restaurants, *see* the Downtown Disney section of Chapter 8.

Entertainment

Downtown Disney provides a number of entertainment venues, from sports to movies, with music thrown in as well. In addition, in the evenings and especially on weekends, local entertainers will perform live—as well as sell their latest recordings.

AMC Theatres

Showing the latest movies, this 12-screen theater is designed in the style of Hollywood's golden era. If your family wants to catch a movie during your vacation, this is a great place to go. If you plan on seeing a show after leaving the parks in the evening (especially on weekends), it's a good idea to purchase your tickets earlier in the day to avoid the lines and to ensure you get seats. For show times, call 714/769–4262 or look them up at www.disneyland.com.

ESPN Zone

Think of this place as a sports bar gone mad. The lower level features a gift shop and two restaurants. The entertainment is on the upper level. Here you can participate in a number of sports-related activities, including video games, a rock-climbing wall, laser skeet, hoop shooting, and much more. There's also a racing simulator where two guests can sit in actual-size cars and race against each other as well as computer-driven opponents. To play the games, you'll need to purchase a Zone card. This is like a credit card that stores points. Each game requires a certain number of points to play. You buy a card with

Helpful Hint

Before you leave on your vacation, visit www. disneyland.com and use the "Calendar" feature. Here you can enter the day of your arrival and the number of days you'll be staying. The Web site will then give you a list of what's going on at Disneyland, Disney's California Adventure, and Downtown Disney during your stay.

Insider's Secret

Annual Passholders receive discounts at many places in Downtown Disney. Discounts vary from 10% to 20% off merchandise or markdown entertainment venue tickets.

a set number of points, and you can add points to the card at ATM-like machines throughout the building. If you'll be playing as a family or group, we recommend getting one card for everyone to share. You get more points for each dollar spent: the more money you spend, the more points you get on that card. For example, $5 will get you a card with 15 points; $10, 40 points; and $100, 600 points.

In addition to the games, you can also catch the day's sporting events on the large-screen monitors down in the Screening Room. The largest has a 16-foot screen. For a schedule of events, either check www.espnzone.com/anaheim or call 714/300–3776.

House of Blues

In addition to being a restaurant, House of Blues features a theater that can seat nearly 1,000 people. Every night of the week, there's some type of entertainment here, and some of them are big names. Ticket prices range from $15 to $50 and up, depending on the show. Check www.disneyland.com for shows, times, and ticket prices. If you plan on seeing a popular show, you can purchase tickets in advance by calling 714/778–BLUE (714/778–2583) or visiting their Web site at www.houseofblues.com. In addition to blues music, House of Blues features rock, reggae, hip-hop, Latin, and R&B. The Sunday Gospel Brunch serves an all-you-can-eat buffet along with live gospel music. Brunch and the show together run around $38 per person.

Ralph Brennan's Jazz Kitchen

This establishment features live entertainment nightly at the downstairs restaurant, Flambeaux's. There's no charge, and although the music is intended for guests of the restaurant, you can sit outside the open-air dining area and enjoy it without having dinner. For a schedule of entertainment, check www. disneyland.com.

Shopping

Downtown Disney is filled with a large variety of upscale shops carrying household items, clothes, toys, and much more. Even if you don't have the money to spend, it's still fun to browse through them. There are also a number of carts and booths set up around the area that sell specialty items.

Anne Geddes

At the Australian photographer's (famous for her photos of adorable babies) flagship store, you can shop for more than just coffee-table books and calendars. Also available in the Anne Geddes line are baby clothing and accessories, wristwatches, bedding, and silver keepsakes and jewelry.

Basin

This London-based shop sells unique bath and body products, including bath bombs for fizzy baths, massage and shampoo bars, as well as lots of fresh soaps in a wide variety of fragrances.

Build-A-Bear Workshop

Create your own teddy bear at this kid-friendly shop. Customers select from dozens of basic bears and then customize them with different outfits and accessories.

Compass Books

This branch of the West's oldest independent bookseller offers books, magazines, and newspapers, and includes a small café selling specialty coffees and baked goods.

Disney Vault 28

Looking for a contemporary boutique that sells trendy fashions with a Disney theme? Then check out this new shop in Downtown Disney. You can find clothes, accessories, and even art and collectibles that you won't find in other places. Disney Vault 28 also has exclusive merchandise based on the latest Disney movies.

ESPN Zone Studio Store

In the ESPN Zone, the Studio Store offers a variety of ESPN merchandise, team jerseys, collectibles, and other professional sports-team items. Of course, the Anaheim Angels and the Mighty Ducks are the two featured teams.

Fossil

Visit the flagship Fossil store for their line of watches as well as other accessories including purses, handbags, shirts, sunglasses, and more.

House of Blues Store

Pick up House of Blues shirts, caps, and other souvenirs. The "Jake and Elwood" collection is a favorite for Blues Brothers fans. You can even find Cajun-theme food items such as hot sauce and bread mixes to take the House of Blues experience back to your kitchen.

Island Charters

This is a fun shop with a nautical-aviation theme. It sells clothing items as well as a variety of other items for your home or office.

LEGO Imagination Center

Designed for kids, this shop sells the entire line of LEGO products. Some of the products are often not available in local toy or department stores. The LEGO Imagination Center also has several workstations where kids can try out the building blocks before you buy them. LEGO-related items such as clothing and software are also available. This is a great place to pick up sets for your children to play with in the hotel or gifts to take home.

Little Miss Matched

This unique store is known for its socks, which are sold in sets of three-each different so you can mix them up. While most of the offerings are girls' apparel, the store also carries clothing for women and socks and flip-flops for boys and men.

Marceline's Confectionery

A standard candy shop designed like one from the past, this confectionery was inspired by Marceline, Missouri—Walt Dis-

Insider's Secret

Marceline's Confectionery sells the same items as the candy shop inside Disneyland, and is often less crowded. We love the delicious caramel apples, which come in several varieties, including an apple of the month. They will even cut them up for you so you can share—or at least not be as messy. Be sure to stop by and try one. It's one of our family traditions.

ney's hometown. You can watch cooks make candies and other treats throughout the day.

Quicksilver Boardriders Club Store

This shop sells clothing, footwear, and accessories from the Quicksilver brand as well as other related brands. Whether you are looking for surfer wear or an outfit for relaxing on the beach, you can stay in style here.

Rainforest Retail Shopping Village

Inside the Rainforest Café, this shop sells clothing and other items with the restaurant's logo as well as toys, jewelry, and other items.

Sephora

This French cosmetics store not only sells all types of cosmetics and fragrances but also offers complimentary makeovers and product application demonstrations.

Something Silver

Something Silver carries all types of silver jewelry and accessories, including bracelets, necklaces, earrings, chains, and rings in a variety of styles.

Studio Disney 365

Does your daughter want to be the next Hannah Montana? At Studio Disney 365, girls can get one of several different makeovers—and even purchase a wardrobe to go along with it. (Boys can also get rock star makeovers.) Makeovers start at $20 and go up to $60. It's a good idea to make an appointment (call 714/781–7895).

Insider's Secret

While you may think a travel office is the last place you would go during your vacation, the Walt Disney Travel Company Guest Services can actually be quite helpful. Not only can the staff book reservations for your next vacation, but they can also assist with any changes you may need to make to your current package. For example, if you want to add another day to your trip or add a character dining meal to your package, they can take care of it for you—often saving you money. This office can also make arrangements for visiting other Southern California attractions and help you find transportation if needed.

World of Disney

Containing California's largest selection of Disney merchandise, this is essentially a super Disney Store. In addition to souvenir items for the Disney theme parks, you can find all types of apparel, household items, and more emblazoned with Disney characters, as well as plush toys, books, DVDs, and much more.

CHAPTER

8

Disney Dining

During your vacation to the Disneyland Resort, your family will have to eat. No matter what your budget, you can eat some of your meals, if not all, at the resort. Therefore, we have included this handy guide to each and every restaurant at Disneyland, Disney's California Adventure, the Disney hotels, and even Downtown Disney.

Although many people think primarily of fast food such as burgers and hot dogs when they consider dining at a theme park, the Disneyland Resort offers much, much more. Of course, you can still find burgers and hot dogs, but because your family is on vacation, try taking a culinary vacation as well. Instead of eating the same quick foods you would at home, try something different. Several families we have talked to told us they plan where they want to eat before they leave on their vacation.

There's a popular misconception that eating at the resort is extremely expensive. Although some things are pricier, you can still find good deals to fit your budget. Fast-food items are probably the main thing that is higher. Although you can get a combo meal at McDonald's for $5 to $6, a similar meal at the resort may be $8 to $9. But keep in mind that you may also spend an extra 30 to 60 minutes walking out of the park, across the street to McDonald's, and then back into the park when you could have been riding attractions instead. You do pay for the convenience of some things. However, some dinners at the restaurants are comparably priced to those outside the park. For example, one family told us they spent less on a big lunch at the Blue Bayou restaurant in Disneyland than they did on dinner at Tony Roma's the following night.

Eat for Less

There are several ways you can enjoy Disney dining without spending a lot of money. First off, schedule your meals so you eat only one or two at the park. If your hotel offers a complimentary breakfast, that takes care of one meal. If you leave the park during the afternoon to return to your hotel for naps or a swim, you can eat at an off-site place along the way. Or if the park closes early, you can eat dinner off-site.

If you plan on dining at a nice restaurant in the resort, do so in the afternoon, usually around 1:30 to 2 PM. You'll miss the lunch crowds, and during the summer you'll be inside during the hottest part of the day. Because this will be your main meal for the day, you can get by with a light breakfast and light dinner.

Another way to save money is to eat two meals and then have snacks in between. A late character breakfast with a buffet will last you into the afternoon. Precede it with some snacks in the morning, then more in the afternoon. Finally, have dinner a bit early before the crowds do and then have snacks or a dessert if needed later in the evening.

The key is to budget your meal expenses for the vacation as well as for each day. How strictly you adhere to this budget is up to you, but no matter what, it's a good starting point to saving money. For example, don't eat at a nice restaurant on the same day you do a character breakfast.

Money-Saving Tip

If you drink tap water with some of your meals instead of buying soft drinks, you can save a bundle over the course of your vacation. For example, a family of four can save $10 to $12 per meal by skipping the drinks.

Instead of buying a lot of snacks at the resort, bring some from home and carry them in a fanny pack or a pocket. During warm weather, don't bring things that will melt, such as chocolate. Instead, bring nuts, dried fruit, granola bars, fruit snacks, pretzels, crackers, and cookies. Candy may recharge you quickly, but the energy you get is fleeting, and candy is not as filling as the snacks just mentioned. Don't forget drinks, either. Water bottles or juice boxes are much cheaper than drinks purchased inside the park. In fact, we use our water bottles everywhere except at restaurants with table service.

Money-Saving Tip

You can also save money on meals through discounts that come with the Disney Club card, American Express, or an Annual Passport at various restaurants throughout the resort. Certain restrictions apply, so check with the appropriate credit-card company or group for more information.

Definitions for Restaurant Ratings

We've categorized and rated the Disneyland Resort restaurants based on the type of restaurant, price, whether you will need reservations, and the restaurant's suitability for children.

Types of Restaurant

Fast Food: Here you'll find sandwiches, hamburgers, and other light meals. This category also includes snack or dessert places.

Buffeteria: At what Disney calls its cafeterialike restaurants, you order a meal at a counter, pay for it, and then carry it to your table.

Buffet: This is an all-you-can-eat meal where you can choose from a variety of items.

Restaurant: Here you're seated and someone takes your order and then brings the food to your table.

Price

$ *Inexpensive*: adult meals about $8 or less

$$ *Moderate*: adult meals about $9–$15

$$$ *Expensive*: adult meals about $16 and up

Reservations

Few restaurants in the theme parks accept reservations. However, most restaurants at the Disney hotels, as well as those in Downtown Disney, do. You can use the following notations to help make your decision:

Suggested: Although you can usually get in without reservations, especially if you come at an off hour, it's still a good idea to make reservations in order to minimize the wait.

Recommended: You'll need reservations here unless it's off-season or you'll be dining at an off hour.

Necessary: You'll almost always need reservations here and may have to make them up to several days in advance.

Time-Saving Tip

You can make reservations at Disneyland Resort restaurants up to 30 days in advance by calling 714/781–DINE (3463). The earlier you make reservations, the better your chance of getting the time you want—especially for weekends or holidays.

Suitability for Children

The following icons in this chapter tell you how suitable an eating place is for children:

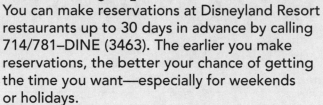 This kind of restaurant is great for kids. It's informal and has several menu items that appeal to kids. It has either some type of entertainment or interesting and fun surroundings that keep kids occupied while waiting for the meal to be served.

☺☺ This kind of restaurant is fairly casual and family-oriented.

☺ This restaurant and its menu are designed mainly for adults. Although it may offer a children's menu, the restaurant is not really suitable for families with young children.

Knight Choice

Our family picked our favorite restaurant in each area: Disneyland, California Adventure, Disney Resorts, and Downtown Disney. These restaurants were selected based on the fact that they offer the best overall experience for the entire fam.

Disneyland Restaurant Descriptions

No alcoholic beverages are served or may be consumed within Disneyland.

Quick Guide to

Name	Description	Location
Ariel's Grotto	Three-course meals including appetizer, entrée, and a dessert	Paradise Pier
Award Wieners	Hot dogs, sausage sandwiches	Hollywood Pictures Backlot
Baker's Field Bakery	Baked goods, specialty coffees, salads, sandwiches	DCA Entry Plaza
Bengal Barbecue	Skewers with meat or vegetables; no children's meals	Adventureland
Blue Bayou	Fine dining; Cajun-style food, prime rib, seafood	New Orleans Square (inside Pirates of the Caribbean)
Blue Ribbon Bakery	Cinnamon rolls, muffins, scones, cookies, specialty coffees	Main Street, USA
Bountiful Valley Farmers Market	Chicken strips, fish and chips, salads, sandwich wraps	Golden State
Bur-r-r Bank Ice Cream	Ice cream cones, sundaes, shakes	DCA Entry Plaza
Café Orleans	Creole-style dinners; salads, crepes	New Orleans Square
Captain's Galley	Sandwiches, salads, boxed lunches, snacks	Disneyland Hotel
Carnation Café	Light breakfasts, sandwiches, salads, home-style dinners	Main Street, USA

$ Inexpensive: adult meals about $8 or less
$$ Moderate: adult meals about $9–$15
$$$ Expensive: adult meals about $16 and up

Disneyland Resort Dining

Type	Price	Reservations	Kids	Details on
Restaurant	$$$	Recommended	☺☺☺	Page 265
Fast Food	$		☺	Page 266
Fast Food	$		☺☺	Page 266
Fast Food	$		☺	Page 252
Restaurant	$$$	Recommended	☺☺	Page 252
Fast Food	$		☺☺	Page 255
Fast Food	$–$$		☺☺	Page 266
Fast Food	$		☺☺☺	Page 267
Restaurant	$$–$$$	Recommended	☺	Page 256
Fast Food	$		☺☺	Page 272
Restaurant	$	Recommended	☺☺	Page 256

☺☺☺ Great for kids, informal, and fun.
☺☺ Fairly casual and family oriented.
☺ Mainly for adults.

(continues)

Quick Guide to

Name	Description	Location
Catal and Uva Bar	Tapas bar, Mediterranean-style meals, soups, salads, sandwiches	Downtown Disney
Catch a Flave	Soft-serve ice cream with flavored swirls, also floats	Paradise Pier
Clarabelle's	Salads, sandwiches, frozen treats	Toontown
Cocina Cucamonga Mexican Grill	Fajitas, tamales, tacos, burritos, grilled chicken	Pacific Wharf
The Coffee House	Baked goods, specialty coffees, drinks	Disneyland Hotel
Corn Dog Castle	Large corn dogs, corn-dipped cheese stick, spicy corn dogs	Paradise Pier
Croc's Bits 'n' Bites	Chicken sandwiches and tenders, burgers, fries	Disneyland Hotel
Daisy's Diner	Individual-size pizzas	Toontown
Disney's PCH Grill	Character breakfast, sandwiches, pizza, salads	Paradise Pier Hotel
Don Tomas	Chimichangas, turkey legs	Paradise Pier
ESPN Zone	Salads, sandwiches, pizza, pasta, chicken, steak, seafood	Downtown Disney
Enchanted Cottage, Sweets and Treats	Bavarian sausages, snacks	Fantasyland

$ Inexpensive: adult meals about $8 or less
$$ Moderate: adult meals about $9–$15
$$$ Expensive: adult meals about $16 and up

Disneyland Resort Dining

Type	Price	Reservations	Kids	Details on
Restaurant	$$–$$$	Recommended	☺	Page 281
Fast Food	$	Recommended	☺☺☺	Page 267
Fast Food	$	Recommended	☺☺☺	Page 256
Fast Food	$	Recommended	☺☺☺	Page 267
Fast Food	$	Recommended	☺☺	Page 273
Fast Food	$	Recommended	☺☺	Page 268
Fast Food	$	Recommended	☺☺☺	Page 273
Fast Food	$	Recommended	☺☺☺	Page 257
Restaurant	$–$$$	Recommended	☺☺☺	Page 274
Fast Food	$		☺	Page 268
Restaurant	$$–$$$	Recommended	☺	Page 281
Fast Food	$		☺☺	Page 257

☺☺☺ Great for kids, informal, and fun.
☺☺ Fairly casual and family oriented.
☺ Mainly for adults.

(continues)

Quick Guide to

Name	Description	Location
Fairfax Market	Fruit, snacks	Hollywood Pictures Backlot
French Market Restaurant	Chicken, roast beef, salmon, pasta, salads	New Orleans Square
Gibson Girl Ice Cream Parlor	Ice cream cones, sundaes	Main Street, USA
Golden Horseshoe	Chicken strips, cheese sticks, chili cheese fries, desserts	Frontierland
Goofy's Kitchen	Character dining, buffet	Disneyland Hotel
Häagen-Dazs	Ice cream cones, sundaes, frozen drinks	Downtown Disney
Harbour Galley	Soups, salads	Critter Country
Hearthstone Lounge	Snacks, alcoholic drinks	Grand Californian Hotel
Hook's Pointe and Wine Cellar	Pasta, pizza, seafood, steak, chicken	Disneyland Hotel
Hot Dog Hut	Hot dogs, corn on the cob	Paradise Pier
House of Blues	BBQ ribs, steak, chicken, seafood, sandwiches, pizza, salads, burgers; Sunday Gospel Brunch	Downtown Disney
Hungry Bear Restaurant	Burgers, chicken sandwiches, salads, vegan patties available	Critter Country

$ Inexpensive: adult meals about $8 or less
$$ Moderate: adult meals about $9–$15
$$$ Expensive: adult meals about $16 and up

Disneyland Resort Dining

Type	Price	Reservations	Kids	Details on
Fast Food	$		☺☺	Page 268
Buffeteria	$$		☺☺	Page 258
Fast Food	$		☺☺☺	Page 258
Fast Food	$–$$		☺☺	Page 258
Buffet	$$$	Recommended	☺☺☺	Page 275
Fast Food	$		☺☺☺	Page 282
Fast Food	$		☺	Page 259
Fast Food	$–$$$		☺	Page 276
Restaurant	$$–$$$	Recommended	☺☺☺	Page 276
Fast Food	$		☺	Page 269
Restaurant	$$–$$$	Necessary	☺	Page 282
Fast Food	$–$$		☺☺☺	Page 259

☺☺☺ Great for kids, informal, and fun.
☺☺ Fairly casual and family oriented.
☺ Mainly for adults.

(continues)

Quick Guide to

Name	Description	Location
Jamba Juice	Smoothies, juice, baked goods	Downtown Disney
La Brea Bakery	Soup, salad, sandwiches, pasta, chicken, seafood, baked goods	Downtown Disney
Little Red Wagon	Corn dogs; nearby cart sells turkey legs and chimichangas	Main Street, USA
The Lost Bar	Hamburgers, sandwiches, appetizers, alcoholic drinks	Disneyland Hotel
Main Street Cone Shop	Ice cream cones, sundaes, sliced caramel apples	Main Street, USA
Mint Julep Bar	Mint juleps, specialty coffees, fritters, baked goods, ice cream bars	New Orleans Square
The Napa Rose	Formal dining, seafood, steak, chicken, pasta	Grand Californian Hotel
Naples Ristorante e Pizzeria	Gourmet pizzas, pasta, chicken, seafood, salads	Downtown Disney
Pacific Wharf Café	Soups and salads in bread bowls, pastries, bread breakfast	Pacific Wharf
Pizza Oom Mow Mow	Pizzas, pasta, salads	Paradise Pier
Plaza Inn	Character breakfast; fried chicken, roast beef, pasta, salads	Main Street, USA

$ Inexpensive: adult meals about $8 or less
$$ Moderate: adult meals about $9–$15
$$$ Expensive: adult meals about $16 and up

Disneyland Resort Dining

Type	Price	Reservations	Kids	Details on
Fast Food	$		☺☺	Page 283
Fast Food	$		☺☺	Page 284
Fast Food	$		☺☺☺	Page 260
Fast Food	$		☺	Page 277
Fast Food	$		☺☺☺	Page 260
Fast Food	$		☺☺☺	Page 260
Restaurant	$$$	Necessary	☺	Page 277
Restaurant	$$–$$$	Recommended	☺☺	Page 284
Fast Food	$–$$		☺	Page 269
Fast Food	$–$$		☺☺☺	Page 270
Buffeteria	$–$$$		☺☺☺	Page 260

☺☺☺ Great for kids, informal, and fun.
☺☺ Fairly casual and family oriented.
☺ Mainly for adults.

(continues)

Quick Guide to

Name	Description	Location
Pluto's Dog House	Hot dogs, chips, drinks	Toontown
Rainforest Café	Breakfast, salads, sandwiches, seafood, pasta, steak	Downtown Disney
Ralph Brennan's Jazz Kitchen	Three separate dining areas all featuring Cajun-style dishes; Sunday brunch	Downtown Disney
Rancho del Zocalo	Burritos, tacos, enchiladas, chicken	Frontierland
Redd Rockett's Pizza Port	Pizza, pasta, salads	Tomorrowland
Refreshment Corner	Hot dogs, chili dogs, pretzels, drinks	Main Street, USA
Rita's Baja Blenders	Margaritas and nonalcoholic drinks	Pacific Wharf
River Belle Terrace	Breakfast; sandwiches, salads	Frontierland
Royal Street Veranda	Gumbo, clam chowder, fritters	New Orleans Square
Sam Andreas Shakes	Ice cream shakes, soft-serve cones	Golden State
Schmoozies	Fruit smoothies, juices, specialty coffees	Hollywood Pictures Backlot
Stage Door Café	Chicken strips, fish and chips, mozzarella sticks	Frontierland
Steakhouse 55	Formal dining, steaks, prime rib, chicken, seafood	Disneyland Hotel

$ Inexpensive: adult meals about $8 or less
$$ Moderate: adult meals about $9–$15
$$$ Expensive: adult meals about $16 and up

Disneyland Resort Dining

Type	Price	Reservations	Kids	Details on
Fast Food	$		☺☺☺	Page 261
Restaurant	$$–$$$	Recommended	☺☺☺	Page 285
Restaurant and Fast Food	$$–$$$	Recommended	☺☺	Page 286
Buffeteria	$–$$		☺☺☺	Page 261
Buffeteria	$		☺☺☺	Page 262
Fast Food	$		☺☺	Page 262
Fast Food	$		☺☺	Page 270
Buffeteria	$–$$		☺☺	Page 263
Fast Food	$		☺	Page 264
Fast Food	$		☺☺	Page 270
Fast Food	$		☺☺	Page 271
Fast Food	$–$$		☺☺	Page 264
Restaurant	$$$	Recommended	☺	Page 278

☺☺☺ Great for kids, informal, and fun.
☺☺ Fairly casual and family oriented.
☺ Mainly for adults.

(continues)

Quick Guide to

Name	Description	Location
Storytellers Café	Character breakfast buffet, pasta, pizza, chicken, steak, seafood	Grand Californian Hotel
Surfside Lounge	Specialty coffees, snacks, alcoholic drinks	Paradise Pier Hotel
Taste Pilot's Grill	Burgers, BBQ ribs, salads, sandwiches	Condor Flats
Tiki Juice Bar	Pineapple spears, juice sorbet	Adventureland
Tomorrowland Terrace	Breakfast, cheeseburgers, sandwiches, salads	Tomorrowland
Tortilla Jo's	Mexican food, tacos, burritos, salads	Downtown Disney
Village Haus Restaurant	Individual-size pizzas, cheese-burgers, sandwiches, salads	Fantasyland
Wetzel's Pretzels	Pretzels, hot dogs, drinks	Downtown Disney
White Water Snacks	Breakfast, sandwiches, burgers, pizza, snacks, desserts	Grand Cali-fornian Hotel
Wine Country Trattoria	Sandwiches, snacks	Golden Vine Winery

$ Inexpensive: adult meals about $8 or less
$$ Moderate: adult meals about $9–$15
$$$ Expensive: adult meals about $16 and up

Disneyland Resort Dining

Type	Price	Reservations	Kids	Details on
Restaurant	$$–$$$	Recommended	☺☺☺	Page 278
Fast Food	$		☺	Page 279
Fast Food	$–$$		☺☺	Page 271
Fast Food	$		☺☺☺	Page 264
Fast Food	$–$$		☺☺☺	Page 264
Restaurant	$$–$$$	Recommended	☺☺	Page 287
Fast Food	$–$$		☺☺☺	Page 265
Fast Food	$		☺☺☺	Page 287
Fast Food	$–$$		☺☺☺	Page 279
Restaurant	$–$$		☺	Page 272

☺☺☺ Great for kids, informal, and fun.
☺☺ Fairly casual and family oriented.
☺ Mainly for adults.

Healthy Meals

In order to provide healthier meals for children, kids' meals are now served with fresh fruit or vegetables with juice, milk, or bottled water for a beverage. However, if the venue serves them, you can substitute fries for the fruit or veggies as well as a soft drink for the choice of beverage. Though this is not listed on the menu, it's an easy substitution and does not change the price of the meal.

Bengal Barbecue
Adventureland　　　　　　　　　　　☺　$　Fast Food

The Bengal Barbecue serves skewers cooked over a flame for around $3.75 each. You can choose from beef in either a spicy or sweet sauce, chicken in a Polynesian sauce, bacon-wrapped asparagus, or just veggies. You can also get breadsticks, cinnamon twists, Mickey Mouse pretzels, and fruit and yogurt parfaits here. If you like spicy treats, be sure to try the jalapeño cheese–stuffed pretzels. For a meal, adults will probably want a couple of skewers or a skewer and a bowl of chowder or gumbo from the Royal Street Veranda. There are no children's meals here.

Blue Bayou
New Orleans Square　　　　　　　　☺☺　$$$　Restaurant

The Blue Bayou is Disneyland's most elegant restaurant. The dining room is inside the boarding area of the Pirates of the Caribbean, and the tables overlook a bayou with the sounds of frogs croaking in the background. Reservations are highly recommended and can be made at the restaurant for the same day. You can also make advance reservations by calling Disney Din-

Our Favorites

After visiting the Disneyland Resort and its various restaurants over the years, we have developed favorites we like to enjoy again and again. Here are some foods we look forward to when visiting the resort.

Food	Restaurant	Location
Monte Cristo Sandwich	Cafe Orleans	Disneyland
Crème Brûlée Trio	Blue Bayou Restaurant	Disneyland
Breakfast Buffet	Goofy's Kitchen	Disneyland Hotel
Jambalaya	French Market	Disneyland
Pancake Breakfast	River Belle Terrace	Disneyland
Carne Asada and Enchilada Platter	Rancho del Zocalo	Disneyland
Pineapple Whip Float	Tiki Juice Bar	Disneyland
Mint Juleps	New Orleans Square	Disneyland
Cheese and Chili Burgers	Taste Pilot's Grill	California Adventure
Corn Dogs	Corn Dog Castle	California Adventure
Shrimp Louie Salad	Pacific Wharf Café	California Adventure
Root Beer Float	Catch-a-Flave	California Adventure

Kids' Picks

Our children have their favorite foods as well. Here are what our 7- to 13-year-olds look forward to:

Child	Age	Food	Location
Tanner	7	Soup Bowls	New Orleans Square Disneyland
Connor	10	Tostada Salad	Rancho del Zocalo Disneyland
Sarah	11	Chicken Soft Taco	Rancho del Zocalo Disneyland
Beth	13	Fried Chicken Dinner	Plaza Inn Disneyland

ing at 714/781–DINE (3463) or from any resort pay phone by dialing *86. If you plan on dining here, either arrive early or call ahead. Although some tables are set aside for standby, the wait can be quite long. If you plan to dine here on a busy day such as Thanksgiving, Christmas, or another holiday, make reservations well in advance.

The menus for lunch and dinner are similar and include jambalaya, prime rib, blackened and roasted chicken, filet mignon, and seafood. A favorite is the Monte Cristo sandwich, made of turkey, ham, and Swiss cheese on bread. The sandwich is then dipped in batter, deep fried, and served with blackberry preserves. Lunch is served from 11 AM to around 3:45 PM, with dinner beginning immediately after. Lunches range in price from $22 to $34, and dinners are from $28 to $40. Sides here include shrimp gumbo, clam chowder, and crab cakes. Desserts include crème brûlée, key lime pie, and similar treats. The kids'

meals include macaroni and cheese, roast beef, chicken breast, and salmon. In addition, soft drinks are refillable (this is the only restaurant in Disneyland at which they are).

Insider's Secret

The lunch and dinner menus are nearly the same, except at dinner you can get filet mignon and lobster, but not the Monte Cristo sandwich. Even with reservations, the best time for dining at the Blue Bayou is around 2 to 3 PM. This is after the lunch rush but before the dinner menu goes into effect. Make reservations for the Blue Bayou before you leave on your vacation or as soon as you check into your hotel. It can be tough to get same-day reservations at the restaurant, especially during the summer or holidays.

Blue Ribbon Bakery	$
Main Street, USA	**Fast Food**

The Blue Ribbon Bakery is a great place to pick up breakfast while you're on Main Street waiting for the park to officially open. You can find all types of baked goods, including cinnamon rolls, scones, sticky buns, cake, cookies, and much more, all from $3 to $5. To wash it down, several types of specialty coffees are available. You can also get sandwiches here on fresh folded bread. Although the bakery does not have a children's menu, kids like the baked goods and the crispy rice treats dipped in chocolate.

Café Orleans
New Orleans Square
☺ $$–$$$
Restaurant

This is another table service restaurant in the park and also offers reservations. It features a variety of Creole-style dishes, including ratatouille, Monte Cristo sandwiches, salads, and a traditional French onion soup. Crepes are also available, both savory for a meal and sweet for dessert. Prices range from $14 to $17. Options for kids include salmon, chicken, and cheesy macaroni. For breakfast you can get three-cheese Monte Cristo French toast, egg scrambles, or even Creole Eggs Benedict.

Carnation Café
Main Street, USA
☺☺ $
Restaurant

The Carnation Café is a table-service restaurant in the park, serving up light breakfasts, including croissant sandwiches, French toast, waffles, and a scramble—all under $9—as well as delicious sticky buns and cinnamon rolls. For lunch and dinner, you can find loaded baked potato soup, a variety of salads, sandwiches, and some hot meals (including potpies and meatloaf). All are between $7 and $11. Children can have a Mickey Mouse waffle for breakfast or macaroni and cheese, hot dogs, or a create-your-own peanut butter and jelly for lunch and dinner. All are about $6. You can dine indoors or outdoors.

Clarabelle's
Toontown
☺☺☺ $
Fast Food

This counter serves sandwiches, salads, and a fruit and yogurt parfait, as well as ice-cream bars and frozen treats. This is a good place for lunch or an afternoon snack if you're in Toontown. Prices range from $3 to $8.

Helpful Hint

Most of the dining venues will allow substitutions for those with special dietary needs. For example, at some places you can choose a vegetable or salad instead of french fries or even get roasted chicken instead of fried chicken. Feel free to ask. If the venue can't help you, the cast member will probably be able to point you to a venue that can.

Daisy's Diner	$
Toontown	**Fast Food**

This counter offers individual-size pizzas with sliced apples for $7.50. Although there are no kids' meals, a pizza splits well between two small children. This can be a fun place to eat because the outdoor dining area is surrounded by the comical buildings of Toontown.

Enchanted Cottage, Sweets and Treats	$
Fantasyland	**Fast Food**

Near the Fantasyland Theatre, Enchanted Cottage is usually open only on days when the Disney Princess Fantasy Faire is taking place. You can find bratwurst and knockwurst sandwiches here for $7. If you just want a quick snack, get a pretzel or some popcorn for $3 to $4 or a Kid's Power Pack with string cheese, yogurt, apples, crackers, and a drink for $6. You can also pick up some tasty desserts here—don't miss the German-chocolate-cake brownies or the decorate-your-own-castle-shaped-cookie kit.

French Market Restaurant
New Orleans Square

☺☺ $$
Knight Choice
Buffeteria

The French Market is one of the best values for dinner at the park. The menu includes roasted chicken breast, salmon, roast beef, seafood jambalaya, pasta, salad, and clam chowder in a bread bowl. Prices range from $9 to $12. Kids' meals include roast beef, grilled chicken, or macaroni and cheese. Other than the Blue Bayou or Café Orleans, this is the only restaurant where you can get a nonalcoholic mint julep with your meal. The French Market often features live Dixieland jazz music throughout the day during the busy season.

Helpful Hint
Many restaurants at the Disneyland Resort offer toddler meals such as chicken and rice or macaroni and cheese, served with applesauce and either milk, juice, or a small bottled water for $4.

Gibson Girl Ice Cream Parlor
Main Street, USA

☺☺☺ $
Fast Food

This crowd-pleaser serves sundaes, cones, and waffle cones. Prices range from $3 to $6. Pick up a treat while you're waiting for a parade or on your way out of the park.

Golden Horseshoe
Frontierland

☺☺ $–$$
Fast Food

Inside the Golden Horseshoe Stage, this bar serves chicken strips, fried cheese sticks, chili cheese fries, chili in a bread

bowl, fish-and-chips, and some tasty desserts including ice cream sundaes. Be sure to arrive at least 15 to 20 minutes before a show so you can find a good seat and get your food. The bar is also a great place for a snack during the day. Prices range from $5 to $9.

Harbour Galley	☺ $
Critter Country	**Fast Food**

This counter, near the dock of the *Columbia,* serves clam chowder, broccoli and cheddar soup, and vegetarian chili in sourdough bread bowls, as well as steak- or salmon salads. The seating looks out over the Rivers of America, making this a nice spot for a lunch or light dinner.

Hungry Bear Restaurant	☺☺☺ $–$$
Critter Country	**Fast Food**

This place along the Rivers of America is great for lunch. The menu includes cheeseburgers, country-fried chicken sandwiches, turkey club sandwiches, grilled chicken Caesar salad, and onion rings. Prices range from $6 to $9. Kids' options include chicken breast tenders for $6. This is one of the few places where you can substitute a vegan patty for meat in the cheeseburgers.

Insider's Secret
This restaurant has a lower level down by the river. The restrooms and telephones here are rarely busy—many people don't know they exist!

Little Red Wagon   ☺☺☺ $
Main Street, USA   **Fast Food**

Near the Plaza Inn, this red truck is the only place in the park
you can get a regular corn dog. There's often a cart nearby that
sells smoked turkey legs and chimichangas. The Little Red
Wagon is usually open only during busy days. Prices range from
$5 to $7.

Main Street Cone Shop   ☺☺☺ $
Main Street, USA   **Fast Food**

Behind the fruit cart, by the lockers, this shop can be hard to
find. Because of its hidden location, this can be a faster spot to
get some ice cream than the often-busy Gibson Girl Ice Cream
Parlor. It serves ice-cream cones, sundaes, and sliced apples with
a caramel dipping sauce. Prices range from $3 to $6.

Mint Julep Bar   ☺☺☺ $
New Orleans Square   **Fast Food**

This counter near the French Market serves the famous Disneyland nonalcoholic mint julep as well as other drinks and specialty coffees. You can also get ice-cream bars, fritters, funnel
cakes, and other baked goods here. Prices are from $3 to $6.

Plaza Inn   ☺☺☺ $–$$$
Main Street, USA   **Buffeteria**

In the morning, the Plaza Inn offers a Disney Princess character-breakfast buffet with several Disney characters. It's $24 for
adults and $12 for children, and the all-you-can-eat buffet in-
cludes an omelet bar, eggs, meats, potatoes, French toast,
blintzes, waffles, fresh fruit, biscuits and gravy, bagels, muffins,
and cereal.

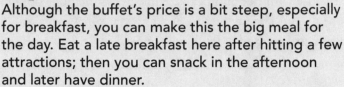

Helpful Hint

Although the buffet's price is a bit steep, especially for breakfast, you can make this the big meal for the day. Eat a late breakfast here after hitting a few attractions; then you can snack in the afternoon and later have dinner.

For lunch and dinner, the Plaza Inn becomes a buffeteria, serving fried chicken, roast beef, pasta, and salads for $12 to $16. Children can choose from chicken and pasta.

Money-Saving Tip

When our family eats at Plaza Inn for dinner, the kids often like to share a fried chicken dinner, which gives them each more food—for less than the price of two kids' meals.

Pluto's Dog House	☺☺☺ $
Toontown	**Fast Food**

This counter serves hot dogs with chips or sliced apples for around $6. Kids' meals have either a hot dog or mac and cheese. With Daisy's Diner next door, it makes a decent place to have lunch while in Toontown.

Rancho del Zocalo	☺☺☺ $–$$
Frontierland	**Buffeteria**

Next to Big Thunder Mountain Railroad, this restaurant serves Mexican fare including burritos, tacos, grilled chicken, salads, carne asada, and cheese enchiladas, all for $10 to $14. Most of these come with rice and beans. Kids' meals include your choice of a bean-and-cheese burrito or a chicken soft taco, along with rice, a fruit cup, and a drink, all for $6.

 ## Helpful Hint

This is a great restaurant for families. The portions are large, and most adults may have trouble finishing a dinner by themselves. To save money, we recommend sharing an adult meal with a small child (especially if they like beans and rice) or having two kids share a meal.

Redd Rockett's Pizza Port	☺☺☺	$
Tomorrowland		**Buffeteria**

Redd Rockett's offers something for everyone. You can get a whole pizza for around $32 or by the slice for about $6. There's a selection of pasta dinners, for around $9, plus a kid's meal with a kid-size pizza or spaghetti for $6. You can also find some interesting and tasty salads for $7 to $9. For dessert, try the cookie dessert pizza for $4. Children like the atmosphere at this place. The pizza slices are fairly large, so two small children could easily split one. If your family can agree on one type of pizza, get a whole one: this is usually cheaper than buying pizza by the slice.

Refreshment Corner	☺☺	$
Main Street, USA		**Fast Food**

This place was originally called Coke Corner when Disneyland first opened in 1955. Here you can find regular or foot-long hot dogs and chili dogs for $5 to $6, as well as Mickey Mouse pretzels. If you just want the chili without the dog, you can also

get it in a bread bowl. This is a good place for a quick lunch or light dinner, and there's often a pianist playing ragtime. Considering the entertainment, this is a good deal.

Helpful Hint
Across the street from the Refreshment Corner, you'll often find the Little Red Wagon (which sells corn dogs) and a cart that sells turkey legs and chimichangas. You can pick up a meal from them and then return to Refreshment Corner to get a drink and to sit down to eat and enjoy the music.

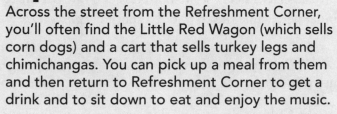

River Belle Terrace	☺☺	$–$$
Frontierland		Buffeteria

The River Belle Terrace serves a good breakfast. You can get pancakes or potatoes, eggs, and meat for around $8, a large Mickey Mouse pancake for about $7, and big cinnamon rolls. The lunch and dinner menus feature hot sandwiches, including carved roast beef, turkey, and barbecue pork as well as salads. The restaurant has a fixings bar where you can customize your sandwich with a variety of toppings. Prices range from $12 to $13. Children can choose from roast beef, turkey, and peanut butter and jelly sandwiches.

Insider's Secret
Walt Disney himself used to enjoy eating Sunday breakfast at the River Belle Terrace. The outdoor seating also provides a good vantage point from which to watch *Fantasmic!*—if you get there early enough. When Disneyland first opened, this restaurant was called Aunt Jemima's Pancake House.

Royal Street Veranda
New Orleans Square   ☺   **$**
Fast Food

This counter serves steak or vegetable gumbo and clam chowder in bread bowls for about $9. You can also find fritters and other sweet snacks here. Some families send one parent to go get dinner here while the rest hold a spot for *Fantasmic!*

Stage Door Café
Frontierland   ☺☺   **$–$$**
Fast Food

Next to the Golden Horseshoe, this counter serves finger food including mozzarella sticks, chicken tenders, and fish-and-chips. Try a funnel cake for dessert—they come in different varieties. Kids can get a meal with chicken nuggets. Prices range from $5 to $9.

Tiki Juice Bar
Adventureland   ☺☺☺   **$**
Fast Food

The Tiki Juice Bar is at the Enchanted Tiki Room. If you don't like pineapples, don't come here, because that's all they have. Choose from pineapple spears and pineapple juice for $2.75 each, or a very tasty pineapple Dole whip, a soft-serve sorbet, for $3. (Or try the Dole whip float, which features the sorbet in a cup with pineapple juice.) The juice bar is a good place for a refreshing snack, especially while you're waiting for the show, and you can also take food into the Tiki Room with you.

Tomorrowland Terrace
Tomorrowland   ☺☺☺   **$–$$**
Fast Food

For lunch and dinner, the Terrace serves cheeseburgers, sandwiches, and salads, with prices ranging from $6 to $9. Kids' meals include a turkey wrap or chicken nuggets. Breakfasts of

French toast sticks, breakfast burritos, and scrambled eggs with meat and potatoes are also served here. On most weekend evenings and all during the summer, there are live musical performances.

Village Haus Restaurant		$–$$
Fantasyland		**Fast Food**

The menu here includes salads, cheeseburgers and sandwiches, and individual-size pizzas. All are $7 to $9. Kids' meals offer a choice of a turkey wrap, chicken nuggets, or mac and cheese for $6. If you decide to eat here, do it in the evening, when the area begins to slow down. During the day it's usually quite busy and noisy, with Fantasyland around you.

California Adventure Restaurant Descriptions

When you decide to dine inside California Adventure, be prepared. It's nothing like Disneyland. Although you can still find the basic fast-food standbys, California Adventure offers a variety of different cuisines to tempt your taste buds. Just about everything here has a touch of California.

Unlike Disneyland, California Adventure sells beer, wine, and cocktails at some of its restaurants. Such beverages must be consumed where they are bought.

Ariel's Grotto		$$$
Paradise Pier		**Restaurant**

You can participate in Ariel's Disney Princess celebration, complete with a princess table visit, when you dine here. The menu, unique to the Disneyland Resort, has set prices for lunch and dinner. Each consists of three courses, including an antipasti tower and salad, an entrée, and a dessert platter for

the table to share. Guests select from many options to create their own meal. Entrées include pasta, chicken, tri-tip, fish, and cioppino. The price is reasonable, considering that it buys a full meal at a sit-down restaurant with character dining. Both lunch and dinner are around $28 for adults and $16 for children. Reservations are recommended, especially in summer or on weekends.

Award Wieners ☺ $
Hollywood Pictures Backlot   **Fast Food**

Right on Hollywood Boulevard, this hot dog stand serves gourmet sausages. In addition to a chili cheese dog, you can also get a hot link, Sicilian sausage, or a portobello mushroom Philly all on a bun with apples or chips for $6 to $7. These are large meals, so expect to be filled up. The kids' meal includes a plain hot dog, apple slices, and a drink for $6.

Baker's Field Bakery ☺☺ $
Entry Plaza   **Fast Food**

This small bakery sells muffins, brownies, and other tasty treats, as well as specialty coffee drinks. You can even find sandwiches and salads here. This is a good place for a quick breakfast or a midday snack. Prices range from about $3 to $9.

Bountiful Valley Farmers Market ☺☺ $–$$
Golden State   **Fast Food**

This eatery serves chicken breast nuggets, mozzarella sticks, fish-and-chips, Caesar salads, and a chicken wrap. For your sweet tooth, try the funnel cakes or apple wedges with caramel and peanuts. Prices range from $3 to $9. Kids' meals come with either chicken nuggets or a turkey wrap.

Bur-r-r Bank Ice Cream   ☺☺☺ $
Entry Plaza   **Fast Food**

This ice-cream stand in the California Zephyr train is a great place for a quick treat, especially while waiting for the parade. In addition to standard scooped ice-cream cones, you can also get waffle cones (dipped in chocolate or not) and sundaes. Cones range in price from $4 to $5, and the sundaes are between $5 and $6.

Catch a Flave   ☺☺☺ $
Paradise Pier   **Fast Food**

This ice-cream stand sells vanilla soft-serve cones that are swirled with your choice of flavor. It's not just limited to chocolate either. You can also choose from cotton candy, grape, orange, lemon, butter pecan, or bubble gum. Cones are around $3. Ice-cream floats in root beer or another soda run around $5, or for $6 you can get them in a souvenir mug. The tasty floats are only a bit more than the cost of just the ice cream, and a couple of kids can easily share one. This is a good place for a snack, especially on warm days.

Cocina Cucamonga Mexican Grill   ☺☺☺ $
Pacific Wharf   **Fast Food**

In the Pacific Wharf food court, this eatery serves Mexican-style food. You can choose from beef, chicken, or vegetable fajitas, tacos or burritos; tamales; carne asada; and grilled chicken. Prices range from $10 to $14. The child's meal comes with a bean burrito or chicken taco for $6. For dessert, try the pineapple- or chocolate empanadas for $5. The tortillas for this restaurant come from the nearby Mission Tortilla Factory.

 Helpful Hint
The Pacific Wharf food court, which has a central dining area, is a great place for families; everyone can choose from a variety of menus. Consider getting a little something from each of the surrounding eateries and then sharing it as a family.

Corn Dog Castle	☺☺ $
Paradise Pier	**Fast Food**

Although you might first think $6 for a corn dog is a bit steep, those served at the Corn Dog Castle are large and a meal in themselves. In addition to the standard corn dog, this place also serves a cheese stick dipped in batter and even a hot link corn dog. If you like spicy food, we definitely recommend the latter as an experience you'll not likely find elsewhere. All of these come with your choice of a bag of potato chips or sliced apples. Unfortunately, this eatery does not have a kid's menu, and the corn dogs are probably too large for most small children and are difficult to share.

Don Tomas	☺ $
Paradise Pier	**Fast Food**

This stand near Toy Story Mania offers smoked turkey legs and chimichangas as well as drinks.

Fairfax Market	☺☺ $
Hollywood Pictures Backlot	**Fast Food**

This stand along the main strip sells healthy snacks, including fresh fruit. Prices range from $3 to $5.

Hot Dog Hut	☺ $
Paradise Pier	Fast Food

Near Toy Story Mania, this stand sells hot dogs with chips, corn on the cob, and drinks; prices range from $5 to $6.

Pacific Wharf Café	☺ $–$$
Pacific Wharf	Fast Food

In the Pacific Wharf food court, this is part of the Boudin Bakery, which you can also tour. The café features soups and salads served in freshly baked bread bowls. Soups include clam chowder, corn chowder, and broccoli cheese for about $9. Chicken and apple, Chinese chicken, or shrimp Louie salads run from $9 to $10. Sandwiches are available on fresh-baked bread. The café also sells delicious cream puffs and other pastries and is one of the few places in Disney's California Adventure that serve breakfast. You can choose from scrambled eggs and bacon in a bread bowl, a breakfast croissant, and a bowl of oatmeal for $4 to $6. The kid's meal is a turkey wrap.

Insider's Secret

Stop by this café and ask about Mickey Mouse–shape sourdough bread. The bakers often make it at different times during the day. You can buy it hot out of the oven and take it home as a souvenir. These loaves run about $7. You can also purchase a hot loaf of round bread for about $4 to share as a family after the bakery tour.

Pizza Oom Mow Mow ☺☺☺ $–$$
Paradise Pier   **Fast Food**

This pizza joint serves a variety of pizzas by the slice or whole. You can also get pasta or salads. Prices run from $6 to $9, with a whole pizza going for $32. Kids can choose a kid-size pizza, pasta, or a peanut butter and jelly sandwich with drink for around $6. This is the only place for pizza in California Adventure.

Rita's Baja Blenders ☺☺ $
Pacific Wharf   **Fast Food**

In the middle of the food court, this is the place to get your drinks if you're eating in this area, or just to wet your whistle. Margaritas run about $7. You can also get a nonalcoholic version for $5.

 Helpful Hint
Rather than buying a soda at one of the eateries, just get the food and then buy your drinks from Rita's.

Sam Andreas Shakes ☺☺ $
Golden State   **Fast Food**

This snack stand sells ice-cream shakes (which include a topping and whipped cream) for around $4.50. The toppings vary from crushed candy bars to healthy snacks such as dates. You can also get a soft-serve cone here for around $3 to $4 depending on size and whether you want it dipped in chocolate. Because this stand is along the parade route and the main pathway

through the Golden State, it's easy to stop by and get some quick refreshment.

Schmoozies 😊😊 $
Hollywood Pictures Backlot Fast Food

This drink stand sells a variety of smoothies that come in several fruit flavors as well as mocha. They go for $5 each. You can get specialty coffees and juices here as well.

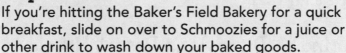

Helpful Hint
If you're hitting the Baker's Field Bakery for a quick breakfast, slide on over to Schmoozies for a juice or other drink to wash down your baked goods.

Taste Pilot's Grill 😊😊 $–$$
Condor Flats Knight Choice
Fast Food

This fun aviation-themed restaurant has a great menu. Choose from a chili burger, blue cheese burger, or cheddar burger, then take it to the condiment bar and add your choice of toppings. This place also serves barbecue pork ribs and chicken sandwiches. Prices range from $7 to $13, and the meals are quite filling. The kids' meals include chicken nuggets or two miniburgers for $6. This eatery contains an indoor dining area, making it a great place for a sit-down meal where you can also rest for a bit. This can also be a great spot for a snack. A family can easily share the chili cheese fries or onion rings while enjoying ice cream shakes.

Wine Country Trattoria   ☺ $–$$
Golden Vine Winery   **Restaurant**

This eatery in the winery district serves soup, salad, sandwiches, and different types of lasagna for $4 to $13. Kids' meals include a meatball sandwich, pasta, or grilled cheese. Finish off your meal with tiramisu. Reservations are available. You can also purchase bottles of wine at the nearby Terrace Wine Tasting. Because you're not allowed to carry the wine bottles around the park, you must buy them a few hours before you leave and then pick them up at the Package Express in the Entry Plaza.

Dining at Disneyland Resort Hotels

The three Disney hotels offer a variety of restaurants and places to pick up a quick bite.

Captain's Galley   ☺☺ $
Disneyland Hotel   **Fast Food**

This poolside shop is like a general store, selling sundries as well as food. The menu features sandwiches, salads, box lunches, and all types of snacks. You can also get a box of sushi (cooked, not raw). Prices range from $1 to $6, making this a quick and inexpensive place for lunch or a snack while at the pool or for something to take back to the hotel.

Helpful Hint

Guests of the Disneyland Resort can make reservations at any of the hotel restaurants by dialing *86 from any resort pay phone. On some phones, there's an autodial for reservations. You can also make reservations before you leave on your vacation or while there by dialing 714/781–DINE (3463). This number is good for all Disneyland Resort restaurants that take reservations, including those at the theme parks, hotels, and Downtown Disney. Most of the restaurants accept reservations up to 30 days in advance.

The Coffee House   ☺☺ $
Disneyland Hotel   **Fast Food**

This shop serves a variety of specialty coffees, hot chocolate, juices, and an assortment of baked goods, including bagels, muffins, scones, Danish, and brownies. Prices range from $2 to $5. This is a good spot to pick up a quick breakfast in the morning. Send one parent while the other and the kids are getting ready.

Croc's Bits 'n' Bites   ☺☺☺ $
Disneyland Hotel   **Fast Food**

Hamburgers, barbecue chicken sandwiches, and chicken nuggets are available at this counter. These are all around $8 and include fries or apple slices. You can even pick up some tasty nachos here. Children's meals include a cheeseburger or chicken nuggets for $6. The place for fast food at the Disneyland Hotel, Croc's Bits 'n' Bites is conveniently located for dining while at the pool.

Disney's PCH Grill	☺☺☺	$–$$$
Paradise Pier Hotel		**Restaurant**

The PCH Grill features the Lilo and Stitch Aloha Breakfast from 6:30 to 11:30 AM. The all-you-can-eat buffet includes an omelet bar, waffles, eggs, meat, and sweet rolls. While guests are enjoying their breakfast, the characters sing and dance around before visiting with guests at each table. The price is $22 for adults and $14 for children. This is the only character breakfast with a show. You can also order breakfast off the menu for about $10 to $15. You should make reservations unless you plan on eating a late breakfast.

Insider's Secret

There are granola bars and juice boxes at the buffet for you to take to the park. In fact, our waiter even invited us to take some boxes of cereal for our children. Cheerios and other cereals are a wonderful way of calming a fussy child when you're in a hurry.

The PCH Grill also serves a variety of dishes inspired by the coast. These include salads and sandwiches as well as wood-fired gourmet pizzas. Most of the meals are fairly light (though you can also get steak or barbeque ribs). Prices range from $8 to $23. The kid's meal is about $8 and offers a choice of macaroni and cheese, grilled chicken breast, a meatball sandwich, and make-your-own pizza. When kids order the pizza, they're brought rolled-out dough with sauce, cheese, and toppings. They then get to assemble the pizza before it's taken back for cooking. Reservations are a good idea for both lunch and dinner, to avoid having to wait. When heading back to the hotel in the evening, stop by for a dessert. The whole family can share the Whole PCH Grill and Kitchen Sink. This sun-

dae has 10 scoops of ice cream and all the toppings you want. Though it runs $22, it's cheaper than everyone getting their own dessert.

This restaurant also provides room service for the Paradise Pier Hotel. To save money, you can walk down to the restaurant and place an order to go. Wait downstairs in the lobby or the gift shop or go back up to your room until it's ready. You can avoid paying the higher room-service prices as well as the service charge and tip. By taking out you can also order from the complete menu rather than the more-limited room-service menu.

Goofy's Kitchen	☺☺☺	$$$
Disneyland Hotel	**Knight Choice**	
	Buffet	

Goofy's Kitchen serves all-you-can-eat buffets for brunch and dinner, complete with characters that come around and visit with guests at each table. This place not only has the most buffet choices, but also the greatest variety of characters. Brunch (7 AM to 2:30 PM) is $26 for adults, and dinner (5 to 9 PM) is $31. Children's meals are all $14. Brunch includes a variety of typical favorites, such as waffles, eggs, a carving station, potatoes, cereal, fresh fruit, sweet rolls, and assorted breads. Dinner entrées include prime rib, chicken, fish, pizza, salad, fruit and sandwich bars, soup, and a variety of delicious desserts. Reservations are a good idea here, but the wait for any of the meals is not too bad if you drop by late. Since the restaurant is less busy at lunch time, your family will also get more personal attention from the characters if you come around 1. Once while we were having a late lunch here, Goofy sat down with our family for more than 10 minutes and played with the children. That in itself was worth the price of the meal—and the food is great, too.

Hearthstone Lounge   ☺ $–$$$
Grand Californian Hotel   **Fast Food**

The hotel's lounge serves coffees and baked goods in the morning, then snacks and light meals (such as spareribs, mini hamburgers, flatbreads, and a chicken quesadilla; prices ranging from $10 to $16) during the remainder of the day. There's also a fully stocked bar. Families can play checkers at some of the tables.

Insider's Secret

All of the woodwork in this lounge—the paneling and the counters—came from the same redwood tree, one that fell naturally rather than being cut down.

Hook's Pointe and Wine Cellar   ☺☺☺ $$–$$$
Disneyland Hotel   **Restaurant**

Hook's Pointe is open for lunch and dinner. You can choose from a variety of pastas as well as steak, chicken, and seafood; dinner prices range from $19 to $32. You can also order assorted appetizers, salads, and desserts. The kids' menu includes macaroni and cheese, salmon, and grilled chicken breast for about $8.

On the lower level of the restaurant is the wine cellar, where guests may taste a variety of California wines and purchase them by the glass or the bottle.

The Lost Bar
Disneyland Hotel

☺ $

Fast Food

Although this is basically a bar serving alcoholic beverages for adults, it also offers hamburgers, chicken sandwiches, and a kid's hamburger meal. Prices range from $6 to $8. You can get delicious nonalcoholic mixed drinks here as well. Although parents can pick up a drink, we don't recommend it for families. After putting the kids to bed, one of the parents can head down to the Lost Bar for refreshments and bring them up to the room to enjoy.

The Napa Rose
Grand Californian Hotel

☺ $$$

Restaurant

This award-winning fine restaurant serves a changing menu that highlights a variety of California-style tastes. Appetizers include scallops, sashimi, salads, soups, and even lobster and caviar from $10 to $43. The entrées include seafood, prime rib, steak, and chicken, and cost $30 to $40. You can also order the Vintner's Table, which is a four-course prix-fixe chef's tasting menu for around $85. For dessert, try the crème brûlée tart, the gourmet cheesecake, and/or the chocolate delicacies. The children's menu varies from pizza to salmon and even beef tenderloin. These run from $7 to $13.

The Napa Rose's wine list features many California wines. You can also purchase various vintages to take home.

Because this is an extremely fancy restaurant, we don't recommend it for families with young children—they can find something more to their taste at the Storytellers Café. However, for couples this is a great restaurant that offers views of the California Adventure park. Parents can enjoy a romantic dinner here alone while their children are supervised at Pinocchio's Workshop (also at the Grand Californian), a fun, entertaining, and safe environment.

 Helpful Hint

If you would like a couple's night out and are staying at the Grand Californian or one of the other Disney hotels, check your children in at Pinocchio's Workshop. This is open from 5 PM to midnight and runs around $13 per child per hour. For more information, *look* under the Grand Californian in Chapter 2.

Adjacent to this fine restaurant is the Napa Rose Lounge, where there's a wide selection of California wines, full-menu service, indoor and outdoor seating, and a crackling firepit.

Steakhouse 55	☺	$$$
Disneyland Hotel		**Restaurant**

This is a formal restaurant that is open only for breakfast and dinner. The menu includes a variety of steaks, prime rib, filet mignon, chicken, lamb, lobster, and other fresh seafood. Dinners range in price from $25 to $35 and even higher for the lobster. Salads, appetizers, and desserts cost $5 to $12. Because of the formal atmosphere and sophisticated menu, this is not a really good spot for families with young children, though one of the kids' meals is a petite cut of prime rib for $12. Breakfast includes the usual favorites of pancakes, egg dishes, and even steak and eggs as well as breakfast burritos and huevos rancheros. These run between $8 and $15.

Storytellers Café	☺☺☺	$$–$$$
Grand Californian Hotel		**Restaurant**

This is the main restaurant in the Grand Californian Hotel. In the morning, Chip 'n' Dale host a character breakfast buffet. It includes fresh fruit, eggs Benedict, bagels with a tray of toppings, potatoes, meat, an omelet bar, biscuits and gravy, and all types of pastries and baked goods. Adults eat for $25, children for $12. The meal includes beverages—juices, soft drinks, hot drinks, and milk (and chocolate milk).

The traditional lunch and dinner menus include sandwiches, soups, salads, pastas, pizzas, seafood, chicken, steak, and so forth. Expect to pay from $12 to $30 per meal. The kids' menu includes pasta and meatballs, chicken nuggets, macaroni and cheese, make-your-own pizzas, and even salmon. All are around $8.

This restaurant also provides room service to the Grand Californian Hotel, so just about anything on the menu can be served in your hotel room for a slightly higher price. If you want to save money, you can walk down to the restaurant and place an order to go and then take it up to your room. You pay the lower restaurant price and also avoid the room-service surcharge and tip.

Surfside Lounge	☺ $
Paradise Pier Hotel	**Fast Food**

This counter serves specialty coffees, hot chocolate, and baked snacks as well as alcoholic drinks. Since the PCH Grill is closed for lunch, you can get burgers, sandwiches, and salads here from 11:30 to 2. They even have kids' meals with either miniburgers or chicken strips.

White Water Snacks	☺☺☺ $–$$
Grand Californian Hotel	**Fast Food**

This snack bar by the pool area is a great place for midday or evening snacks as well as light meals. You can find breakfast sandwiches, breakfast burritos, and French toast here in the morning for around $7, as well as cereals and baked goods. Later, chicken sandwiches, burgers, pizzas, nachos, and hot dogs are served for

Helpful Hint

White Water Snacks is a great place for lunch. While most restaurants in the parks are busy, this one is usually quiet; your family can sit down and relax—in air-conditioning. If you're inside California Adventure, just exit the park through the Grand Californian Hotel entrance near Grizzly River Run and within a minute you'll be there. If you have younger children who are tired from a long day at the parks and are staying at one of the Disneyland Hotels, pick up their dinner from White Water Snacks as you leave California Adventure and take it back to the hotel room. While the kids crash, the adults can order room service and enjoy a nice, quiet dinner together.

$6 to $9. In addition, there are a variety of prepackaged sandwiches, salads, desserts, and snacks, including Mickey Mouse pretzels and candy bars. You can get kids' meals here as well. A small indoor dining area is provided, or you can grab some grub while your family is down by the pool or pick up dessert to take back to your room after a busy day at the parks.

Downtown Disney Restaurant Descriptions

Admission-free, Downtown Disney includes a variety of shops as well as restaurants. Because Downtown Disney remains open several hours after the parks close, as late as 2 AM, you can find a late dinner here after enjoying a day at one of the parks. Or you can have breakfast or lunch here during the day. (For more information about the shops and the entertainment venues, *see* Chapter 7.)

Catal and Uva Bar   ☺ $$–$$$
714/774–4442   **Restaurant**
www.patinagroup.com/catal

This restaurant has two different types of dining. The Uva bar is on the ground floor as well as out in the center of the Downtown Disney walkway. The outdoor bar serves coffees and pastries in the morning, then turns into a wine and cocktail bar later in the day, serving tapas (appetizerlike dishes).

The Catal restaurant, on the second floor, serves a variety of Mediterranean-inspired dishes. In addition to appetizers, you can also order pasta, paella, seafood, chicken, steak, and lamb. The dinners are priced from around $20 to $40. The children's menu includes hamburgers, hot dogs, pasta, chicken, and steak for $7 to $12. Catal serves breakfast in the morning; the menu includes pancakes, quiche, and huevos rancheros. This is also a good place to come for a nice dessert.

Catal is not a very good choice for families with young children because of the atmosphere, though they do offer a children's menu with pasta, chicken, hamburger, and steak for $7 to $12. Reservations are recommended for the restaurant during dinner hours.

ESPN Zone   ☺ $$–$$$
714/300–3776   **Restaurant**
www.espnzone.com/anaheim

ESPN Zone has two restaurants that share the same menu but have different atmospheres. The Studio Grill is set up more like a restaurant and is more appropriate for family dining. The Screening Room is like a sports bar, with all types of games playing on monitors—including one monster that's 16 feet wide.

The menu offers salads, sandwiches, and appetizers for $10 to $16. Entrées include steak, chicken, seafood, and pasta,

with prices ranging from $12 to $25. Even if you're not in the mood for a meal, there are several delicious desserts to sample while watching a game.

This is not a great restaurant for families with small children because of the sports bar atmosphere and the noise. However, if your children are older and enjoy sports, ESPN Zone can be a lot of fun.

Häagen-Dazs   ☺☺☺ $
                                                    Fast Food

---

This ice-cream shop serves ice-cream cones, sundaes, and ice-cream or frozen drinks as well as specialty coffees. Prices range from $3 to $6. This is a great place for a treat after the parks close, before you head back to the hotel.

House of Blues   ☺ $$–$$$
714/778–2583   **Restaurant**
www.hob.com/venues/clubvenues/anaheim

This restaurant feels a bit like a nightclub with a Southern atmosphere. Appetizers include such tasty treats as catfish nuggets, voodoo shrimp, quesadillas, and others, most between $9 and $12. In fact, this is a fun place to just come in for an appetizer and beverage. Soups and salads are also available; seafood gumbo, steak salad, and a Thai chicken salad are among the more interesting choices. They run from about $4 to $15. For a light meal, choose from several sandwiches, including a shrimp po'boy or a pulled pork sandwich. There are also burgers and pizzas. These run around $13. For the main entrées, you can try barbecue ribs, seafood, steak, chicken, or even pasta. Most are reasonably priced, starting around $16 but going up to $33 for some meals. Kids' meals include

grilled cheese, hot dog, pasta, pizza or chicken tenders and run around $7.

Helpful Hint
The Sunday Gospel Brunch is a fun alternative to the character breakfasts for families with older children.

House of Blues also features a live entertainment area that is separate from the dining area. There's something going on there just about every night of the week. Because of the loud atmosphere, we do not recommend this restaurant for families with young children. However, teenagers usually have a great time.

Reservations, especially for dinner, are recommended. If you want to dine here during a holiday or a busy night such as a Friday or weekend, be sure to make your reservations several days, or even a couple of weeks, in advance.

One of the unique experiences at this venue is the House of Blues Gospel Brunch. Served just about every Sunday morning, this Southern-style all-you-can-eat buffet features jambalaya, eggs Benedict, prime rib, barbecue chicken, catfish, and more for guests to enjoy while listening to local gospel singing groups. Be sure to reserve tickets in advance. They run $36 for adults and $16.50 for children 3–9 years old.

Jamba Juice $
                                                          Fast Food

This is the place to pick up a quick meal or snack on the go. Jamba Juice sells not only fresh juice but also smoothies and baked goods. Prices start around $3. If you want your family to have something healthy, these smoothies can be a meal in themselves.

La Brea Bakery
714/490–0233

☺☺ $
Fast Food

Besides breads and pastries, this bakery, which has outdoor seating, serves soups, salads, and sandwiches ranging in price from $6 to $15. Also available are pasta, chicken, and seafood for $18 to $22. A wine bar serves beer and wine by the glass. Unlike some restaurants in Downtown Disney, La Brea Bakery has kids' meals for $6.

La Brea Bakery is the closest place in Downtown Disney to the main gates of both theme parks. In the morning, stop by for a hot drink and a muffin or other pastry; in the evening, get a dessert to take back to your hotel.

Naples Ristorante e Pizzeria
714/776–6200
www.patinagroup.com/naples

☺☺ $$–$$$
Restaurant

A great place for families, this Italian restaurant offers a comprehensive menu of unique as well as traditional Italian foods. One of the specialties is the wood-fired gourmet pizzas. These come in individual as well as family sizes and start at $16 for an individual and go up to $45 for a family size. In addition to the traditional toppings, you can choose from seafood (not just anchovies), goat cheese, and several other things you might not think to put on a pizza. Soups and salads are available for $6 to $14. Several different types of pasta dinners are served, ranging from $18 to $20. You can also order entrées such as veal, chicken, and seafood for $19 to $29.

Although the prices seem a bit high for pizza, you may not find some of these pies served anywhere else, and they are quite filling. The price of the dinners is in line with those at most restaurants in the resort area. The restaurant is family-oriented, and older children will enjoy the place. Younger children can

usually share a meal with an adult or with each other, and they can often find a pizza or meal that meets their tastes.

Next to the restaurant, Napolini is an Italian gourmet deli where you can pick up salads, pasta, pizza by the slice, and sandwiches on the go.

Reservations are recommended at Naples Ristorante e Pizzeria for dinner, especially on weekends and during holidays. You can usually get them a day or two in advance or maybe even the same day. Try this restaurant for a late dinner after the parks close. You can also pick up dinner here and take it back to your hotel.

Rainforest Café	☺☺☺	$$–$$$
714/956–5260		Knight Choice
www.rainforestcafe.com		Restaurant

This restaurant, housed in what looks like an ancient Maya pyramid, also has a great interior. Large aquariums around the dining area and other effects, like rainstorms and animated animals, make guests feel as though they're dining in a jungle.

The menu combines dishes from both North and South America and is quite varied. You can get several different types of salads, including buffalo chicken, for $6 to $14. Appetizers feature pizzas, crab cakes, shrimp cocktail, chimichangas, and much more ($9 to $14). There are also soups, sandwiches, wraps, and pastas. There are a number of interesting seafood dishes, including coconut shrimp, as well as steak, chicken, barbeque pork ribs, and even pot roast. These all range in price from $10 to $26 and higher for king crab and lobster. A children's menu features smaller portions of some of the adult dinners, with prices around $7. Breakfast is also served during the morning hours for around $10. Reservations, especially for dinner, are highly recommended, and you can make them sev-

eral days in advance by calling ahead. This is the most family-oriented restaurant in Downtown Disney.

Ralph Brennan's Jazz Kitchen ☺☺ $$–$$$
714/776–5200 **Restaurant and Fast Food**
www.rbjazzkitchen.com

This establishment is divided into three parts. The Carnival Club, upstairs, is for fine dining. Flambeaux's, downstairs, is more relaxed and often has live entertainment. The Creole Café is the take-out eatery.

The Carnival Club is only open for dinner and serves Southern specialties. The menu changes regularly and includes dishes such as Creole onion soup, pecan-crusted pork, blackened salmon, and poultry dishes. Entrées are priced from $20 to $30. Prix-fixe dinners that include an appetizer, an entrée, and a dessert cost $30 to $40. These are actually a good deal, compared to ordering everything separately.

Flambeaux's serves several Cajun-style dishes, some with seafood. The menu here also changes regularly, but you can expect to pay from $13 to $25 for a dinner. In the evening, you're entertained by live jazz music. Both Flambeaux's and the Carnival Club accept reservations. If you plan to dine here, be sure either to call ahead or to stop by during the day to make a reservation.

The Creole Café is great for a quick bite or for something to take back to the hotel. There are several types of sandwiches, including po'boys (shrimp, pork, or turkey). You can also get jambalaya, gumbo, and red beans and rice. These range from $7 to $10. If dessert is more your speed, try the beignets (doughnuts). The breakfast menu features egg sandwiches, French toast sticks, and a breakfast burrito. The Creole Café's takeout also gives parents an option for taking meals back to the hotel while they pick up dinner elsewhere for the kids.

Ralph Brennan's Jazz Kitchen serves a kids' menu; on some days, kids eat free before 6 PM. In addition to daily lunch and dinner, the restaurant serves a Sunday brunch.

Tortilla Jo's ☺☺ $$–$$$
714/535–5000   Restaurant
www.patinagroup.com/tortillajos

This south-of-the-border restaurant has an inside room for sit-down dining, a cantina for drinks and light meals, and a taqueria for quick orders to eat outside or to take with you.

The restaurant serves traditional favorites (tacos, burritos, and fajitas) as well as specialties (Mayan spiced salmon, chipotle-maple glazed chicken, and several salads and appetizers). The cantina serves a smaller, lighter menu with selections from the restaurant's menu; the taqueria serves tacos, burritos, nachos, and *mexicones* (cone-shape crispy corn tortillas filled with various ingredients). Desserts are good here, and several are available at the taqueria so you can pick them up to take back to the hotel or eat while you're shopping.

Tortilla Jo's offers a good children's menu with tacos, burritos, tacquitos, quesadillas, and chicken fingers all for around $6 to $7. Reservations are recommended for the restaurant during dinner hours.

Wetzel's Pretzels ☺☺☺ $
Fast Food

This is a typical pretzel stand like those often found in shopping malls. In addition to pretzels with a variety of toppings, you can get hot dogs and drinks here. Prices range from $2.50 to around $4.

CHAPTER

9

Knott's®
Berry Farm

Knott's Berry Farm

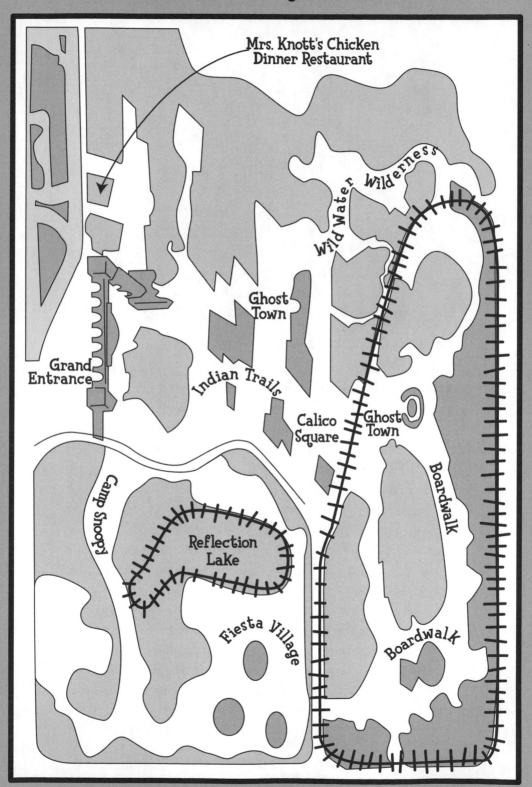

Knott's Berry Farm

Knott's Berry Farm might not be as flashy as other area theme parks, but its simple, down-home appeal still delights visitors young and old. In fact, the park advertises itself as "The Theme Park Californians Call Home." However, this does not mean only those visitors from California will enjoy themselves here. On the contrary, Knott's offers something for everyone, and uses the California Gold Rush and other historical eras as themes. Knott's newest promotion, which slashes children's admission by more than half, makes this theme park even more attractive. If you're considering adding another theme park to your vacation, Knott's prices can't be beat if you have younger children.

Knott's Berry Farm really did begin as a berry farm. Walter Knott was the propagator of the boysenberry—a cross between the red raspberry, blackberry, and loganberry. During the Depression, to help make ends meet, his wife, Cordelia, began serving chicken dinners on their wedding china to customers for 65¢ (the equivalent of about $8 in 2008 dollars). A few years later, the Knotts expanded their business into a restaurant, which steadily became more and more popular. In 1940 Walter Knott began bringing historical buildings to the farm as an attraction to entertain the thousands of customers lining up each day at the restaurant. These buildings became the basis for Knott's first theme park—the Old West Ghost Town. Since that time, more and more attractions, including rides, have been added. Five other theme areas joined the Ghost Town, making Knott's Berry Farm what it is today.

Although its rides and attractions don't always get the publicity and attention of those at other parks, Knott's Berry Farm was truly a pioneer in the theme and amusement park industry. It not only was the first theme park (Disneyland opened several years later), but also featured the first log ride as well as the world's first 360-degree roller coaster.

Adjacent to Knott's Berry Farm is a separate water park, Soak City USA, which is modeled on the 1950s–60s California surfing scene. Families can find a variety of fun-in-the-sun here for all ages. Although it's aimed primarily at young to preteen children, there are a few high-speed slides for older and more thrill-seeking visitors. More information on Soak City USA is at the end of this chapter.

Knott's Berry Farm
8039 Beach Boulevard, Buena Park, CA 90620
714/220–5200
www.knotts.com

Location

Knott's Berry Farm is in Buena Park, 15 minutes from Disneyland. Although it's easy to get there by car, check to see if your hotel offers a shuttle, as this can be convenient and save you the cost of parking. However, depending on how often the shuttle runs, you may prefer the flexibility of driving your own car.

If you're coming from the Disneyland area, take I–5 (Santa Ana) north to the 91 (Riverside) Freeway west. Exit at Beach Boulevard, and turn left at the end of the exit ramp. Proceed south one mile to the auto entrance lanes on your right, past La Palma Avenue.

If you're coming from downtown Los Angeles, take the I–5 Freeway south to Beach Boulevard. Turn right at the end of the exit ramp, and proceed south 2 miles to the car entrance lanes.

Admission

Single-day admission is $53 for adults and $24 for senior citizens (62 and over). Children ages 3 to 11 (and under 48 inches tall) are also only $24. In summer, when the park is open until 10 or 11 PM, you can purchase a discounted pass that allows you to enter after 4 PM. All adults pay $27, but it's still $24 for children ages 3 to 11 and senior citizens.

Tickets can be purchased at the ticket booths outside the main gates. You can also buy tickets in advance at some hotels. Check with the front desk when you make your reservations.

Money-Saving Tip
It's possible to see the park in only half a day. Therefore, the discounted admission after 4 PM can really save your family some money. Consider this if you have small children who will be spending most of their time on the kiddie rides in Camp Snoopy or older children who will be hitting the coasters and other wild rides.

Discounted tickets can also be purchased from AAA (40% off the regular price). As with most theme parks, you can now purchase tickets online and print them at home. This will save you

$8 off the price of an adult ticket. Don't expect any discounts on children's tickets, however. Knott's occasionally offers specials such as two days for the price of one. Be sure to check the Web site to see what promotions are currently running. Several businesses or credit unions may offer discounts to employees and members in the form of the Joe Cool Club. Each club has a card giving discounts not only on admission but also at several restaurants and shops in the park. Also check your hotel or local businesses for coupons. You should be able to save around $5 per adult ticket with coupons.

The cost for parking is $12 for cars and motorcycles and $17 for RVs. Don't forget to write down where you parked your vehicle before heading into the park. After a long day of fun, you don't want to have to wander around looking for your car. There's free three-hour parking for people visiting the restaurants and shops outside of the park.

Several vacation packages are available at the Knott's Berry Farm Resort Hotel. This 321-room hotel includes a pool, a spa, a kids' activity center, two lighted tennis courts, an exercise facility, and an arcade center. For families with young children, the hotel also offers 16 Snoopy-theme rooms and suites. Check the Knott's Web site for details and rates.

Operating Hours

Knott's Berry Farm is open daily, except for Christmas. In summer, the hours are 10 AM to 10 or 11 PM. Nonsummer hours are 10 AM to 6 PM, with later hours on the weekends and during holidays.

Amenities

Knott's Berry Farm's Information Center offers help and answers to all your questions. Guests with disabilities can pick up a guide at this location. This is also where the Lost and Found is located. If you get separated from one or more of your children, ask an employee for assistance. Separated children will be taken to the Lost Child Center in Calico Square. Most restrooms offer baby-changing facilities. In addition, there are three baby stations: one at Camp Snoopy, another in Wild Water Wilderness, and the third in Knott's Marketplace. All include facilities for nursing.

Lockers are available in Ghost Town and near Bigfoot Rapids, allowing you to stash items such as dry clothes in case you plan to take on any water rides. Strollers can be rented for about $10 per day. However, if you'll be visiting another theme park, it might be worth your money, and your child's comfort, to buy an umbrella stroller before your trip. These can usually be found at large discount stores for $10–$15.

If you're traveling with pets, you cannot take them into Knott's Berry Farm and there are no kennel services available on-site. You'll have to make other arrangements before your visit.

Suitability for Children

Knott's Berry Farm does a good job of providing something for everybody. Small children will enjoy Camp Snoopy and some of the milder rides throughout the park, such as the Log Ride and the Mine Ride. Also walk around Ghost Town to see the sights, and check out some of the shows.

Attractions

Knott's Berry Farm is divided into six theme areas. Each offers exciting rides and attractions, though some are designed specifically for certain age groups.

Ghost Town

This is where it all started. Ghost Town is the heart of Knott's Berry Farm, and contains several shops, restaurants, and exhibits. It's fun to just stroll down the streets pretending you're back in the Wild West. Although you can quickly move through this area on to other parts of the park, it can be educational as well as entertaining to explore Ghost Town with your children. Not all the sights here are listed on the map of the park you receive when you enter Knott's Berry Farm, so it's worth your time to wander. Along the way you can peer into an old barbershop, a Chinese laundry, and much more. The buildings here are either re-creations of historical buildings or actual buildings brought here from around the United States. Visit the 19th-century one-room schoolhouse from Kansas. Children will be impressed with how it differs from their own classrooms. A "teacher" is usually there from noon until 5 PM to answer questions and describe how schools functioned more than 100 years ago. You can also watch a blacksmith work his trade in another building.

The Birdcage Theatre, modeled after the original in Tombstone, Arizona (remember the O.K. Corral?), offers seasonal entertainment. Several well-known performers got their start here, including Steve Martin. The Calico Saloon offers daily shows with music, dance, and comedy. There's also a stunt show and street entertainment throughout the day. At the far end of Ghost Town, you can pan for gold in sluice boxes for an additional charge. However, it's worth the price for children who may never get such an opportunity again, especially those who have recently studied the Gold Rush in school. There's also a shooting gallery. Be sure to visit Boot Hill, Ghost Town's cemetery. Behind some shops, it's easily overlooked. The inscriptions on the tombstones are good for a laugh. Plus, don't forget to place a foot on the grave of the man buried alive. Somethin' is a-thumpin'.

There's a lot to look at in Ghost Town, and there are also several rides. Relive Old West travel by riding a real Butterfield Stagecoach around a track circling Camp Snoopy and Fiesta

Quick Guide to

Attraction	Location	Requirement
Balloon Race**	Camp Snoopy	None
Bigfoot Rapids	Wild Water Wilderness	46 inches
Boomerang	Boardwalk	48 inches
Butterfield Stagecoach*	Ghost Town	None
Calico Mine Train*	Ghost Town	None
Calico Railroad*	Ghost Town	None
Camp Bus	Camp Snoopy	42 inches to ride alone
Charlie Brown Speedway	Camp Snoopy	42 inches to ride alone
Dentzel Carousel*	Fiesta Village	None
Dragon Swing	Fiesta Village	42 inches
GhostRider	Ghost Town	48 inches
Hat Dance	Fiesta Village	36 inches
Huff 'n' Puff	Camp Snoopy	Under 52 inches
Jaguar!	Fiesta Village	48 inches
Joe Cool's Gr8 Sk8	Camp Snoopy	36 inches
La Revolucion	Fiesta Village	48 inches
Log Peeler	Camp Snoopy	32–48 inches

*Guests under 46 inches must be accompanied by an adult.
**Guests between 36 inches and 54 inches must be accompanied by an adult.

0 Not scary at all.
! Might be somewhat frightening for some children. Usually either dark or a mild roller coaster.
!! Most young children will find this scary.
!!! This attraction may frighten some adults. This is usually reserved for high-speed roller coasters and other thrill rides.

Knott's Berry Farm Attractions

Duration of Ride/Show	Scare Factor	Age Range
1 minute	0	All
6 minutes	!	5 and up
1½ minutes	!!!	8 and up
6 minutes	0	All
8 minutes	!	5 and up
6 minutes	0	All
1 minute	0	All
1½ minutes	0	All
1½ minutes	0	All
2 minutes	!	6 and up
2½ minutes	!!	7 and up
2 minutes	!	4 and up
1½ minutes	0	All
2 minutes	!	6 and up
1 minute	!	5 and up
1 minute	!!	8 and up
1½ minutes	0	All

(continues)

Quick Guide to

Attraction	Location	Requirement
Montezooma's Revenge	Fiesta Village	48 inches
Peanuts Playhouse	Camp Snoopy	None
Perilous Plunge	Boardwalk	48 inches
Pony Express	Ghost Town	48 inches
Rip Tide	Boardwalk	54–76 inches and 10 years or older
Rocky Road Trucking Company	Camp Snoopy	42 inches
Sierra Sidewinder	Camp Snoopy	42 inches
Silver Bullet	Ghost Town	54 inches
Screamin' Swing	Ghost Town	48 inches
Snoopy's Red Baron Airplanes	Camp Snoopy	32–54 inches
Supreme Scream	Boardwalk	52 inches
Timber Mountain Log Ride*	Ghost Town	None
Timberline Twisters	Camp Snoopy	36–69 inches
Waveswinger	Fiesta Village	48 inches
Wheeler Dealer Bumper Cars*	Boardwalk	42 inches

*Guests under 46 inches must be accompanied by an adult.
**Guests between 36 inches and 54 inches must be accompanied by an adult.

 0 Not scary at all.
  ! Might be somewhat frightening for some children. Usually either dark or a mild roller coaster.
 !! Most young children will find this scary.
!!! This attraction may frighten some adults. This is usually reserved for high-speed roller coasters and other thrill rides.

Knott's Berry Farm Attractions

Duration of Ride/Show	Scare Factor	Age Range
36 seconds	!!	8 and up
10 minutes	0	All
1½ minutes	!!!	9 and up
36 seconds	!	7 and up
Approx. 2 minutes	!!	10 and up
1 minute	0	All
1 minute	!	6 and up
2½ minutes	!!!	10 and up
1 minute	!!!	10 and up
1½ minutes	0	3 and up
45 seconds	!!!	8 and up
4½ minutes	!	3 and up
1 minute	0	2 and up
2 minutes	!	6 and up
2 minutes	!	4 and up

(continues)

Village

Quick Guide to

Attraction	Location	Requirement
Wipeout	Boardwalk	48 inches
Woodstock's Airmail	Camp Snoopy	36 inches
Xcelerator	Boardwalk	52 inches

*Guests under 46 inches must be accompanied by an adult.
**Guests between 36 inches and 54 inches must be accompanied by an adult.

0 Not scary at all.
! Might be somewhat frightening for some children. Usually either dark or a mild roller coaster.
!! Most young children will find this scary.
!!! This attraction may frighten some adults. This is usually reserved for high-speed roller coasters and other thrill rides.

Village. Around since 1950, this is the park's oldest ride. And because it can accommodate only a limited number of guests at a time, waits can be long. Hit this ride either early in the day or later in the afternoon as things begin to slow down. There's also the Calico Railroad. This steam-powered, narrow-gauge railroad originally operated on the Denver and Rio Grande line. During the ride, you may even experience a train robbery. Explain to children that this is just pretend so they are not frightened.

The Calico Mine Ride takes you into a mock gold mine, with miners digging deep into the earth in search of riches. Although there's no height requirement, young children may be scared of some of the ride's dark parts. The entire family can go on this ride together, and even babies are fine. Nearby, the Timber Mountain Log Ride offers a ride through a logging camp in

Knott's Berry Farm Attractions

Duration of Ride/Show	Scare Factor	Age Range
2 minutes	!!	6 and up
1½ minutes	0	All
1 minute	!!!	8 and up

one of the logs. Again, there's no height requirement, so children who could not ride Splash Mountain at Disneyland can enjoy this log ride. Be sure to smile on the way down the final chute. Your picture is taken here, and you can buy a copy at a stand near the exit to the ride. Children under 46 inches tall must be accompanied by an adult on the Mine and Log rides as well as on the Stagecoach and Railroad.

For a little more excitement, try the GhostRider. At 4,533 feet long and 118 feet high, it's the longest and wildest wooden roller coaster in the West. In fact, GhostRider appears on A&E's and the Travel Channel's top 10 lists of the country's best coasters. With an initial banked drop of 108 feet, this coaster includes 13 other drops and races out over Grand Avenue and into the parking area before returning. Riders must be at least 48 inches tall in order to ride this coaster.

Time-Saving Tip

For families with children unable to go on some attractions, Knott's Berry Farm allows for parent swapping. While one adult goes with part of the group, the other waits with the young children. Then when the first group returns, those who waited and want to ride can enter through a special entrance for immediate boarding. Be sure to speak with the attendant at the entrance to the attraction about instructions for waiting and swapping.

Ghost Town's wildest attraction is the Silver Bullet. This roller coaster puts you in ski-lift-style cars, where your feet hang down with no floor. The cars are suspended from a track above. After ascending 146 feet in the air, you head back down into an outside loop. The remainder of the ride features several inversions, including a cobra roll, corkscrew, and other extreme twists, turns, and spirals. Riders must be 54 inches tall for this exciting roller coaster.

Pony Express, Ghost Town's newest ride, is a unique coaster. Riders climb onto a coaster train that consists of 16 horses (like combining a carousel with a roller coaster). The ride—which reaches a top speed of 40 mph—consists of climbs, curves, and shallow drops. Since the ride only climbs up to a maximum of 47 feet high and lasts just 36 seconds, it isn't too extreme for kids, but still offers a unique experience for adults. Riders must be 48 inches tall.

The Screamin' Swing seats riders at the end of two long arms that swing like pendulums in opposite directions. This attraction takes you 70 feet up into the air and exerts four Gs of force for some intense thrills. There's an extra charge for this ride, and riders must be at least 48 inches tall.

Indian Trails

This small area is in between Ghost Town and Camp Snoopy. It has a Native American tribe theme and you can try crafts such as beadwork. There's a fee for materials. In addition, watch Native American song and dance or listen to storytellers pass on the legends of their tribes. Elementary-school-age kids will enjoy seeing an authentic Big House as well as teepees of the Blackfoot, Nez Perce, Cheyenne, Crow, and Kiowa tribes. The best time to visit this area is around show time so you can take in the show and look around before or after.

Camp Snoopy

If you have young children, plan on spending a good part of your day in Camp Snoopy, to the right of the main entrance. These 6 acres feature more than 30 different attractions, all but one scaled for the younger set. Snoopy himself is often around to meet children and take pictures with them.

Sierra Sidewinder is at Camp Snoopy's entrance and is considered a family roller coaster. Traveling at only 37 mph, this ride combines a roller coaster with a spinning motion. Riders sit in pairs back to back with the cars spinning around as they travel 1,400 feet of track in just over a minute. The scariest part is a 39-foot drop. Younger children should pass this ride; however, older children will enjoy it if they like to spin around.

On Joe Cool's Gr8 Sk8, riders sit atop a giant skateboard that tilts and goes up and down to mimic a ride on a half pipe. Riders must be between 36 and 80 inches tall to have a great skate.

The Grand Sierra Scenic Railroad circles Reflection Lake and even crosses a drawbridge over the water. Both of these rides are fine for entire families; however, children under 46 inches tall must be accompanied by an adult.

Helpful Hint
If your family has only younger children, head to Camp Snoopy during the morning after you ride the Stagecoach and Log Ride. (If your children want to do those.) Camp Snoopy is usually not busy in the morning so you'll be able to do the rides without the long waits. As Camp Snoopy gets a bit busier, go to other areas of the park and then come back in the late afternoon if you want to ride these attractions again.

Other rides in this area include the Balloon Races and Snoopy's Red Baron, where riders pilot their craft around in a circle. Woodstock's Airmail is a pint-size version of the Supreme Scream, where riders are lifted up on a giant airmail letter and then released in short, quick drops. The Charlie Brown Speedway takes riders around a course with quick turns, and the Rocky Road Truckin' Co. features small trucks that meander around a trail. Children can ride in the cab while their parents sit on the back of these trucks. The Huff 'n' Puff puts children in little cars that they must propel themselves by pushing a lever back and forth. The Camp Bus takes riders up and down, as does the miniature Ferris wheel. For those too young to ride the big coasters, the Timber Line Twister provides some scaled-down thrills. Likewise, the Log Peeler is a smaller version of the Wilderness Scrambler spinning ride.

In addition to these attractions, kids can burn off some energy at the Snoopy Bounce. Children ages 2 to 9 will enjoy most of the attractions here. A few attractions are wilder and may not appeal to the youngest, and some have height requirements (minimum and/or maximum heights). The Red Baron and the Huff 'n' Puff require children to ride without adults because of the height requirements.

Fiesta Village

Fiesta Village reflects the West's Spanish-Mexican influence. If you're looking for some wild rides, this area should be one of your first stops. Jaguar! is a roller coaster that meanders all over Fiesta Village and around a Maya temple. It even passes through the loop of Montezooma's Revenge. Although it has several quick turns as well as climbs and drops, it's not too fast and has no inversions. It's designed to simulate the stalking of prey by a big jungle cat. If children are unsure about this coaster, let them watch it and judge for themselves. Riders must be at least 42 inches tall to ride. As for Montezooma's Revenge, the other roller coaster in this area, riders accelerate out of the station, reaching 55 mph in only five seconds, and immediately go through a 360-degree vertical loop before climbing to a stop. Then the coaster heads back down through the loop again, in reverse, through the station and up another vertical climb. Finally, the coaster heads back down and ends at the station. Although this ride is short, it is intense. The minimum height requirement for this ride is 48 inches. This is one of the more thrilling coasters at the park. If children have no problem with Jaguar! or GhostRider, then they'll probably also enjoy Montezooma's Revenge.

Fiesta Village also features a number of carnival-style rides. The Waveswinger is a hanging swing ride that twirls you around. The Dragon Swing consists of a Viking longboat that swings back and forth. Up for a spin? Try the Hat Dance, where you control how fast you want to spin your sombrero. This ride is similar to the Mad Tea Party at Disneyland. All three of these rides are fairly tame, though intended for older children and adults. For a bit more excitement, there's La Revolucion, a ride with spinning gondolas that include the swinging action of the Dragon Swing.

Before leaving Fiesta Village, be sure to try the carousel. More than 100 years old, this is one of the world's oldest working Dentzel carousels, and it offers rides not only on horses but also on lions, tigers, and even pigs. Oh my!

Boardwalk

For those of you who haven't been back to Knott's in a few years, the old Roaring 20s area was remodeled as the Boardwalk—a tribute to the California beach scene of the 1950s and 1960s. This area contains the wildest rides and is where teenagers will spend a lot of their time.

The most thrilling ride on the Boardwalk is Xcelerator, a 1950s-theme coaster that launches riders to a speed of 82 mph in only 2.3 seconds. If that isn't enough to get your pulse racing, the cars use this speed to climb 205 feet up and then head back down in a 90-degree drop. The entire ride, which takes less than a minute, is one of the most extreme rides at the park.

The Scare Factor

The Boardwalk features some of the more intense rides at Knott's Berry Farm. While older children who like thrills will want to hit this area early, families with younger children can skip it altogether—unless you want to try out the bumper cars.

Another extreme ride is the Perilous Plunge, which claims to be the tallest, steepest, and wettest ride on the planet. Riders take boats up 127 feet and then drop down a 115-foot water chute at a revolutionary 75-degree angle. The 45-foot splash at the bottom drenches not only the passengers but also any nearby observers. This ride is very intense and scary. Even many adults don't want to ride it. Just watching others go down the chute can be heart-stopping. Did we also mention you will get very wet? Although this ride appears quite simple, it's the most thrilling ride at Knott's Berry Farm.

For a drier rush, the Supreme Scream is a completely vertical ride. Riders are quickly carried 30 stories straight up in a matter of seconds. Then they drop all the way back down to the launch pad in only three seconds, reaching a speed of 50 mph and experiencing 1.5 Gs. The riders then rebound halfway back up the tower before returning to Earth a final time. Another roller coaster in the area is the Boomerang. This one takes riders through a vertical loop as well as a boomerang corkscrew. Then the coaster reverses and takes the riders through the loops again backward. Riders experience six inversions and a lot of thrills, ranking this one of Knott's more intense rides.

Rip Tide is a rotating, swinging ride that lifts riders 82 feet into the air and then spins them head over heels in a 360-degree arc. All the twisting and turning make this another intense ride. Wipeout is a spinning ride that's mild by comparison with those previously mentioned in the Boardwalk area. The Wheeler Dealer Bumper Cars are a lot of fun, and the Sky Cabin takes you on a leisurely ascent to overlook the park and the surrounding community.

The Boardwalk features the Charles M. Schulz Theatre, formerly known as the John Wayne Theatre, and the Goodtime Theatre, which offers a variety of shows seasonally. You can also find midway games, arcades, and a Lazer Runner game where players can battle with one another using phasers and fiber-optic vests. There's a $3 fee for this attraction. You can also try rock climbing on the Boardwalk for a $5 fee.

Wild Water Wilderness

There's only one main ride in the Wild Water Wilderness area: the Bigfoot Rapids. This thrilling river-raft ride takes you down a white-water river full of drops, bumps, spins, and lots of splashes. It's similar to the Grizzly River Run at Disney's California Adventure. The fact that this ride has its own lockers nearby is a sure sign you can get wet. In fact, near the entrance to this ride you can buy ponchos to help keep you dry. The action is fairly mild, and the height requirement is 46 inches. It's designed as a family ride, as long as your children are all tall enough. If the air is chilly or you want to stay dry, skip this one.

At the Ranger Station, a naturalist will introduce you to snakes, spiders, insects, and other creepy-crawly critters. Finally, be sure to check out the Mystery Lodge. We cover it in more detail in the "Shows" section below.

Shows

Knott's Berry Farm offers a variety of entertaining shows throughout the park. When you purchase your ticket or enter through the main gates, be sure to pick up an entertainment schedule listing all the shows as well as their times and locations. Most of the shows are performed several times each day. However, a few may show only once. If you want to see one of these shows, make sure you schedule it into your day and arrive early.

Helpful Hint

No matter the ages of your family, there's at least one show that everyone will enjoy. The shows also offer a break from rides and waiting in queues, allowing you to sit down and enjoy a snack and a drink.

The Bird Cage Theatre

This theater features various seasonal performances. During the Christmas holidays, for example, Christmas plays are presented.

The Calico Saloon

Here you can sip a sarsaparilla while watching shows that range from Old West singing to a cancan dance show. Most shows are around 20 minutes in length.

Camp Snoopy Theatre

This theater puts on seasonal performances starring Charlie Brown and the rest of the *Peanuts* gang. It's aimed at young children and their families.

Charles M. Schulz Theatre

This large 2,100-seat theater hosts musicals and seasonal ice shows throughout the year. When the park is not open late, the shows are often only on Friday or Saturday.

Indian Trails Native Song and Dances

This show, at the Indian Trails Stage, features both Native American and Aztec dancers, singers, and musicians who share their cultural heritage with the audience. The show can last from 15 to 30 minutes and is good for all ages.

Mystery Lodge

In this mystical, multisensory show, the Old Storyteller relates Native American folklore; the smoke from the fire illustrates the story. Lasting about 20 minutes, this show keeps all ages fascinated with the special effects as well as the stories.

The Wild West Stunt Show

Inside the Wagon Camp Theater, this Western stunt show lasts about 20 minutes and is a lot of fun. If you're expecting something like Universal Studios' Western stunt show, however, you may be disappointed. The Knott's show focuses on humor rather than amazing stunts. All ages will enjoy this show, but the sound of cap guns can startle some young children. Warn them in advance, and sit toward the rear of the theater to lessen the effect of the noise.

Tips for Touring Knott's Berry Farm

Although Knott's Berry Farm is a fairly large park, it's possible to see and do everything in a single day. If you want to save some money and are content with just hitting certain types of attractions, such as just the rides for small children or just the coasters and wild rides, consider visiting the park after 4 PM and paying reduced admission.

There are two main strategies for touring Knott's Berry Farm. The difference is your focus. Do you want to hit all the roller coasters and thrill rides, or do you have small children and want to do only the attractions they can ride? Both strategies assume you'll be arriving in the morning. A third strategy takes into account families with children of mixed ages, and there's a late-entry plan as well.

Time-Saving Tip

Most families spend only a single day at Knott's Berry Farm. That is all the time it really takes to see everything. Therefore, you'll probably not want to leave the park to rest at your hotel and then return later. Instead, you can rest for a bit in the park by hitting the shows or riding the train. Or you can just wander around Ghost Town while sipping on a refreshing drink.

The Younger Children Plan

With younger children, a lot of your time will be spent in Camp Snoopy. The lines in Camp Snoopy never get as long as some of the more popular rides in the park because there are so many different rides in this area. Therefore, when you first get to the park, bypass Camp Snoopy and head straight back through Ghost Town toward the Stagecoach ride. Because this ride can have a long wait, hit it early. If there's already a long line, continue on to the Log Ride and the Calico Mine Ride. Both can handle guests much more quickly. After getting both of these out of the way, make your way back to Camp Snoopy. You can easily spend several hours here. When the children begin to get tired or hungry, pick up a snack and head off to one of the shows. This will give you a chance to sit down and rest for a bit. When you are ready to go again, try Bigfoot Rapids to help cool you off on a warm day. By now it should be mid-afternoon. Consider eating an early dinner or strolling around Ghost Town. If you missed the Stagecoach ride earlier, try it now as well as the steam train. Then go back and do any of the attractions again that the children liked and watch some more shows.

The Teenager Plan

If your children are older and want to hit the wild rides, veer to the left after you enter through the main gates and make your way to the GhostRider. It's the only coaster on the southern side of the park, so ride it early while you're already nearby. Next, head west across Ghost Town to the Pony Express. (Since it's one of the newest rides and is quite popular, it will be busier if you wait until later.) Next make your way toward the middle of the park and ride the Silver Bullet, then head to the Board-walk area and—if you're feeling brave—try the Xcelerator, Supreme Scream, the Boomerang, and Perilous Plunge. Continue on to Fiesta Village for the Jaguar! and Montezooma's Revenge. By this time, you have gone on all the major thrill rides and the lines for these are probably getting long. So try out all the smaller carnival-style rides now, as well as the Calico Mine Ride, the Log Ride, and Bigfoot Rapids. During mid-afternoon, take in some shows or shop around Ghost Town. As people begin to leave and things start to slow down late in the afternoon, start going back to the coasters. The later it gets, the shorter the lines on most nights.

The Mixed Ages Plan

If you want to take in the roller coasters as well as the kiddie rides, you'll have to use a plan combining the previous two. Start off with one or more of the popular roller coasters—GhostRider, Pony Express, the Silver Bullet, or Xcelerator. The lines should be short, so the little ones won't have to wait long, especially if you do a parent swap. Next, try the Mine and Log rides before making your way through Fiesta Village to Camp Snoopy. Hit any rides with short lines along the way. As the little ones get tired, try a show or the attractions on the other side of the park, such as Bigfoot Rapids. When things begin to slow down in mid- to late afternoon, the younger children will usually be content to munch on a snack as they watch the older children go on the wilder rides you skipped earlier.

This is actually one of the more difficult plans to follow because there are times when only part of the family is riding attractions. The key is to minimize the downtime for each age group. Try to go from thrill rides to kiddie rides and back, with family rides thrown in between.

The Late-Entry Plan

The late-entry plan is best suited to families with older children: after 4 PM, most younger children are starting to get tired. If you want to save money with your younger children by coming late, make sure they get a nap and are well rested before entering the park. This plan does not work well for families with children of mixed-age groups because there's usually not enough time to see everything.

Unlike the other plans, the late-entry plan works in reverse. You begin by hitting the less popular rides first and then work your way to the coasters as the night progresses and the lines shorten. Because many of the shows do not continue late, see those you want early so you won't miss them. Also, because you don't want to waste time eating inside the park, have a good dinner before entering. Mrs. Knott's Chicken Dinner Restaurant is a good choice. Get there around 2:30 PM, and by the time your family is finished it will be time to enter the park. Just don't eat too much if you plan on hitting the coasters!

Dining and Shopping

Knott's Berry Farm started out with a restaurant, so you should definitely try Mrs. Knott's Chicken Dinner Restaurant. In fact, this is probably the best meal deal you can find at a theme park during your vacation. This restaurant is just outside the main gate in Knott's Marketplace. Lunches are around $7 to $10, and children's meals are $6 to $8. However, the best deals are the dinners, which are served from 11 AM to close. For around $15 you can get four pieces of fried chicken, a salad, your choice of chicken soup or an appetizer, mashed potatoes and gravy, vegetable, biscuits, and your choice of dessert (including boysenberry pie as well as other tasty treats). There's so much food that an adult can usually share a dinner with a small child. In addition to fried chicken, you can get ribs, chicken potpie, pot roast, and other home-style meals for the same price. Mrs. Knott's Chicken Dinner Restaurant is quite popular, and you don't have to go to the park in order to eat here. In fact, you can park for three hours free near the restaurant.

Knott's Berry Farm also has other great restaurants and eateries. You can get fried chicken to go or in boxed meals at several other locations. Spurs Chop House is a steak-house restaurant that also serves sandwiches, burgers, and salads. Fireman's Brigade Barbecue has great chicken and ribs. Ghost Town Grill offers burgers, sandwiches, chicken, and chili. All of these are in Ghost Town.

For south-of-the-border fare, head to Fiesta Village, where Fiesta BBQ serves carne asada, enchiladas, and chicken, and the Cantina offers fajitas, tacos, and burritos. The Boardwalk area features several places to eat, including a new Johnny Rockets, the ever-popular shakes and burger joint. Coasters offers similar fare while Hollywood Hits is the place for pizza. In addition to these places, Knott's offers several spots to find a quick bite or snack. Funnel cakes, somewhat like a Belgian waffle, are very popular and are found around the park.

Helpful Hint

You do not have to eat your meals in the park. Knott's Marketplace, just outside the front gate, features several dining venues including Mrs. Knott's Chicken Dinner Restaurant, a T. G. I. Friday's, and places to get burgers and fries or even ice cream. These eateries can be less busy for lunch than those inside the park.

Part of the Knott's experience is the shopping. Although you can find typical souvenirs as at most other theme parks, Ghost Town offers some unique and interesting shops. You can find pioneer bonnets, Native American beaded items, and other Western goods. Whether you buy anything or not, just browsing can be a good way to rest during the busiest part of the day. Of course, you'll have to go home with some Knott's Berry Farm preserves. Several shops in the park offer these goods, but it's best to wait and buy them in Knott's Marketplace outside the gates of the park or, if you buy them in the park, when you're ready to leave. Jars of jam can be quite heavy to carry around. The country-store-style shop in Knott's Marketplace offers a variety of preserves, including hard-to-find sugar-free selections as well as varieties not available in stores back home. Even if you're not going into the park, you may want to stop by the market to pick up gifts for others or yourself.

The Boysenberry Experience

When you visit Knott's Berry Farm, you have several opportunities to try one of the fruits of their labor—the boysenberry. Just about every restaurant and eatery offers some type of boysenberry product. Thirsty? Try some boysenberry punch. (You can also buy the concentrate to make it at home.) If you're eating pancakes in the morning or funnel cakes throughout the day, drizzle them with boysenberry syrup. Spread some boysenberry jam on your biscuits. There are several baked goods featuring the boysenberry, and for dessert try either boysenberry pie or boysenberry sherbet. Although boysenberry isn't the only flavor at Knott's, it is the most popular.

Visiting During the Holidays

If you'll be visiting Knott's Berry Farm near Halloween or Christmas, be ready. During October, the park becomes Knott's Scary Farm. Camp Spooky combines daytime trick-or-treating, costume contests, fun mazes, Camp Snoopy Sidewalk Theater shows, and children's hands-on craft activities. Not recommended for children under 13, Halloween Haunt features hundreds of monsters, lots of mazes, and several scare zones, as well as creepy shows and other entertainment. If you have teenagers who like to be scared, it's worthwhile to check this out.

In late November and December, get ready for Knott's Merry Farm, when Ghost Town is transformed into the Christmas Crafts Village. There are Victorian carolers walking around and lots and lots of crafts. If you want to go just for the shopping during this time, you can purchase a separate admission to the crafts village for only $5 for adults. Children 11 and under are free. It makes for good Christmas shopping even if you don't want to see the other attractions, and you still get to experience Ghost Town and its shows as well. For more information on these and other seasonal events, check the Knott's Web site or call the number listed at the start of this chapter.

Soak City USA

Like many other Southern California theme parks, Knott's has an adjacent water park. Soak City USA's 13 acres host 16 speed, tube, and body slides leading down from four platforms between 39 and 62 feet high. In addition to the slides, Soak City USA has a large wave pool, a lazy river on which you can ride inner tubes, and a beach-house fun house with water activities for the entire family. For younger children, the lagoon area has a small pool and an activity area. There are changing rooms for men and women, as well as locker rentals. Meals and snacks can be purchased at two dining locations and from snack carts.

Soak City USA admission includes unlimited use of all rides and attractions in the park. Adults pay $30, and admission for children 3 to 11 is $20. After 3 PM, adults pay $20. The park is open from Memorial Day through Labor Day, 10 AM to 7 PM in summer. It closes earlier in spring and at the end of summer. For $95 on weekdays or $115 on weekends a family can rent a private cabana right off the wave pool with four lounge chairs, a dining table with four chairs, and a shade umbrella. Also included are free inner-tube rentals and walk-up food service (though food charges still apply). This price is for up to eight people. For a family, especially on a weekday, the cabana can be a great place to set up camp. If you plan on renting a cabana, be sure to make reservations at least 24 hours in advance; you do this via the Knott's Web site. Small and large lockers can also be rented at $7 and $22 per day, respectively. Knott's also operates Soak City USAs in San Diego and Palm Springs.

CHAPTER

10

Universal Studios Hollywood

Universal Studios Hollywood

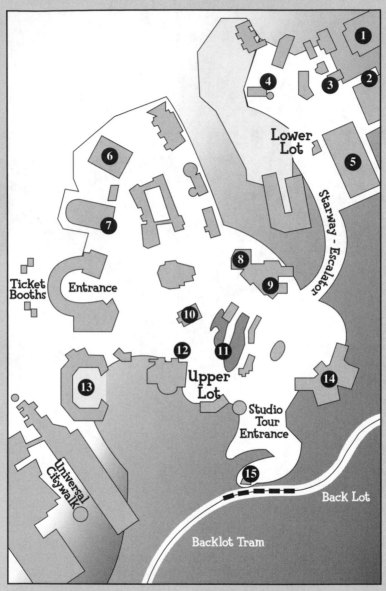

Lower Lot

Starway - Escalator

Ticket Booths

Entrance

Upper Lot

Studio Tour Entrance

Universal Citywalk

Back Lot

Backlot Tram

niversal Studios is a fun-
filled theme park that captures the glamour and thrill of Hollywood. Everything here is related to the moviemaking
industry. In themes from some of the greatest Universal films,
Universal Studios Hollywood features rides and attractions as
well as live-action shows, taking guests from the prehistoric to
the future.

When Carl Laemmle founded his movie studio Universal
City in 1915, he invited the public to visit. It was such a success that he had special bleachers constructed at the studio—for
25¢ spectators could watch movies being filmed. This ended
when talkies arrived, since the spectators might make noise during the recording. Universal Studios Hollywood reopened in
1964, once again giving the public the chance to observe
moviemaking firsthand.

Universal Studios Hollywood is the only Southern California theme park that is also part of a working movie studio.
Unlike other theme parks, the rides are not the major attractions. In fact, there are only a few rides in the park. Instead,

Universal concentrates on making you feel like you are in the movies. The special effects are incredible.

> 100 Universal City Plaza,
> Universal City, CA 91608
> 818/622–3801
> www.universalstudioshollywood.com

Location

Universal Studios Hollywood is just off the Hollywood Freeway (U.S. 101). Take the Universal Center Drive or Lankershim Boulevard exit, in between Hollywood and the San Fernando Valley.

Admission and Package Deals

Admission to Universal Studios Hollywood costs about the same as that of the other area theme parks. Single-day admission is $67 for adults and $57 for children under 48 inches tall. Check Universal's Web site for details on seasonal specials. For $79, you can purchase a Regular Annual Passport. This allows visits to Universal Studios Hollywood for 12 months (there are about 25 blackout days). The Deluxe Annual Passport, which costs $99, has no blackout dates. The Premium Annual Passport ($119) includes all of the features of the Deluxe and adds on free parking and front-of-line access to the Studio Tour. All annual passes include a 10% discount on park food and merchandise.

If you're a big movie buff, you may want to take the VIP Experience. For $199 per person, adult and child alike, guests are given a behind-the-scenes guided tour of the studios, access to production facilities to see movies and television shows currently being filmed on one of the 35 soundstages, and priority boarding on all rides. The priority boarding allows you to go to the front of the line for most rides and puts you ahead of other guests in a shortened queue for the rest of the attractions. You also get an All You Can Eat Pass for unlimited meals at selected restaurants. This includes an entrée, side, and a dessert each time you use it; the pass is $27 for adults and $16 for kids. If you just want priority access for rides and shows, for $119 you can purchase the Front of the Line Pass.

If you plan on visiting SeaWorld in San Diego during your vacation, the 2-Park Flex Ticket allows unlimited admissions for a period of 14 consecutive days. This is a good deal and can save you money. These tickets are $105 for adults and $95 for children ages 3 to 9.

All these passes and tickets can be bought at Universal Studios Hollywood from the box offices near the park entrance. They can also be bought in advance from the Universal Studios Web site. At times, the studios run specials or offer discounts for online tickets. You can print out tickets bought online at home, so that you're ready to enter the park as soon as you arrive. Discounted tickets can also be purchased from AAA, giving you a discount of around $10. Several businesses offer coupons for their employees, or you can check at area supermarkets for coupons. The Box Offices open an hour before the park, so if you have to buy tickets there, you can get there early and have your tickets in hand when the park opens.

More than 75 acres of adjacent parking serve not only

Money Saving Tip

If you know ahead of time that you'll be visiting Universal Studios, purchase your tickets online. The Universal Studios Web site has deals that are not available at the park, such as discounts on the various tickets and passes and bonus deals. You can then print out your tickets at home, or have them sent to you.

Universal Studios Hollywood and CityWalk but also the Universal Amphitheater. Normal parking costs $12; preferred parking, which is closer, is $20. Before heading into the park, remember to write down where you parked your vehicle. After a long day of fun, you don't want to have to wander this large parking area looking for your car.

Operating Hours

Universal Studios is open daily, except for Thanksgiving and Christmas. From mid-June through September, the hours are 9 AM to 8 PM (until 9 PM on Saturday and Sunday). Nonsummer hours are 10 AM to 5 PM. The box offices open an hour before the park does and close at 5 PM in summer and at 4:30 PM the rest of the year. If you plan on arriving later in the afternoon, make sure you already have your ticket or get there before the box offices close.

Amenities

At Guest Services, near the main gate, you can find visitor information on the local area, guides for guests with disabilities, audio assist units, TDD phones for the hearing impaired, and travel assistance. This is also the location for the lost and found as well as for lost children. Any purchases you make during the day can be sent to Studio Styles, near the main gate, to be picked up when you're ready to leave later in the afternoon. Lockers are available to store items you don't want to carry around all day. Strollers can be rented for about $7 a day. However, if you'll be visiting for more than one day or you'll be going to another theme park, it might be worth your money and your child's comfort to purchase an umbrella stroller before your trip. These can usually be found at large discount stores for around $10–$15.

Universal Studios Hollywood has a complimentary kennel service if you're traveling with pets. Go to Guest Services at the main gate outside the park, and a representative will take care of your pet for the duration of your visit.

Universal Studios also has a Guaranteed Rain Check. On any day on which the park receives ⅛ inch or more of rain before 2 PM, you'll be offered a rain check allowing you to return to the park anytime during the next 30 days. In addition, on rainy days complimentary coffee and hot chocolate are served at designated covered or indoor areas where you can also meet characters.

Suitability for Children

Although children under 6 will enjoy some shows here, most will be bored for much of the day, waiting while their parents and older siblings take turns doing things the little ones can't. Many of the rides and attractions have either height requirements or are too intense for the younger set. However, children 6 and up, especially teens, will have a blast. If you have both young and older children, it's often a good idea to split up when doing age-appropriate attractions.

Helpful Hint

You can check your strollers at two different locations inside the park. One is at the entrance to the Studio Tour boarding area. The second is next to the Starway at the Lower Lot. Because most of the attractions are close to each other on this level, small children can walk or be carried from place to place. The attendant will give you a claim tag for picking up your stroller when you're ready to go again. For the shows and attractions on the Upper Lot level, there's plenty of stroller parking.

Attractions

Universal Studios Hollywood is divided into two main areas. You begin at the Upper Lot when you walk in through the main gates. Most of the shows as well as some of the attractions, including the Studio Tour, are here. Down the hill is the Lower Lot. To get there you take the Starway. This series of very long escalators takes you down the hill and over to the second area, where you can find more rides and attractions.

If you're pushing a stroller, you can take it on the Starway escalators as long as you first remove the child and carry the child or have him or her walk next to you. There's an elevator for handicapped guests and strollers. However, because the Starway carries you over a distance as well as down, arrangements need to be made for a van to pick you up at the bottom and take you to the Lower Lot. This method can often take around 30 minutes. There's an attendant by the elevator to help out and to make arrangements.

The Upper Lot

The Upper Lot is the main level of Universal Studios Hollywood. Its several streets look like avenues from around the world. Although you begin on New York Street, turning one of the corners takes you to London, Paris, Cape Cod, or even the Old West. The streets are lined with restaurants and shops, with the shows and attractions located primarily along the periphery.

As you're wandering the streets, be on the lookout for famous Universal stars. You may see Woody Woodpecker, Lucy, Groucho Marx and his brothers, Laurel and Hardy, Charlie Chaplin, Marilyn Monroe, as well as the Universal monsters: Dracula, the Wolfman, the Phantom of the Opera, the Mummy, and, of course, Frankenstein's monster. Some of the stars walk around, and others drive around in automobiles, but

Helpful Hint

For families with children unable to go on some attractions, Universal Studios Hollywood allows for parent swapping. While one adult goes with part of the group, the other waits with the young children. Many of the attractions even have waiting areas for parents. When the first group returns, those who waited can then enter through a special entrance for immediate boarding. Be sure to speak with the attendant at the entrance to the attraction for directions to the waiting area and any other instructions for waiting.

all are willing to have their photos taken with you. For a great shot, get your picture taken next to the 24-foot hanging shark.

If you're interested in seeing the live taping of a television show, be sure to visit the TV Audience Ticket Booth. Here you can get free tickets to shows taped not only at Universal Studios but also at other studios in the area. *The Tonight Show with Conan O'Brien* is also filmed at Universal Studios. You can request tickets four to six weeks in advance at www. tonightshowwithconanobrien.com/tickets. Standby tickets are also available at Universal Studios, but you are not guaranteed a seat. Guests must be at least 16 years of age. Visit the Web site for more information.

The Simpsons Ride

Universal Studios' newest attraction is based on *The Simpsons Movie* and TV show. You'll get to ride along with Homer, Marge, Bart, Lisa, and Maggie Simpson as they visit Krusty the Clown's new low-budget fantasy amusement park. Riders make their way through a queue area themed like a midway before

Quick Guide to

Attraction	Location	Requirement
The Adventures of Curious George	The Upper Lot	None
Backdraft	The Lower Lot	None
The Blues Brothers	The Upper Lot	None
Creature from the Black Lagoon: A Raging Rockin' Show	The Upper Lot	None
Jurassic Park: The Ride	The Lower Lot	46 inches
Revenge of the Mummy: The Ride	The Lower Lot	48 inches
Shrek 4-D	The Upper Lot	None
Simpsons Ride	The Upper Lot	40 inches
Special Effects Stages	The Lower Lot	None
The Studio Tour	Tram Level	None
Terminator 2: 3-D	The Upper Lot	None
The Universal Experience	The Lower Lot	None
Universal's Animal Actors Show	The Upper Lot	None
Universal House of Horrors	The Upper Lot	None
WaterWorld	The Upper Lot	None

0 Not scary at all.
! Might be somewhat frightening for some children. Usually either dark or a mild roller coaster.

Universal Studios Attractions

Duration of Ride/Show	Scare Factor	Age Range
N/A	0	All
Approx. 12 minutes	!	5 and up
20 minutes	0	All
Approx. 25 minutes	!	8 and up
5½ minutes	!!!	7 and up
3 minutes	!!!	10 and up
11 minutes	!	All
6 minutes	!	7 and up
Approx. 30 minutes	0	All
Approx. 50 minutes	!	All
12 minutes	!!!	8 and up
N/A	0	All
15 minutes	0	All
N/A	!!!	10 and up
15 minutes	!!!	8 and up

!! Most young children will find this scary.
!!! This attraction may frighten some adults. This is usually reserved for high-speed roller coasters and other thrill rides.

Insider's Secret
You can experience some of the fun of The
Simpsons Ride at home before you even leave on
vacation. Visit www.simpsonsride.com to play some
arcade games from the ride's midway.

being seated in roller coaster–like cars. However, there is no
track. Instead, the Simpsons Ride is a motion theater attraction
with a large IMAX screen. The cars move up, down, and tilt so
riders feel like they are actually moving along with the movie.
As you follow the Simpson family up and down the track of a
roller coaster, Sideshow Bob tries to hit them with a wrecking
ball. The cars are knocked off the track and then continue
crashing through various lands and rides within Krustyland as
they are chased by Bob. The ride includes smoke, fire, mist, and
even water spray to add realism to the ride. Most children 7 or
older will like this ride. Use Star Tours or Soaring Over California at the Disneyland Resort as guides. Riders must be 40
inches tall.

Terminator 2: 3-D

Terminator 2: 3-D incorporates Universal's well-done special
effects and live actors. The attraction begins in a lobby of a robotics company named Cyberdyne. Your hostess welcomes
you and begins to give a presentation on the company. However, the hostess's video introduction is interrupted by Linda
Hamilton and Edward Furlong, reprising their roles from the
movie. After they warn the audience to "Get out while there
is still time," the hostess regains control and opens the doors
to the 700-seat theater. No one directs you to your seats, so
try to sit in the middle of the theater. Although sitting up
front gives you a closer view of the actors, you have a limited
view of the side screens and their action. Even if you have to

sit in the very back, you will still be able to see everything. And don't worry—the 3-D effects will reach you, no matter where you sit.

The show includes loud gunfire (both on screen and live), explosions, lasers, smoke, jolting seats, and, of course, things coming at you from the screen. James Cameron, the director of the *Terminator* movies as well as *Titanic,* also directed this production. The interaction between the screen and the live action is incredible. Be sure to watch as the Arnold Schwarzenegger look-alike rides a motorcycle through the screen and then enters the 3-D movie.

The Scare Factor

Although there's no age limit or height requirement, Universal Studios recommends this attraction for children 8 years and up. There's no blood or gore, and the violence is limited to the destruction of robots, but the show is quite intense and may frighten even older children. You should judge its appropriateness for your children based on the type of movies you let them watch.

The Studio Tour

No one can go to Universal Studios Hollywood without taking the Studio Tour. In fact, for many years in the beginning, this was about the only attraction at the park. If you have not been to the park in the last several years, you're in for a surprise. The trams are new and feature state-of-the-art audio and video technology, with Whoopi Goldberg as your virtual guide. Each tram is outfitted with four LCD flat-screen monitors (so everyone can see the tour guide), a state-of-the-art audio system, and a DVD player that stores numerous film clips and interviews.

This adds a new dimension to the tour. After seeing some of the actual sets, you then get to see the sets as they appeared in the movie.

During the course of the 50-minute tour, the trams will take you all around the studios' production lot. This is no ordinary tour, with the tour guide just pointing out buildings. In several areas, you experience Hollywood special effects first-hand. If you don't think a heavy, multicar tram can be shaken and jolted, you'll be in for quite a surprise.

The tram enters a soundstage while the guide explains how the buildings are used for filming movies. The one you enter is set up like Skull Island from the latest incarnation of *King Kong*. The tour also takes you through movie sets from such films as *War of the Worlds* and *Jurassic Park*. You'll even get to experience a chase sequence inspired by *The Fast and the Furious: Tokyo Drift*. Other sets include Wisteria Lane from the TV show *Desperate Housewives* and Whoville from the movie *Dr. Seuss's How the Grinch Stole Christmas*.

Another soundstage you visit is a re-creation of a modern subway station. Now for a California experience—a magnitude 8.3 earthquake. The pavement above cracks, and an 18-wheeler carrying flammables comes crashing down amid sparking power cables. Just when you think it's over, a subway train

Insider's Secret

It's best to sit as close to the front of the tram as possible. The front car is usually reserved for those with Front of the Line Passes or the VIP Experience. However, if you do not have one of these passes, still try to get in the second car so you'll be able to see the attractions earlier than those at the rear.

comes speeding out of control into the tunnel and 60,000 gallons of water begin flooding the area.

Another shaker is a bridge that begins to collapse as the tram drives over it. However, after crossing over safely, look back and watch the bridge amazingly rebuild itself. The tour will eventually take you by Jaws Lake, which features an animatronic great white shark that terrorizes the lakeside village before swimming over to the tram and lunging up, with jaws wide open. At another part of the tour, you'll enter the ruins of the lost Egyptian city of Hamunaptra, where you face the Curse of the Mummy's Tomb. Based on the movie *The Mummy*, the walls of the tunnel begin to rotate, causing the illusion of motion, as if the tram were beginning to tip to one side. However, the tram does not move at all. The guests are just experiencing vertigo. If the special effects are too stomach turning, just close your eyes and the illusion disappears.

Speaking of vertigo, many of Hitchcock's classics were filmed at Universal Studios. The tour takes you by the Bates Motel and the house where *Psycho* was filmed. Also, along the way you go through many sets from a host of movies. They allow filmmakers to represent many different locations worldwide and at different time periods. You'll even see the waters part for the tram so it can get through a flooded area.

Even though there are some pretty intense and amazing rides at Universal Studios Hollywood, many people say that the Studio Tour is their favorite part. We recommend it for all ages. Remind your children that none of it is real. It's just make-believe. Although some parts of the tour can be scary, it's mostly visual. Therefore, tell children who don't like it to just close their eyes. Most scary parts are over quickly. Our 2-year-old slept through the entire tour, and our 4-year-old just closed her eyes when she got scared. If a child does have a hard time, the tour guide will allow you to get off and will arrange a ride back to the start. Certain tours during the day are presented in Spanish.

To get to the trams, you must descend an escalator to the boarding area. For those with strollers or wheelchairs, there's an elevator for getting down and back up again—a stroller check-in is at the entrance to the attraction.

Shrek 4-D

In this 3-D movie, Shrek and Donkey are back for another adventure, and they're taking the audience along for the ride. Although the special effects are similar to those in *Terminator 2: 3-D* in that you not only see and hear the action but also feel it, this attraction is a little less intense and can be enjoyed by the entire family. And although the 3-D effects and noise might be frightening for some children, most will enjoy it. A good judge of whether your children will like it is how they liked the movie *Shrek.* If you're unsure, sit toward the rear and near an exit so you can leave in the middle if necessary. However, some children may want to just close their eyes to avoid effects that might be frightening.

Universal's House of Horrors

This walk-through attraction is based on Universal's horror movies. You'll experience classics such as Dracula, the Werewolf, and Frankenstein's monster as well as scenes from newer films. Watch out for the zombies from *Dawn of the Dead.* Preteens and older will usually enjoy it, but younger children will

Scare Factor!

Universal's House of Horrors is pretty scary—even for some adults and teenagers. It's not a wax museum or Disneyland's Haunted Mansion, but more like a maze with characters and scary things that pop out at you. If you're still unsure whether your children will like it, send an adult through first to check it out.

be scared. Again, use the original movies as a guide. If you would not want your children to see the movie, don't take them into this attraction.

The Adventures of Curious George

Although many of the Universal Studios attractions seem to be geared toward older children and adults, the Adventures of Curious George is aimed at younger children. Modeled on the popular books and animated series, this area features fountains, water activities, and a fun-house area with balls; kids can also meet the famous monkey himself. Highlights include a 500-gallon water dump and water cannons for shooting at other people. For preschoolers, there's a slower-paced area, which gives younger children a place to play without having to worry about being run over by older children and preteens. Since many of the other attractions in the park require sitting and being still, the Adventures of Curious George gives young children a place to run around and use up some of their energy. It's also a good place to cool down during a hot day at the park, if you want to get wet!

Coke Soak

Near the exit to the *Terminator 2: 3-D* show, the Coke Soak is a series of fountains in which guests can cool off. Unlike the Jurassic Park ride, this one lets you control how wet you want to get.

The Lower Lot

Down the hill from the Upper Lot, the Lower Lot contains several rides and attractions in close proximity to one another. This area often opens later than the upper level. Try to get down here as soon as possible after it does open—some of the most popular attractions are here.

Revenge of the Mummy: The Ride

One of Universal Studios' newer attractions is an indoor roller coaster based on the *Mummy* movies. You're taken on a journey

The Scare Factor

Revenge of the Mummy is the scariest ride in the park because it combines a fast roller coaster ride in the dark with frightening scenes and events. It's definitely not for young children, and older children should try the House of Horrors first to see if they like that type of attraction before combining it with a thrill ride. We recommend ages 10 and older.

into the cavernous tomb of Imhotep, Egypt's legendary Keeper of the Dead. Think of this ride as a roller coaster through a haunted house. The designers worked to create a psychological adventure that taps into a number of different fears, including such classics as the dark, insects, height, speed, and death. The cars are propelled along tracks using electromagnetic propulsion and move both forward and backward throughout the ride. You'll encounter warrior mummies, scarabs, and even Imhotep himself as you trigger the curse by entering the tomb and begin your race back out to safety. You must be 48 inches to ride.

Jurassic Park: The Ride

Based on Steven Spielberg's popular movies, this ride is fantastic. Let us warn you now: you will not get wet—you will get soaked! One of our Studio Tour guides recommended just jumping in the lagoon. "You will get just as wet and not have to stand in a line," he said. As you enter the queue area, there are some vending machines off to the right side. For 75¢, you can purchase a poncho to keep your clothes somewhat dry. There's a locker room to the left where you can store backpacks and other items you want to keep dry. A waiting area is adjacent to the lockers for guests with small children.

You board 25-passenger rafts for your trip through Jurassic Park. You pass by three-story-tall dinosaurs, and one suddenly rises out of the water right next to you. However, just as in the movies, something goes wrong. Your raft begins to drift through the back area of the park, where some dangerous dinosaurs have gotten loose. A truck comes falling down toward you, spitting dinosaurs launch

Helpful Hint

If you want to stay dry but don't want to pay for a poncho, check the locker room and waiting area. You can often find ponchos there, left by previous riders.

water right at your face, and raptors lunge at you. However, for the finale a giant T. rex comes out at you just before an exhilarating 84-foot drop. By the time you reach the lagoon below, you're traveling nearly 50 mph and it feels as if someone has thrown a bucket of water at you. The drop is the fastest, steepest water-ride drop in amusement park history.

The ride has a minimum height requirement of 46 inches. However, even if your child is tall enough, the dinosaurs can be quite intense, not to mention the drop, which can be terrifying by itself. Children who were not scared by the movies and who like roller coasters should do fine. As usual, if they do get scared on the ride, just tell them to close their eyes.

Insider's Secret

When your raft takes a turn into the area where the dinosaurs have escaped, take a look at the ravaged raft to the left. Can you find the mouse ears from an unlucky tourist?

Backdraft

This interesting attraction features a behind-the-scenes look at the making of the movie *Backdraft*. The attraction is narrated by the director of the film, Ron Howard, with help from some of the actors, including Scott Glenn and Kurt Russell. This walk-through attraction is made up of three different rooms. In the final room, you confront an inferno in a chemical plant. It starts as a small fire in an office and gradually spreads until the whole stage is ablaze. Then at the end, the platform everyone is standing on jerks, as if it were about to collapse and throw everyone into the blaze below.

There's no age limit for this ride, and you can take a stroller inside. The final scene can be quite intense, with loud explosions, and you can really feel the heat of the flames in front of you. However, most kids do fine in this attraction. The best time to hit Backdraft is just after going on the Jurassic Park ride: the heat here will help you dry off.

Special Effects Stages

The Special Effects Stages take you behind the scenes, immersing you in the magic of the movies. As you progress through a series of stages, you're shown how different types of special effects are created for some of the biggest blockbuster hits—each stage showing a specific effect or technique. Volunteers from the audience are often used in the process. Once you learn how these effects are created, you're then shown how they appear in the actual movie. It's really amazing how some high-tech scenes in movies use very low-tech techniques for sound and visual effects.

Although certain scenes in these movies may be somewhat scary for young children, this attraction is usually fine for all ages, since children can see that the monsters and other scary things are just pretend. If you want to be selected as a volunteer, show the staff that you're not afraid to act. Although they often pick teenagers, they also pick adults.

The Universal Experience

This walkthrough exhibit features props, wardrobes, and artifacts from past, present, and upcoming Universal productions, such as Russell Crowe's armor from *Gladiator* and miniatures from *Apollo 13*. Interactive kiosks add some technology to this attraction, and this is a good place for some downtime from the more thrilling attractions. While adults and older children will enjoy seeing the exhibits, younger children may get bored—so bring snacks or something to keep them occupied.

Shows

Universal Studios Hollywood has just about as many shows as it does attractions, with several different shows each day. For show times, check the *Studio Guide* you'll receive when you enter the park or look them up on one of the Digital Directories around the park. All shows are at several different times, so you should be able to catch all of them in between seeing the other attractions. Most of the shows are also offered in Spanish, although those usually run only on Sunday. Check Universal's Web site for times and dates.

Helpful Hint

Be sure to see all of the shows you can while at Universal Studios. These are unlike the shows at any other theme park and often feature lots of special effects. Although most shows have plenty of seating, try to get in line at least 20 minutes early. Once a show begins, no further seating is permitted.

Creature from the Black Lagoon—A Raging Rockin' Show
Universal Studios' newest attraction is a musical stage show based on the old Universal monster movie. The show features romance and comedy as well acrobatics as it tells the story of a beast who falls in love with a beauty in the Amazon jungle. The music is fast and loud, and some small children may be scared. However, there is more singing and dancing than action. While it is billed as a Broadway-style musical, it is not as good as the

Aladdin show at Disney's California Adventure. If you're short on time, you may want to skip it so you can enjoy the park's other shows and attractions.

WaterWorld: A Live Sea War Spectacular

Based on the Kevin Costner movie from 1995, WaterWorld is Universal Studios Hollywood's biggest show and features some great action and special effects. The audience witnesses a battle featuring the Mariner and Helen (the good guys) against Deacon and his cronies. The stunt-filled battle uses firearms, cannons, Jet Skis, hovercraft, and much more. The show is filled with gunfire, explosions, and pyrotechnics, including giant fireballs rising 50 feet into the air, then cascading down to create a wall of fire. The finale includes a seaplane that comes swooping down over the audience, skidding across the water to an explosive crash landing, all up close to the audience. You'll be amazed at what Universal fits into a 15-minute show.

The loud gunfire and explosions in this show make it unsuitable for most small children, who are often frightened by all the fighting. As for the violence factor, the actors shoot at each other with guns—the show is basically a big battle. Therefore, you should decide on this show based on the type of television programs and movies you deem appropriate for your kids. Also note that the green seats in the front rows are colored for a reason: if you sit in them, you'll probably get wet. This show is popular and fills up quickly, so get in line early, not only so you can get a good seat but also just so you can get in.

Universal's Animal Actors

Unlike many of the animal shows you see at other parks or zoos, Universal's Animal Actors is pure entertainment. Don't expect to learn how animals are trained. Instead, get ready for a fast-paced show featuring more than 100 animals of various types. The cast includes dogs, pigs, primates, birds, and more crazy critters. Many of these animals are movie or television stars. A few volunteers, usually younger children, are selected from the audience to take part in some of the acts. The 15-minute show leaves most people wanting more.

This show is great for all ages, and everyone seems to love it. In fact, several families go to more than one showing during the day because the kids want to see the animals again. The popular show holds a lot of people, but be sure to get in line early to secure a good seat.

The Blues Brothers

Jake and Elwood Blues have just arrived from Chicago, and they're getting the band back together. If you liked the movies, you'll love this rhythm-and-blues show. It's appropriate for all ages, and younger children will enjoy the music and dancing. This show runs on weekends only year-round and some weekdays in summer.

Tips for Touring Universal Studios Hollywood

A little advance planning goes a long way. Go to the Universal Studios Hollywood Web site and look up show times up to a week in advance. Decide which shows you would like to see and when. If you have enough time before you leave on your vacation, purchase your tickets online so you don't have to wait in line at the park.

If you have to buy tickets at the park, get there early. The box offices open an hour before the park. Even if you already have your tickets, still arrive early so you can get a good parking spot and then get in line to enter the park when it opens. While in line, do some planning. Too often families walk into the park and then stop to plan what they'll do first. At least know where you want to go first when you get through the main gate.

Time-Saving Tip

Try to see everything at the Lower Lot at once. Trips down and back up the Starway can take a lot of time. Aim for only one trip, especially if you're on a tight schedule.

The Simpsons Ride, *Terminator 2: 3-D,* and *Shrek 4-D* can all have long waits later in the day, so they're good attractions to head to first. While waiting to get in, pick up a *Studio Guide* at the main gate to see when the Lower Lot opens. In summer or other busy times, you'll want to head down the Starway as early as possible.

After the Simpson's Ride, *Terminator 2: 3-D,* and/or *Shrek 4-D,* take the Starway down to the Lower Lot.

As soon as you get down to the Lower Lot, take a left and go to Revenge of the Mummy. This is usually the longest wait, so get on early. Next go for the Jurassic Park ride. You might even be able to ride these two a second time if the lines aren't long yet. You'll already be soaked, so a little more water won't hurt.

Helpful Hint

If you plan on eating lunch on CityWalk, head there after finishing up on the Lower Lot. Then you can experience the Upper Lot when you get back to the park.

While at the Lower Lot, catch all the attractions here. Be sure to catch Backdraft, the Special Effects Stages, and the Universal Experience. By now it's probably lunchtime. If you're going to eat at the Jurassic Cove Café, do it now. Otherwise, head back up the Starway.

Back up at the Upper Lot, take in a show or two, then head for the Studio Tour. Because it lasts nearly 50 minutes, it gives families a chance to rest from the busy morning. In addition, younger children can use this as a nap time. After the tour, catch another show or walk through Universal's House of Horrors. Although you can go from one show to the next, most children may get restless with all the sitting. Stop by the Adventures of Curious George or the Coke Soak to let them burn off some energy.

Dining and Shopping

Universal Studios Hollywood offers a variety of dining options, from hot-dog stands to nice sit-down restaurants. Between the park itself and Universal CityWalk, you won't have to leave the studios to find a meal.

Within the park, there are some good choices. Some of the fare offered includes hamburgers and hot dogs, fried and rotisserie chicken, pizza, and Chinese food. Kids' meals are available at most of the restaurants. In addition to the restaurants just listed, there are several spots where you can pick up fast food or a quick snack.

In addition to the dining venues at the park, Universal CityWalk contains several great restaurants, with nearly 30 choices from fancy dining to fast food. Because it's just outside the main gate, it's easy to leave the park for lunch or dinner, then return for more excitement.

Although most families think of having a quick lunch, then a nice dinner, while you're at Universal Studios Hollywood, the opposite is a better idea. Most of the nice restaurants, especially on CityWalk, get busy in the evening because many local residents go there to eat, and that's when most tourists have their main meal. Instead, try having your main meal of the day in the early afternoon, usually after 1:30 PM. By that time the lunch crowd is leaving, so you don't have much of a wait, and the lunch menu is often less expensive. Then in the evening, have your quick meal while everyone else is dining.

Money-Saving Tip

If you plan on eating more than one meal in the park, consider purchasing an All You Can Eat Pass: one day of unlimited trips through the food service lines at the five participating restaurants. Each trip includes an entrée, side, and a dessert. Drinks are not included. Kids get a kid's meal. Prices are $27 for adults and $16 for kids. You can order these passes online when you purchase your admission tickets (and discounts are often available). If you have picky eaters, be sure to check which restaurants are included.

Because you're having lunch later, either take some snacks along to tide the children over or get a treat in the park.

Universal Studios Hollywood has a lot of fun shops where you can buy souvenirs. All of the main attractions have a shop dedicated entirely to the attraction and movie. In fact, *Terminator 2: 3-D* exits right into the T2 Gear and Supply shop. You can also find places to buy Universal DVDs, all types of clothing, and anything else the Universal logo can be put on. A favorite souvenir is a Universal Studios clapboard. All the merchandise can also be purchased from home through the Universal Web site. So you can either browse to see what you want in advance or see what you like while you're there and purchase it after you get home.

Universal CityWalk

Universal Center Drive
Universal City, CA 91608
818/622–4455
www.citywalkhollywood.com

Just outside the main gate to Universal Studios Hollywood, Universal CityWalk is a glamorous promenade with dining, shopping, and entertainment establishments that can easily take up half a day. CityWalk does not require admission, so you can come back later.

Along the walk, you can find many different types of restaurants, including the Hard Rock Cafe, Saddle Ranch Chop Shop, Bubba Gump Shrimp Co., Wolfgang Puck's Café, Buca Di Beppo, and Tony Roma's Ribs. There are also several fast-food venues and snack spots.

There are also a number of shops on CityWalk. Most of these are "fun" shops and places to buy treats or souvenirs. With all the different types of shops, there's something for everyone. Even if you don't want to spend any money, just browsing around CityWalk is enjoyable in itself.

There's an 18-screen movie theater, an IMAX theater, a virtual-reality NASCAR racing arcade, and much more. The Jon Lovitz Comedy Club, the Rumba Room, and Howl at the Moon feature nightclub entertainment for adults.

Gibson Amphitheater

100 Universal City Plaza
Universal City, CA 91608
818/622–4440
www.livenation.com/venue/gibson-amphitheatre-tickets

The Gibson Amphitheater, also in the Universal Studios area, features concerts and other types of shows. Before you leave on your vacation, check Universal's Web site to see if anything will be going on while you're there. You can purchase tickets online or by calling Universal.

CHAPTER

11

Six Flags® Magic Mountain

Magic Mountain

Magic Mountain's slogan—"Where the rides ARE the attraction"—pretty much says it all. Even though there are some shows and an assortment of Looney Tune characters and DC Comics superheroes running around, people come here for the rides. Self-proclaimed as the "world's first and only Xtreme Park," Magic Mountain features some of the greatest roller coasters, and is constantly adding bigger, faster, and better rides to keep up its reputation. Currently there are 16 coasters and a number of other thrilling rides.

> 26101 Magic Mountain Parkway
> Valencia, CA 91385
> 661/255–4100
> www.sixflags.com/magicmountain

Location

Six Flags Magic Mountain is west of Interstate 5 in Valencia. Take the Magic Mountain Parkway exit. It's about an hour and a half from Anaheim, depending on time of day and traffic.

Admission and Package Deals

Admission to Magic Mountain is similar to that of most other area theme parks. Single-day admission is $54 for adults, $30 for children under 48 inches tall. Children 2 years old and younger are free. A combo ticket to both Magic Mountain and the Hurricane Harbor water park on the same day is $70. For only Hurricane Harbor, admission is $25 for adults and $20 for children under 48 inches tall, with children 2 years old and under getting in free.

Magic Mountain also offers a season pass good for the calendar year. Depending on what specials are running, you can get a season pass for $10–$20 more than the cost of a single-day admission. With this, you get unlimited admission not only to Magic Mountain but also at all the other 15 Six Flags theme parks throughout the United States and even the parks in Montréal and Mexico City. The season pass does not include Hurricane Harbor or any other water park. If you plan on spending more than one day at Magic Mountain or will be visiting any of the other Six Flags theme parks during the year, the season pass is the way to go. Check the Six Flags Web site or

Money-Saving Tip

If you plan ahead a bit, you can avoid paying full price for admission to Magic Mountain. Many employers, credit unions, and travel clubs offer coupons for admission. Local supermarkets or fast-food restaurants may also have discounts. Some will save you from $15 to $20 off each adult admission to Magic Mountain and around $4 to Hurricane Harbor. These discounts can really add up for families. Also check the Web site. Sometimes you can bring a specific brand of coupon-bearing soda can and get a free admission with one paid admission.

call for the current pricing. Magic Mountain also accepts season passes to other Six Flags parks.

Tickets can be purchased at the gate or online. For online purchases, you can either have your tickets mailed to you (with a shipping and handling fee added) or print them out at home. Sometimes you can save up to $26 per ticket by purchasing your tickets online in advance. Magic Mountain also features ATM-like ticket dispensers that take either credit cards or some ATM cards. Although this is usually a quick way to avoid the lines at the ticket booths, the ATM machines do not accept coupons or discounted admission.

Magic Mountain has a Flash Pass which reserves your place in line electronically for 17 of the more popular rides. Flash Passes vary in price depending on how many riders you have and the level of service. A single person starts at $34, while a family of four can use a Flash Pass for $91. (This price is in addition to admission.) The Flash Pass is an electronic device similar to a pager. You check in at a ride and then come pack at a later time based on how long the current wait is. You can also wait for more than one ride at a time. The Gold Flash Pass, which costs almost twice as much, actually reduces your wait time by up to 75%. (On busy days, you can easily wait for one to two hours for a popular ride. Therefore, if you want to ride all of the popular rides, a Flash Pass is a must.)

There's a large parking lot at Magic Mountain, but it's a good walk from the lot to the main gate, especially if you have

Helpful Hint

As a security precaution, Magic Mountain has metal detectors near the main gate. Leave all pocketknives, including the little ones on key chains, and other potential weapons in your car. All backpacks and bags are also searched.

to park at the far end. A tram provides transportation from the lot to the gate, though it's often quicker to walk. The cost for parking is $15. Don't forget to write down where you parked your vehicle before heading into the park. After a long day of fun, you don't want to have to wander around looking for your car.

Operating Hours

Magic Mountain is open daily April through August. During the rest of the year, it's open only on weekends and certain weekdays. Either call or check the Web site for hours and dates. It usually opens at 10:30 AM, but closing time varies. If you're staying in Anaheim, you don't have to get up very early to get to the park as it opens, so this might be a good choice after a few early-morning days.

Amenities

Magic Mountain offers several amenities for its guests. At Guest Relations, near the main gate, you can pick up a copy of the *Guests with Disabilities Guidebook,* which provides detailed information on the accessibility of rides and attractions. Here you can also find audio-assist units and TDD phones for the hearing impaired. This is also the location for the lost and found as well as for lost children. Lockers are behind the Guest Relations building. Strollers rent for $10 a day, with a $10 deposit. Wheelchairs are also available for rental.

If you're traveling with pets, Magic Mountain offers free pet boarding. Just go to the kennel in the parking lot, and a representative will take care of your pet for the duration of your visit.

Although food cannot be brought into the park, Magic Mountain provides a picnic spot in the parking area if you want to bring your own meals.

Suitability for Children

When you're deciding whether to include Magic Mountain as a part of your family's vacation, it's important to know that more than half of the rides at the park have a minimum height requirement. Despite the shows and kiddie rides, if none of your children is over 42 inches tall, it isn't worth the drive or the cost. However, if you have teenagers who love roller-coaster thrills, they'll usually want to try out the latest and greatest rides here. For families with children, both younger and older, you can divide into two groups and let the older kids hit the coasters while the younger ones do the less-intense rides.

Attractions

Magic Mountain is divided into nine theme lands, arranged in a circular pattern. The park contains four main types of rides. There are the monster roller coasters, which are scattered about the park. Filling in the spaces between the coasters are carnival-style rides. Then there are kiddie rides and, finally, the water rides. Unlike most other theme parks, which have only one or maybe two water rides, Magic Mountain has five.

Helpful Hint

For all the roller-coaster rides: you can choose where you want to sit in the cars. The queues widen out at the boarding area, letting you get in line for the different seats. The line for the front is usually the longest. Although sitting in the front gives you a better view of what's ahead, the best ride is usually in the back, since the momentum builds when you're going down drops. Plus, the line for the back is usually short.

Quick Guide to

Attraction	Location	Requirement
Atom Smasher	Gotham City Backlot	42 inches
Batman: The Ride	Gotham City Backlot	54 inches
Buccaneer	Colossus County Fair	None*
Circus Wheel	Colossus County Fair	None*
Colossus	Colossus County Fair	48 inches
Cyclone 500	Cyclone Bay	58 inches
Déjà Vu	Cyclone Bay	54 inches
Dive Devil	Cyclone Bay	48 inches
Freefall	Movie District	42 inches
Gold Rusher	Movie District	48 inches
Goliath	Colossus County Fair	48 inches
Goliath Jr.	High Sierra Territory	Must be under 54 inches
Grand Carousel	Six Flags Plaza	None*
Granny Gran Prix	High Sierra Territory	48 inches*
Grinder Gearworks	Gotham City Backlot	42 inches
Jet Stream	Cyclone Bay	None*
Kiddie rides	Bugs Bunny World and Thomas Town	None

Guests under 42 inches must ride with an adult.
Guests under 48 inches must ride with an adult.
Guests under 54 inches must ride with an adult.

Magic Mountain Attractions

Duration of Ride	Scare Factor	Age Range
1½ minutes	!	6 and up
2 minutes	!!!	8 and up
2 minutes	!!	6 and up
2 minutes	!!	6 and up
2½ minutes	!!	6 and up
3 minutes	!	9 and up
2½ minutes	!!!	8 and up
2½ minutes	!!!	9 and up
1 minute	!!	8 and up
2½ minutes	!	6 and up
3 minutes	!!!	8 and up
1½ minutes	0	6 and up
2 minutes	0	All
3 minutes	0	4 and up
1½ minutes	!	6 and up
5 minutes	!	5 and up
Varies	0	All

0 Not scary at all.
! Might be somewhat frightening for some children. Usually either dark or a mild roller coaster.
!! Most young children will find this scary.
!!! This attraction may frighten some adults. This is usually reserved for high-speed roller coasters and other thrill rides.

(continues)

Quick Guide to

Attraction	Location	Requirement
Log Jammer	Six Flags Plaza	None*
Ninja	Samurai Summit	42 inches
Revolution	Baja Ridge	48 inches
Riddler's Revenge	Movie District	54 inches
Roaring Rapids	Rapids Camp Crossing	42 inches
Sandblasters	Movie District	42 inches***
Scrambler	Movie District	36 inches
Scream!	Colossus County Fair	54 inches
Sierra Twist	High Sierra Territory	42 inches
Spin Out	Movie District	36 inches
Superman: The Escape	Samurai Summit	48 inches
Swashbuckler	Colossus County Fair	42 inches
Tatsu	Samurai Summit	54 inches
Terminator Salvation: The Ride	Cyclone Bay	48 inches
Tidal Wave	Movie District	42 inches
Viper	Baja Ridge	54 inches
X2	Baja Ridge	48 inches
Yosemite Sam Sierra Falls	High Sierra Territory	None*

Guests under 42 inches must ride with an adult.
**Guests under 48 inches must ride with an adult.*
***Guests under 54 inches must ride with an adult.*

Magic Mountain Attractions

Duration of Ride	Scare Factor	Age Range
4½ minutes	!	5 and up
1½ minutes	!!	6 and up
2 minutes	!!	6 and up
3 minutes	!!!	9 and up
3 minutes	0	5 and up
3 minutes	0	5 and up
2 minutes	!	6 and up
3 minutes	!!!	9 and up
2 minutes	!	6 and up
1½ minutes	!	6 and up
1 minute	!!!	9 and up
2 minutes	!	5 and up
2 minutes	!!!	9 and up
3 minutes	!!	6 and up
2 minutes	!	5 and up
2 minutes	!!!	8 and up
3 minutes	!!!	8 and up
N/A	!	5 and up

0 Not scary at all.
! Might be somewhat frightening for some children. Usually either dark or a mild roller coaster.
!! Most young children will find this scary.
!!! This attraction may frighten some adults. This is usually reserved for high-speed roller coasters and other thrill rides.

Roller Coaster Heaven!

Since 2001, Six Flags Magic Mountain has held the world record for the most roller coasters in a single park. This tradition continues with the opening of Terminator Salvation: The Ride—a new wooden roller coaster themed after the Terminator movies—which replaces the old Psyclone roller coaster.

Six Flags Plaza

Once you enter Magic Mountain through the main gate, you're in Six Flags Plaza. The Grand Carousel is the centerpiece of the plaza, where Looney Tunes characters roam about and are available for pictures with guests.

If you don't feel like walking all the way up to Samurai Summit, you can go on the Orient Express. This people mover takes you from Six Flags Plaza to the top of the hill.

High Sierra Territory

The next land, as you head around the park counterclockwise from the entrance, features most of the rides for young children. The hallmark is the 140-foot General Sam Tree, the largest man-made tree in the world. A tunnel at its base allows you to walk through to Bugs Bunny World, where you can find a number of kiddie rides. There's a Tour Bus ride that takes kids up and down, and Taz's Lumber Co. is a car ride. Plus, there are airplane and balloon rides, mini spinning cups, and even a fun house. To help get the youngsters ready for the big coasters, Bugs Bunny World offers two small ones. The Canyon Blaster is a mini roller coaster with some small hills and easy drops. Parents and children can ride this one together. For children 7 and under, Bugs Bunny World is the place to be for small adventures. Young children will also enjoy Critter Canyon, a petting zoo with a variety of farm and exotic animals. Thomas Town features the Thomas the Tank Engine ride, which takes you on a round-trip tour of the Island of Sodor. This area also includes a small kiddie coaster called Percy the Small Engine, which goes only about 10 mph with a maximum height of 10 feet. Riders must be under 54 inches tall.

In addition to the kiddie rides, there's also the Granny Gran Prix, which allows you to drive around in electric antique cars. Although this may seem like a ride for small kids, they must be 48 inches to drive alone or 42 inches if riding with an adult. Yosemite Sam Sierra Falls is one of two water rides in this land. You ride in two-person rafts down a waterslide; it's pretty tame compared to the other water rides in the park. The Log Jammer is a larger and higher flume ride for the older kids and adults; it features a couple of drops.

Colossus County Fair

This land is home to Goliath, the behemoth billed as the first large coaster of the millennium. Riders begin when their car climbs to the top of the first hill, which is 255 feet high. Even though the car climbs quickly, it seems as if you just keep going up and up. The biggest thrill occurs as you cross over the top and begin your descent down at a 61-degree angle. To take the drop even farther, the track at the bottom goes underground for 120 feet. However, riders—now traveling at 85 mph—will hardly notice the tunnel before heading back up again to float over camel backs and speed down through a spiraling curve and breathtaking dives. The minimum height requirement is 48 inches.

If you're looking for a hair-raising good time, the ride Scream!'s name says it all. You board trains connected to a track

Scare Factor!
Scream! is definitely a ride for experienced coaster riders. Goliath can also be pretty thrilling; though it does not have loops and sharp turns, its long, steep dives make this a fairly intense coaster.

below. However, there are no floors, so your feet hang in the open air. Starting with a 150-foot drop, the coaster reaches a speed of 65 mph and immediately enters a 128-foot vertical loop, the first of seven inversions, including a high-speed helix and two interlocking corkscrews. With 4,000 feet of track, this three-minute ride is indeed extreme and will have you shrieking. Riders must be at least 54 inches tall in order to fly around on this attraction.

The namesake of this land, the Colossus, is a dual-track wooden roller coaster that takes you up and down hills over a 2-mile track. Compared to the other coasters here, this one is pretty tame, so it's a good thrill-ride introduction for kids taller than 48 inches. The Buccaneer, a swinging pirate-ship ride, and the Swashbuckler, a spinning swing ride, round out the attractions in this land.

Gotham City Backlot

Appropriately enough, the featured coaster here is Batman: The Ride. What makes this ride so unique is that you ride in ski-lift-style cars suspended from the track above with your feet dangling in thin air. As the world whooshes by, you'll accelerate through vertical loops, corkscrews, and a heartline spin (a spin in which riders are spun inward, toward the centers of their bodies). Because your feet hang, visitors wearing sandals or other footwear that may come off must carry them on the ride. If you have to do this, just sit on them. The attendants will not let you leave your shoes behind at the station. This

Insider Tip
Although you may have to wait longer, try to sit in the front for Batman: The Ride. Otherwise all you will see throughout the ride are the seats in front of you. The wait is worth it.

ride is moderately intense, with a minimum height requirement of 54 inches.

Also in Gotham City Backlot are the Atom Smasher and the Grinder Gearworks, a couple of carnival-style rides. For a good picture-taking spot, stop by the replica of the Batmobile near the entrance to Batman: The Ride.

The Movie District

This land continues the Batman theme with Riddler's Revenge. What makes this ride different from the rest is riders stand up while on this coaster, which includes loops and drops. Currently the world's tallest and fastest stand-up coaster, it has a minimum height requirement of 54 inches. The second coaster here is the Gold Rusher. The first coaster at Magic Mountain, it's quite tame compared to the rest. There are no loops, just drops and tight turns, which make this another good introductory thrill ride. Riders must be at least 48 inches tall. Freefall is a unique ride in that the seated guests are raised to the top of a 10-story tower, then dropped unrestricted, reaching 55 mph in only two seconds. The minimum height requirement is 42 inches.

In the Movie District you'll find yet another water ride, the Tidal Wave. This simple ride takes 20-passenger boats up a hill, then plunges them down a 50-foot waterfall, getting everybody wet as the boat creates a wall of water at the bottom. You must be at least 42 inches tall to ride this. Finally, you can take in a few more carnival-style rides here, including bumper cars.

Samurai Summit

On the top of the hill at the center of the park, Samurai Summit is a challenge just to get to. If you decide to get to the top on foot, it's a steep walk. Pushing a stroller is really difficult. Therefore, if you have small children, take the Orient Express from Six Flags Plaza or the Metro Monorail.

Scare Factor!

Tatsu is one of the most extreme coasters at the park and can be very scary for younger children. Even though Superman: The Escape looks fairly simple, it too is quite intense.

But the trek is well worth it; this summit hosts one of the park's newest coasters—Tatsu (also the world's tallest, fastest, and longest flying coaster). Riders actually lie down on the coaster cars when boarding, then are suspended once the ride begins, flying head first through 3,602 feet of track and reaching up to 62 miles per hour. The track takes you up, down, and around the park's central hill as you go through other rides as well. Because of the way you ride this coaster, it's one of the most thrilling attractions in the park—and one no coaster aficionado should miss.

If you're up for a big thrill, try Superman: The Escape. This is the world's tallest and fastest thrill ride. Using electromagnetic force, guests in 15-passenger vehicles accelerate from 0 to 100 mph in only 7 seconds, rocketing to the top of a 41-story tower where they experience 6½ seconds of weightlessness before heading back down backward to the station. Riders on this intense coaster must be at least 48 inches tall.

Also at the top of the hill is Ninja. Riders sit in cars suspended from an overhead track. Although there are no loops and the ride is fairly tame, the cars swing 180 degrees from side to side as the coaster goes around fast turns. The minimum height for this ride is 42 inches. Towering 38 stories above the summit, the Sky Tower gives you a scenic view of the park and surrounding hills. Just the elevator ride to the top alone is a lot of fun.

Cyclone Bay

This land, themed like a California boardwalk, is home to two coasters and a few other rides, including a water ride.

Terminator Salvation: The Ride is the park's newest coaster. This wooden roller coaster starts off with a 100-foot lift, followed by a series of drops and turns; it reaches a top speed of 55 mph. During the course of the ride, you'll also travel through tunnels and pass through the area right above the track where people are boarding. Since the track is not as banked as some of the steel coasters, expect to get pushed to the sides of the car as you take some of the turns. This coaster is not as intense as some of the others in the park, though it's a bit wilder than the Colossus. Riders must be at least 48 inches tall.

Déjà Vu is a boomerang-style coaster with vehicles that hang from the track above, making it similar to a ski lift. The coaster starts off by carrying the riders, with their feet dangling in the air, backward up a 196-foot tower and then drops them in a 20-story vertical free fall facedown. Reaching a speed of 65 mph, the coaster then takes you around the outside of a 102-foot vertical loop, followed by a butterfly turn, after which it climbs a second tower, 200 feet tall. Then you descend backward down the drop, going through the turn and loop again in reverse before stopping at the station. This is another intense ride and requires riders to be at least 54 inches but under 76 inches (6 feet 4 inches) tall.

On the Jet Stream water ride, passengers board colorful jet boats that take them up the hillside and circle around the area before dropping down a 57-foot plunge into Jet Stream Lake. Small children can ride this if they're accompanied by an adult.

Cyclone Bay also features a couple of attractions that require an additional fee. The Dive Devil combines the thrills of hang gliding and bungee jumping as riders are attached to a cable, hoisted up 150 feet, then released to swing forward, reaching speeds of 60 mph. Guests 48 inches or taller can ride solo or with up to two other people. The price for a single person is $28 and goes up from there. Reservations are required, and the ride is weather dependent. The Cyclone 500 raceway lets riders drive small gas-powered race cars. Drivers must be at least 58 inches tall, and the price is $6. And for $5, you can practice your rock climbing on a climbing wall.

Rapids Camp Crossing

This land has just one ride, the Roaring Rapids. You ride in 12-passenger boats along an artificial whitewater river. Expect waves, crosscurrents, and—you guessed it—rapids. This is a fun ride for those at least 42 inches tall. As with most of the water rides, expect to get wet.

Baja Ridge

Completing the Magic Mountain circle, this land features the Viper and X2. Voted California's number one coaster, Viper is the world's largest looping roller coaster. Riders experience a breathtaking 18-story drop, three vertical loops, a double-barrel boomerang, and a classic corkscrew with speeds approaching 70 mph. To ride the Viper, riders must be at least 54 inches tall. It's very intense, with one loop, turn, or drop after another.

The other extreme coaster in this land is X2. If you have been to Magic Mountain before, the X2 was previously named the X; the revamped ride features new trains and audio-visual special effects. The seats on the X2 can rotate 360 degrees independently of the vehicle's motion, and unlike most rides,

Scare Factor!
Both X2 and Viper are fast, thrilling coasters that can be scary for younger children. Try out the less intense coasters first to see how your children do before taking them on the more advanced rides.

they are positioned off the sides of the track rather than directly over or under the track. Along with the rotations of the seat, you do not know what to expect next, thus increasing the thrill. The ride reaches speeds of 76 mph and includes a 200-foot first drop. Since there's no other coaster like this around, you should definitely try it—if you dare! Riders must be at least 48 inches tall to go on this extremely intense ride.

Also in this area is the Revolution, the first 360-degree looping steel coaster ever built. This is a moderate coaster and a good introduction to loops, with some fast turns and steep drops thrown in for thrills. The minimum height requirement is 48 inches.

Shows

Magic Mountain offers several shows throughout the day. These vary from year to year and can include stunts, animals, and audience participation. Most shows only run from mid-May through the end of August. Also, during the summer months you can catch the parade as it passes through the plaza area.

All the shows are seasonal and subject to change. The best way to see what shows are on is to check the Six Flags Web site. Also, many shows seem to take Tuesday off. Others may be put on only during the summer or on weekends.

Tips for Touring Six Flags Magic Mountain

If you plan on hitting the roller coasters at Magic Mountain, get there early. Unlike other parks where the lines get longer during the day and then shorter toward night, the roller-coaster lines here get continuously longer as time goes by. Because Magic Mountain attracts a lot of local residents, especially teens and young adults who either get out of school or off work in the afternoon, the coasters can be quite busy at night.

However, if you don't plan on riding the coasters, you don't have to rush to the park. Most of the carnival-style rides and some of the kiddie rides don't start up until an hour or more after the park opens. This is especially true during off-peak weekdays.

Helpful Hint

For families with young children, we recommend a stroller. All the walking you must do at Magic Mountain will soon wear out little legs and feet. Having to carry a tired child will quickly wear out parents. Although you can rent a stroller at the park, a lightweight umbrella stroller will work just as well.

Magic Mountain is a big park. Its circle arrangement around a center hill makes getting from one point to another time consuming. To minimize walking time, there are two strategies.

If your family has small children, plan on making one lap around the park. As you get to each land, do everything you can there before moving on to the next area. The only downside to this strategy is that if you want to do some of the rides that are not yet running when you get there, you'll have to come back. Right at the beginning, head to High Sierra Territory and hit the kiddie rides at Bugs Bunny World and Thomas Town. This is fairly close to the main gate, so you can get the kids riding right away. Then make your way counterclockwise around the park. After you do this, the rest of the rides around the park should be open. Once you've made the full circuit, you can head back to Bugs Bunny World to hit the rides that open later and for a repeat of the kiddie rides before leaving the park, if the little ones are game.

The second strategy applies to older children who want to take in all the coasters. This will require two trips around the park. As soon as you get to the park, head straight to X2 and the Viper since they're close to the entrance. Then hit Tatsu and Superman: The Escape. Now make your way around the park in a clockwise direction, taking in Terminator Salvation: The Ride, Déjà Vu, Riddler's Revenge, Batman: The Ride, Scream!, and then Goliath. These are all the rides that will get long lines later in the day. Once you have ridden them all, make another lap around, taking in the rides you skipped the first time, including the older coasters, the water rides, and the carnival-type rides.

It can get quite hot at Magic Mountain, even when it's cool in the Los Angeles area. Be sure to drink lots of fluids. Several of the dining venues offer refillable sports bottles. (Although these can be expensive, you'll get free refills throughout the day.) It's also a good idea to take along some water bottles of your own. These can be refilled at drinking fountains as needed. Nighttime can get cold at the park, even if it was hot during the day. If you're staying until closing time, you may need jackets or sweatshirts. Keep these in the car or in the lockers, and get them when needed.

Dining and Shopping

With one exception, the dining venues at Magic Mountain offer primarily fast-food fare, such as burgers, pizza, chicken, and the like. Eatery chains in the park include Papa John's Pizza, Cold Stone Creamery, and Johnny Rockets. If you want more of a sit-down meal, head to the Mooseburger Lodge. The restaurant also features entertainment, music, and air-conditioning—a real bonus on hot days. Because most guests will be at the restaurant around noon or 5 to 6 PM, the best time to go is between 2 and 3 PM. Eat a hearty breakfast before you arrive

Helpful Hint

There are several ways to save money on food. Some venues offer family meals, which include chicken strips or pizza along with sides and two refillable sports bottles. Though these meals run about $40, they are cheaper than buying the food individually along with the sports bottles. (The meals are intended for a family of four.) You can also purchase a bucket of popcorn or cotton candy for around $8, and you can get free refills throughout the day. If you purchase a season pass at Magic Mountain, you often receive a coupon book with lots of food discounts.

at the park, and then have a good lunch with a light meal or snacks in the evening.

If you want to bring your own lunch, there's a picnic area in the parking-lot area. This can save you some money. Don't try to leave the park to eat—there's nothing close by. The walk to the car, the drive to the off-site restaurants, the wait to get back into the parking lot, and then the walk back to the park can take a big chunk out of your day.

There are a number of shops throughout the park. In addition to the standard theme-park souvenirs, you can also purchase Looney Tunes and DC Comic superhero paraphernalia.

Hurricane Harbor

Right next to Magic Mountain is Hurricane Harbor, a water park with waterslides and other related activities for the whole family. Tickets for the park are available at the same booths as for Magic Mountain. A combo ticket to both Magic Mountain and the Hurricane Harbor water park on the same day is $70. For only Hurricane Harbor, admission is $25 for adults and

$20 for children under 48 inches tall, with children 2 years old and under getting in free.

Hurricane Harbor is divided into a number of areas and features seven towers with more than 20 slides among them. The newest slide, the Tornado, has guests ride in four-person rafts down a tunnel into a funnel where they bank back and forth. Black Snake Summit features five speed slides, including two of the tallest, fully enclosed speed slides in Southern California, as well as two enclosed twisting slides and a near-vertical open drop slide. The Bamboo Racer has a six-lane slide where you race head first down the slide to the finish line. Reptile Ridge is another tower, with three twisting slides, a straight drop slide, and a gentle slide. Taboo Tower has three slides: a 45-degree straight drop, a bumpy slide, and a spiraling slide. Lighting Falls has three twisting and turning slides. Tiki Falls takes riders down three slides that end with the rider coming out through the mouths of three tikis. Finally, the Lost Temple Rapids puts you into four-passenger rafts and sends you down an ancient-looking aqueduct. Black Snake Summit, Reptile Ridge, and Taboo Tower each have 48-inch minimum height restrictions. However, anyone can ride the rest. Some slides require rafts; others are body slides.

In addition to the water slides, Hurricane Harbor has several other attractions. Castaway Cove is for children under 54 inches in height. It has small slides, waterfalls, a fortress, swings, and a tide pool at Octopus Island. Shipwreck Shores is for families with children of all ages. There are more than 30 interac-

Helpful Hint

If you plan on wearing shorts over your swimsuit, make sure they don't have rivets or metal buttons. These are not allowed on the slides because they might get caught on the way down.

tive activities here. The River Cruise takes you in rafts along a lazy 1,300-foot river past many of the park's sites. The Forgotten Sea is a wave pool with a constant tide of two-foot waves. This pool begins at a depth of zero and goes down to 6 feet.

Helpful Hint

You should always be safety conscious, especially with small children. Even though there are lifeguards all around, it's hard for them to keep track of every child, especially when it's busy. Stay close to your children. If you let your older kids go off on their own, make sure they use the buddy system and go in a group of at least two.

Rafts can be rented for the day. However, all the rides that require rafts have them available for use. If you rent rafts, you then have to keep an eye on them and drag them around with you. There are men's and women's changing rooms with showers and lockers near the entrance plaza and lots of lounge chairs throughout the park.

Dealing with money can be a real hassle at a water park. Therefore, Hurricane Harbor offers Play Money. You can wear a waterproof, bar-coded wrist band, which acts like prepaid gift cards. Play Money can be purchased in several different denominations, and unused balances are fully refundable. This is great for families that split up or want to give each child an amount of spending money for the day. The park has a number of dining venues with fast-food-type fare on the menu.

CHAPTER

12

LEGOLAND California

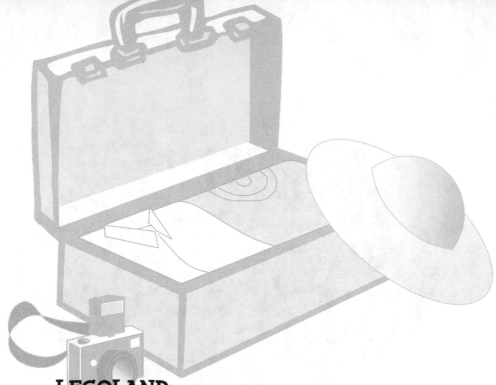

LEGOLAND

Unlike most other area parks, LEGOLAND is designed especially for children under 12. In addition, most attractions are interactive, so kids get to take part in the fun instead of just being passive riders or observers.

The first LEGO bricks were introduced by Ole Kirk Christiansen in 1958, in Denmark, and they arrived in the United States three years later. Since that time, LEGOs have spread around the world and have become a favorite of children everywhere. In fact, in 1999 *Fortune* magazine designated LEGO a "Product of the Century." The word *LEGO* was formed by contracting the Danish words *leg godt,* meaning "play well." Later, it was learned that LEGO in Latin means "I put together" or "I assemble." The first LEGOLAND opened in Billund, Denmark, in 1968. It was such a huge success that a second park opened in Windsor, England, in 1996. LEGOLAND California, which opened in 1999, is the third park. There's also one in Germany.

Reviews on LEGOLAND can be mixed. We find that most families who have visited LEGOLAND have one of two opinions: either they love it or they feel they should have spent the day elsewhere. There are several factors that affect a family's enjoyment at LEGOLAND. One is the age of the children. Although LEGOLAND was designed for children from 2 to 12 years of age, 3 to about 10 years is a bit more realistic, according to the families we talked to (children up to 12 will still be fascinated if they're really into LEGOs). Older children will probably be bored unless they enjoy taking their younger siblings around the park. Another factor affecting enjoyment is expectation. There are nearly 30 rides in the park, and all are quite mild. Only a few could even be considered somewhat scary. Therefore, many families used to the large number of fast, wild rides at other parks will be

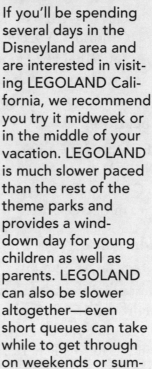

Insider's Secret

If you'll be spending several days in the Disneyland area and are interested in visiting LEGOLAND California, we recommend you try it midweek or in the middle of your vacation. LEGOLAND is much slower paced than the rest of the theme parks and provides a wind-down day for young children as well as parents. LEGOLAND can also be slower altogether—even short queues can take while to get through on weekends or summer days.

disappointed. The final factor is LEGOs themselves. Because everything at LEGOLAND is based on the toy-building system, children who are not familiar with the product will miss out on some of the excitement.

SEA LIFE Aquarium opened adjacent to LEGOLAND in 2008. This 36,000-square-foot, two-story building houses 36 displays showing the fish indigenous to California streams and lakes as well marine animals found off the coast of California.

SEA LIFE is a separate venue, but combination tickets to the aquarium and LEGOLAND are available.

> One LEGOLAND Drive
> Carlsbad, CA 92008
> 760/918–LEGO (5346)
> www.legoland.com

Location

LEGOLAND California is about 45 minutes south of the Disneyland area and 30 minutes north of San Diego. Take I–5 to Carlsbad and exit at Cannon Road. Go east, following the signs to LEGO Drive.

Admission

Admission to LEGOLAND California is similar to that of most other area theme parks. Single-day admission is $63 for adults and $53 for senior citizens and children 3 to 12. SEA LIFE Aquarium admission is $19 for adults, $16 for seniors, and $12 for children. Park hopper tickets that allow visits both venues on the same date run $73 for adults and $63 for seniors and children. Two-day tickets are also available. LEGOLAND offers discounts to AAA members; ask your employer or credit union about discounts as well.

LEGOLAND has a large adjacent parking lot. Parking is $10 for cars and $11 for RVs. Preferred parking is available for $20. Remember to write down where you parked your vehicle before heading into the park. Although the parking lot is not as big as at other theme parks, with tired children you don't want to have to search all over for your vehicle. There's also a complimentary kennel where you can keep your pets during your visit. Space is limited, so get there early during the busy season if you need to use this service.

Operating Hours

LEGOLAND is open daily from 10 AM to 8 PM from the end of June through mid-August. During the rest of the year, the park closes at 5 PM, with later hours around Halloween and Christmas. LEGOLAND also closes on Tuesday and Wednesday during most of the year, with the exception of spring break, summer, and the last weeks of December. Therefore, be sure to check the Web site for the days the park will be open before heading down. Nothing is more frustrating than taking the hour drive from Anaheim, only to discover the park is closed. In summer, Tuesday and Wednesday tend to be the least busy days.

Amenities

LEGOLAND offers a number of services for its guests. Lockers can be rented for $5 at the Marketplace, near the entrance. Strollers, wheelchairs, and electric wheelchairs are also available. A single or infant stroller rents for $9, a double is $15, a wheelchair is $10, and an electric wheelchair is $35.

Following LEGOLAND's focus on families with young children, you'll find many things at the park designed with children in mind. All the restrooms have low sinks for washing small hands as well as diaper-changing stations in both men's and women's restrooms. There are also family restrooms at var-

Helpful Hint

You'll be hard pressed to find much shade at LEGOLAND, especially when waiting in lines. Remember to bring hats and sunscreen. Several food stands sell drinks in souvenir sports bottles. Although they cost around $9, you can refill them for free over and over again throughout the park at the various places to eat.

ious locations. In all the interactive attractions, buttons and other controls are at lower levels, and even the restaurants have low counters that allow children to push their own trays and see what's available without needing an adult to pick them up. The Model Mom Baby Care Center, in Fun Town, provides a microwave, high chairs, rockers for nursing mothers, and diaper-changing facilities. Entire families are welcome, and there are LEGO stations where children can play while their baby brother or sister is being fed. If you run out of diapers or happen to forget them, the Baby Care Center provides complimentary size-3 diapers and diaper wipes. If you're traveling with pets, you can check them into the kennel to the east of the front gate. There's no charge for this service.

LEGOLAND Vocabulary

To help you better understand the LEGO lingo, here are a few terms with which you should be familiar:

Model Citizen: A LEGOLAND employee. The park security personnel are known as Park Rangers.

Block: LEGOLAND is divided into several theme areas known as blocks.

Buddy: The life-size LEGO man who wanders around LEGOLAND greeting guests.

DUPLO: The series of LEGO toys designed for younger children.

Mindstorms: LEGO's product line that allows builders to create actual working robots.

LEGO Maniac: Anyone crazy about LEGOs.

Attractions

LEGOLAND is divided into nine "blocks." The Beginning block, just inside the front gate, contains only shops and restaurants. Here's a rundown of the fun in each of the other blocks.

Dino Island

Just to the left of the Beginning, Dino Island is made to look like a prehistoric jungle, with life-size and scale models of dinosaurs throughout the block. The ride here is the Coastersaurus. This junior coaster reaches speeds of up to 21 mph and features curves and dips as riders move past animated LEGO dinosaurs. Another fun attraction here is Dig Those Dinos. Kids love this large sand pit where they can unearth the skeletal remains of dinosaurs. Tool kits with a bucket, shovel, and fossil brush can be rented for $3. When you return them, you'll get a souvenir surprise egg to take home with you. Finally, at the Raptor Splash, families can man battle stations and launch water balloons at each other. A bucket of balloons costs $3, or two for $5.

Explore Village

Explore Village is designed for younger children. The Safari Trek takes you around in little jeeps through a jungle, savanna, and waterway, where more than 90 life-size animals made entirely out of LEGOs roam. These include lions, monkeys, flamingos, crocodiles, and elephants. Fairytale Brook is a boat ride that takes you through scenes from classic fairy tales with music and animation. Several of the stories have a modern

Insider's Secret

There are more than 15,000 LEGO models in LEGOLAND. The largest, "Bronty" the giant dinosaur, is made up of more than 2 million bricks!

Quick Guide to

Attraction	Location	Requirements
Aquazone Wave Racers	Imagination Zone	40 inches**
Beetle Bounce	Land of Adventure	36 inches
BIONICLE Blaster	Imagination Zone	42 inches**
Captain Cranky's Challenge	Pirate Shores	34 inches *
Cargo Ace	Land of Adventure	36 inches
Coast Cruise	Miniland USA	None*
Coastersaurus	Dino Island	36 inches*
The Dragon	Knight's Kingdom	40 inches*
Dune Raiders	Land of Adventure	36 inches
Fairy Tale Brook	Explore Village	None*
Flight Squadron	Fun Town	34 inches*
Fun Town Fire Academy	Fun Town	34 inches
Kid Power Towers	Fun Town	40 inches*
Knight's Tournament	Knight's Kingdom	40 inches***
LEGO Show Place	Imagination Zone	None
LEGOLAND Express	Explore Village	None
Lost Kingdom of Adventure	Land of Adventure	34 inches
Royal Joust	Knight's Kingdom	36 inches
Safari Trek	Explore Village	34 inches*
Skipper School	Fun Town	34 inches*
Sky Cruiser	Fun Town	36 inches*
Sky Patrol	Fun Town	34 inches*

 * Guests below this height must be accompanied by someone 48 inches or taller.
 ** Guests below this height must be accompanied by someone 52 inches or taller.
 *** Guests below this height must be accompanied by someone 55 inches or taller.

LEGOLAND Attractions

Duration	Scare factor	Age range
1½ minutes	!	4 and up
1 minute	!	3 and up
1 minute	0	3 and up
1 minute	!	4 and up
2 minutes	0	3 and up
8 minutes	0	All
1 minute	0	3 and up
3 minutes	0	3 and up
1 minute	0	3 and up
5 minutes	0	All
1 minute	0	3 and up
10 minutes	0	All
2 minutes	!	4 and up
1 minute	!–!!!	4 and up
10–15 minutes	0	All
2 minutes	0	All
6 minutes	!	3 and up
2 minutes	0	4 to 12
5 minutes	0	All
2 minutes	0	All
2½ minutes	0	All
1 minute	0	All

0 Not scary at all.
 ! Might be somewhat frightening for some children. Usually either dark or a mild roller coaster.
 !! Most young children will find this scary.
!!! This attraction may frighten some adults. This rating is usually reserved for high-speed roller coasters and other thrill rides.

Quick Guide to

Attraction	Location	Requirements
Splash Battle	Pirate Shores	36 inches *
Technic Test Track	Imagination Zone	42 inches**
Treasure Falls	Pirate Shores	36 inches *
Volvo Driving School	Fun Town	6 to 13 years
Volvo Junior Driving School	Fun Town	6 to 13 years

   * Guests below this height must be accompanied by someone 48 inches
     or taller.
  ** Guests below this height must be accompanied by someone 52 inches
      or taller.
*** Guests below this height must be accompanied by someone 55 inches
       or taller.

twist. Look for Prince Charming with a cell phone and the Big Bad Wolf with a boom box.

The rest of Explore Village uses DUPLO bricks as its theme. At the Water Works, children can play with water without getting wet. All the activities here are interactive. By pressing buttons, turning handles, and pulling levers, children shoot water cannons that animate various characters and animals when the water hits the target. The DUPLO Playtown features 13,000 square feet of fun. Children can climb on and explore several different types of buildings in the town, go through a maze, and activate various features such as lights and sirens or talk on a phone. The Legoland Express is just the right size for toddlers and takes them around a little farm. They can even

LEGOLAND Attractions

Duration	Scare factor	Age range
3 minutes	0	3 and up
2 minutes	!	5 and up
2 minutes	!	3 and up
4 minutes	0	6 to 13
3 minutes	0	6 to 13

0 Not scary at all.
! Might be somewhat frightening for some children. Usually either dark or a mild roller coaster.
!! Most young children will find this scary.
!!! This attraction may frighten some adults. This rating is usually reserved for high-speed roller coasters and other thrill rides.

ride it on their own. This is where children ages 3 to about 6 will want to spend some time.

Fun Town

Fun Town is where children go to do adultlike activities in a town scaled down to their size. One of the most popular rides here is the Volvo Driving School. Children from 6 to 13 years of age can drive electric cars through a layout of roads. There are stop signs and traffic lights to obey, and the drivers actually steer, accelerate, and apply the brakes as they drive around without the confinement of tracks. For children 3 to 5, there's the Volvo Junior Driving School, where little tikes drive smaller, slower cars around an oval, also without tracks. A Model Citizen is right there to help teach children how to operate the cars and to help keep them around the course. At the Skipper School, you ride propeller-powered boats through a maze of buoys. As with the cars, the boats are not on tracks and can be steered freely within the confines of the course.

The Fun Town Fire Academy is an attraction that can be enjoyed by the entire family. In fact, it's a contest where you must compete against other families to put out a fire fastest. First a family climbs aboard their fire engine and must drive to the fire by pumping levers to make it move. Then they must man pumps and water cannons to douse the "flames." Win or lose, everyone will have a great time.

For young aviators, Fun Town offers two rides that let them take to the sky. The Sky Patrol features helicopters with two joysticks that allow you to control the helicopter as it goes up and down and also turn it right and left. On the Flight Squadron, children pilot small planes, controlling their up-and-down motion as they fly around in a circle.

Fun Town also includes kid-powered rides that allow you to view the entire park. The Sky Cruiser lets you pedal your way down a track that wraps around a ridge in the center of the park. If you get tired, don't worry. An electric motor will take over and keep your vehicle moving. Also here, the Kid Power Towers seats two guests and allows them to pull themselves up to the top of 30-foot towers. When the rope is released, you return to the bottom in a controlled free fall. Because their legs dangle below the seat, younger children may find this ride too much, especially if they do not like heights.

Fun Town also contains a couple of interesting walk-through attractions. The LEGO Factory shows you how the popular bricks are manufactured and boxed into sets. The self-tour even has "quality control" games. The Adventurer's Club is also a lot of fun. You wander through a jungle, an ancient pyramid, and the Arctic on a quest for keys. The club is filled with interactive games, but some areas are dark and may frighten younger children.

Pirate Shores

Pirate Shores is one of the more popular blocks at LEGOLAND—but be warned—ye may get wet, arrrh!

The main attraction here is Splash Battle. You climb aboard miniature pirate ships, which seat four people with a water cannon for each person. As you sail through pirate-infested waters, you can take aim at targets as well as other riders and even spectators. However, these targets can also fire back at you! Captain Cranky's Challenge tests your sea worthiness. The pirate ship sways back and forth along a U-shape track while rotating in two different directions. Treasure Falls is a flume ride where logs take you around and then down a 12-foot drop. This is much milder than any flume or log ride at other parks and fine for young children.

Helpful Hint
If you're planning on visiting Pirate Shores, it's a good idea to bring swimsuits for the kids as well as towels. Either have them wear the suits under their clothes or change while in the park. Swim diapers are required for all children under age 4.

In addition to the rides, there are also a couple other activities in Pirate Shores. Soak-N-Sail is a water fun park for kids. There's a waterslide, water cannons, lots of interactive gadgets, and even a large bucket that dumps 300 gallons of water all at once. For the younger kids there's Swabbies Deck, which features water fountains, pop-up water jets, and squirt cannons.

Pirate Shores often opens later than the rest of the park and can be closed because of cold and inclement weather. Therefore, check to see when it opens so you don't rush to Pirate Shores right at the start of your visit only to find it closed until later in the day.

Castle Hill

Castle Hill's rides and attractions are themed after LEGO's popular castle series. Knight's Tournament is the first Robocoaster attraction in the United States. It consists of six robotic arms, each of which holds seats for two riders. You can select which level of thrill you want. Level 1, the only one available to riders under 48 inches tall, is limited to rotating around with some up-and-down motion. Level 2 is a bit more exciting. Beginning with Level 3, you go upside down; Level 4 is similar to an extreme roller coaster, with quick drops and spins. Level 5 is only for the most daring, since it has you cartwheeling and pulling some Gs. The nice feature about this ride is it's for both young children at least 40 inches tall and their older siblings. Everyone can choose how much of a thrill he or she wants. Since this is one of the most popular attractions, try to get to Knight's Tournament early, before the lines get long.

The Dragon roller coaster begins with a tour of the castle, with Merlin as your host. As you're given an animated depiction of life in a fortress, you'll suddenly come across a large dragon guarding the treasure. You're then whisked out of the castle, and the roller-coaster part of the ride begins. This coaster is quite mild compared to most coasters elsewhere and consists of one climb, after which it twists and turns back down to the end of the ride. A fun ride for children 12 and under is the Royal Joust. Each child mounts his or her own "horse," which trots along a track through a knight's training area. At the end, they charge against another knight as their picture is taken. These photos can be bought near the exit of the ride.

Near the Royal Joust is the Hideaways. This giant jungle-gym castle contains towers to climb up, balance beams, curvy slides, and net and wall climbs. For younger children who cannot climb up into the castle, there are several types of equipment to play on. Wild Woods Golf is an 18-hole miniature golf course complete with several interactive features. There's an additional $6 fee for each round of golf. The Enchanted Walk is a short nature path where you can view indigenous plants of the California foothills and mountains, as well as LEGO re-creations of the wildlife that lives in those regions. Finally, at the Builder's Guild, children 5 years and older can build with LEGO castle products, while younger ones can play with DUPLO blocks. During the year, there are building contests and seminars. Check your daily program to see if any will be held during your visit.

Land of Adventure

Land of Adventure is the newest block at LEGOLAND. It is themed like Egypt in the 1920s, with hidden tombs and treasure waiting to be discovered.

The main attraction in Land of Adventure is the Lost Kingdom Adventure. Guests board roadsters and make their way through a dark ride where they fire laser pistols at targets. This interactive ride is very popular, so try to hit it early. Another ride, Beetle Bounce, lifts riders 15 feet into the air and then takes them down and up again for a mild ride. Cargo Ace lets kids fly around in small airplanes suspended from above. (Unlike Flight Squadron, they have no control over their planes in this ride). Dune Raiders lets guests ride carpets down a 50-foot-long slide from a height of 30 feet. Finally, kids can burn off some energy as they run around inside Pharaoh's Revenge—a large playhouse area where kids can explore a maze and fire soft foam balls at targets.

Miniland USA

If you have ever built with LEGOs, Miniland USA is something you can't miss. New Orleans; New York City; Washington, D.C.; the California coast; and a New England harbor are all re-created here with LEGO bricks in 1:20 or 1:40 scale. New to this block is Las Vegas, featuring the "strip" with several of the city's landmark hotels, including the Luxor, Treasure Island, MGM Grand, and a model of the Stratosphere, which stands 20 feet tall. In addition to admiring the detail, you can press buttons or turn handles to animate scenes or activate sounds. Model Builders often add new features to Miniland USA during the day. To see what new projects they're working on, check out the Model Shop, where you can watch the Model Builders in action. They'll also show you the basics of building models.

Insider's Secret

The New York area of Miniland USA features the Freedom Tower—even though it will not be completed for several years. At 28 feet tall, it's the tallest Miniland building. The smallest model in the park is also in this area. Look for the pigeon on a building in the Washington, D.C. area. It's made of only four bricks.

The Block of Fame is also here. It features busts of historical figures and pop icons as well as LEGO models of famous works of art. The only ride in Miniland USA is the Coast Cruise. Large boats take you around a lake on a short ride. The cruise is the only way you can get a close-up view of some of the models and areas in Miniland USA.

Imagination Zone

The Imagination Zone offers a variety of attractions for all age groups. The BIONICLE Blaster is based on the popular line of action toys. This attraction features 12 cars, each of which can hold up to five guests. As the cars spin around on large platforms, you can make the ride even wilder by spinning the wheel in the middle as fast as you desire. This ride is similar to the Mad Tea Party at Disneyland. The LEGO Technic Test Track is a roller coaster with a number of tight turns and quick drops; the cars are designed like life-size TECHNIC vehicles. The Aquazone Wave Racers is the first power-ski water ride in North America. You board power-ski craft that move around in a circle on the water. You can steer the craft left and right, allowing you to weave through water blasts triggered by spectator stations outside the ride. Children too small for this ride still have a lot of fun pressing the buttons for the water blasts as they try to get the riders all wet. While in the area, be sure to stop in at the LEGO Show Place and see three different movies. *LEGO Racers 4-D* is a 12-minute 3-D movie that features a number of special effects along with computer animation to make the audience feel like they're racing along with Max Axel. Also showing here is *Spellbreaker,* another 4-D movie. This one is a medieval adventure with sorcerers, swords, and a princess in need of rescue. For younger children, *Bob the Builder in 4-D* follows the popular worker and his friends as they learn about teamwork and following a plan.

The main part of the Imagination Zone is the building area. Here children and adults alike can get their hands on LEGO products. For youngsters under 6 years of age, the DUPLO Play Area provides thousands of DUPLO bricks and toys. Bionicle Evolution provides the backstory for this LEGO line and lets you build your very own Bionicle creation. At the Build and Test, children can build cars with LEGO TECHNIC elements and then test them for speed. In the Maniac Challenge, you can use LEGO software in a learning-center environment. Finally, for the older children and adults, LEGO Mindstorms teaches the basics of robotics and provides an opportunity to build and program a simple robot. All these building areas can be reserved by schools and groups. However, there's always lots of time left for all guests to use these facilities. See the signs in the area for availability.

Shows

LEGOLAND offers a variety of shows throughout the park. Each show has at least one day off during the week, so you may not get to see every show on a single day. Shows also vary seasonally. Fun Town features *The Big Test,* a great show filled with both slapstick comedy and acrobatics. It includes a working fire truck, which keeps the younger children entertained. Plus, there are inside jokes that make adults laugh as well. Most shows average between 15 and 20 minutes, which make them a good time to sit down and rest. Be sure to check the schedule you receive at the front gate to see which ones are playing during your visit as well as their start times. It's usually a good idea to get seated 15 to 20 minutes before the start of the show on busy days—seating is limited. On slow days, five minutes is plenty of time.

Tips for Touring LEGOLAND California

The best time to visit LEGOLAND is on a weekday. Weekends can be much busier, since that's when the park gets a lot of local visitors using their annual passes. However, in summer any day can be busy. On a slow day you can take your time and still be able to see and do everything you want. Busy days take a bit more planning. Normally the busiest time is between noon and around 4 PM, so try to avoid the more popular attractions during these hours any day.

Most families take a left at the Beginning and head straight to Dino Island when they enter the park. Be different and take a right, toward the Imagination Zone. If you have older children who want to do any of the activities in this area, such as the Mindstorms, be sure to make reservations and check to see when the other activities will be open. Then continue up to Land of Adventure to ride the Lost Kingdom Adventure and any of the other rides in this block. After that, make your way to Castle Hill. Because Knight's Tournament has one of the longest lines in the park, hit it first. Next head to Fun Town for the Skipper School, followed by the Driving Schools. Finish off this block with the Sky Cruiser and the Kid Power Towers. Try to go on most of these rides before noon. By then, Pirate Shores should be open. Head over to cool down. Afterward, visit Explore Village, Fun Town, Miniland USA, and Dino Island. This is also a good time to see the shows, though you'll need to arrive early. As things begin to slow down in the late afternoon, head back to the more popular rides and do them again.

Dining and Shopping

When you decide to have a meal at LEGOLAND, be prepared for a change: most of the food is fresh and made to order. This continues LEGOLAND's philosophy of nourishing the child in all areas of development—including nutrition. LEGOLAND has four sit-down restaurants and numerous other eateries and kiosks. The Upper Deck Breakfast of Champions, in the Imagination Zone, serves breakfast for an hour right after the park opens. Ristorante Brickolini in Explore Village has pastas, salads, and wood-fired pizzas. Fun Town Market serves salads, sandwiches, pastas, and ice cream. The dining area is decorated with antique toys from the LEGO collection. The Garden Restaurant overlooks Miniland USA. Here you can find soups, sandwiches, and specialty breads, as well as salads and desserts. The Knight's Table Barbecue offers smoked Danish spareribs and roasted rosemary chicken. These dinners come with all the fixin's as well. You'll pay between $6 and $19 for a meal at LEGOLAND.

There are also several places where you can pick up snacks such as fruit, baked goods, and ice cream. One of LEGOLAND's specialties is Granny's Apple Fries. The fried apple strips are rolled in cinnamon and sugar, then served with a whipped-cream dipping sauce. These are delicious and make a great snack. Of course, you can also find the fast-food standbys. Hamburgers and hot dogs are available at most places as well. For an entertaining snack break, try the LEGO Clubhouse. This ice cream and soda fountain features a LEGO robot band and is popular with children of all ages.

LEGOLAND has several shops with all types of LEGO items. In addition to the usual clothing and other kinds of souvenirs, you can buy LEGO play sets. The Big Shop at the Beginning offers just about every current LEGO toy the company makes. You'll find sets here that most stores never carry, such as LEGO lines for girls and bags of extra parts you would normally have to special-order directly from LEGO. A LEGO set makes a great souvenir that will get used more often than most. In addition, lots of families do

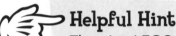

Helpful Hint

There's a LEGO shop in Downtown Disney, so if you don't have time to purchase items at LEGOLAND, you can also find them near Disneyland.

shopping for birthdays or holidays while they're at the park. The prices here are comparable to those at most major stores outside the park. A new feature is the LEGO Bricks by the Pound. At the LEGO Clubhouse in Fun Town, you can choose from more than 400 different bricks in all colors and pay for them based on weight. This is great if you need certain pieces that may have been lost or if you want to create a new masterpiece back at home.

SEA LIFE Aquarium

This aquarium is located just outside the entrance to LEGOLAND and can easily be seen within a couple hours. You can view more than 200 different species of sea creatures, including leopard- and blacktip reef sharks, octopuses, jellyfish, stingrays, sea horses, trout, and much more. One of the

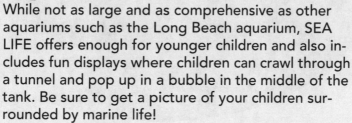

Helpful Hint

While not as large and as comprehensive as other aquariums such as the Long Beach aquarium, SEA LIFE offers enough for younger children and also includes fun displays where children can crawl through a tunnel and pop up in a bubble in the middle of the tank. Be sure to get a picture of your children surrounded by marine life!

main features is the Lost City of Atlantis, where you can walk through a 35-foot-long tunnel and watch sharks and stingrays swim around and above you. There are also areas where you can touch rays, starfish, and other animals. At the entrance, be sure to pick up quiz cards for each person in your party (you'll find the answers at interactive panels throughout the aquarium).

The aquarium often closes before LEGOLAND, so don't wait until the end of the day to visit.

CHAPTER

13

Other
Los Angeles Area
Attractions

The Los Angeles area is filled with great things for families to do in addition to the major theme parks. If you have an extra day or two in your vacation, consider visiting some of the following places.

Orange County

Orange County offers several attractions besides the Disneyland Resort and Knott's Berry Farm. You can see most of them within a few hours.

Medieval Times

> 7662 Beach Boulevard, Buena Park
> 888/935–6878 or 714/521–4740
> www.medievaltimes.com

This fun and entertaining dinner theater takes you back to the days of knights and their ladies. The seating is arranged around an arena, where you watch Andalusian stallions, authentic jousting matches, and hand-to-hand combat between knights using medieval weaponry. Audience participation is a part of the show as you cheer for your favorite knight. Although the performance might be a bit loud for young children, the atmosphere is designed for families. Children love to watch the pageantry from nearly a thousand years ago.

The cost is $56 for adults, $38 for kids 12 and younger (this does not include tax or gratuity). Admission includes the show and a meal (an appetizer, soup, roasted chicken, spareribs, potato, dessert, and a beverage). It's a good idea to make reservations in advance, especially on weekends or during the busy season, and be sure to call for hours and show times.

> ### Insider's Secret
> For a great listing of just about everything to do in Orange County, from attractions to hotels and restaurants, request *The Anaheim/Orange County Official Visitor's Guide*. Call 714/765-8888 or visit www.anaheimoc.org, which also lists deals and coupons to print out.

Depending on the season, there are usually two to three shows a day. Check the Web site or local hotels for discounts and specials. You can often save $5–$10 per person or get free upgrades—sometimes the Web site even offers free admission for kids and teens.

Pirates Dinner Adventure

7600 Beach Boulevard, Buena Park
866/439–2469 or 714/690–1497
www.piratesdinneradventure.com

This swashbuckling dinner theater show includes a lot of audience participation both from adults and kids. Included with the show is an appetizer buffet and the main meal, which features a salad, your choice of chicken, beef, or seafood, a side, a dessert, and a beverage. The cost is $57 for adults and $38 for children ages 3–11. It's a good idea to make reservations or buy tickets three days in advance either by phone or online. There's one evening show daily, plus a late afternoon show Saturday (and sometimes Sunday during summer). The show is loud, so use your judgment with younger children.

Long Beach

Long Beach is California's fifth-largest city, and its port is one of the busiest shipping centers on the Pacific Coast. It hosts a few attractions that are worth a visit if your vacation offers enough time for them.

Long Beach Aquarium of the Pacific

> 100 Aquarium Way
> 562/590–3100
> www.aquariumofpacific.org

This aquarium features 17 major habitats as well as 30 smaller exhibits representing three main regions of the Pacific Ocean: Southern California/Baja, the tropical Pacific, and the northern Pacific. You'll see more than 12,500 ocean animals from nearly 1,000 species. These include leopard sharks, giant Japanese spider crabs, sea lions, seals, a giant octopus, sea stars, and much, much more. An interesting exhibit lets you observe jellyfish (also known as sea jellies). The ever-popular Shark Lagoon lets guests interact with four types of sharks in shallow pools. There are several other interactive exhibits, making this attraction a lot of fun for children of all ages. For an additional $3, catch a 3-D movie. Since seating is limited, it's a good idea to either purchase your tickets in advance or as soon as you arrive at the aquarium.

The aquarium is open most every day of the year (except Christmas day and the Grand Prix of Long Beach weekend in mid-April) from 9 AM to 6 PM. Admission is $24 for adults, $21

Helpful Hint

The Long Beach Aquarium of the Pacific is a great change of pace from theme parks, so you might want to give it a try in the middle of your vacation. Combined with some time on one of the local beaches, this could be a great break for the family.

for senior citizens, and $12 for children 3 to 11. Parking is $7 if you show your aquarium ticket stub. This is a popular attraction with the local community, so the best time to come is during the week in the morning. When it's busy, the aquarium uses timed ticketing so that large groups of people are not crowded into the exhibits. During these periods, you may have to wait until an assigned time to enter.

The *Queen Mary*

> 1126 Queen's Highway at end of I–710
> 800/437–2934
> www.queenmary.com

Take a tour of this former star of the Cunard Line. It first sailed in 1936 and took its last voyage in 1967, after which it docked in Long Beach. The ship is now a museum and hotel and contains several restaurants as well. Basic admission is $25 for adults, $22 for military and senior citizens, and $13 for children 5 to 11. This includes a self-guided tour of the ship and the Ghosts and Legends exhibit, which explores supernatural experiences that passengers and crew members have reported. A guided tour is also available for an additional $8, and takes you other places on board that are not accessible with the self-guided tour. You can also purchase a combo package that also includes admission to the Aquarium of the Pacific for $35 for adults and $19 for children. Parking is $10.

Adjacent to the *Queen Mary* is the Russian Foxtrot submarine *Scorpion*. Admission is $11 for adults and $10 for military, senior citizens, and children 5 to 11. The self-guided tour of the sub requires children to be at least 48 inches tall, and they cannot be carried. You must climb ladders and walk through narrow and cramped passageways. Wheelchairs and strollers cannot be accommodated, and it's not recommended for expectant mothers or people prone to claustrophobia or motion sickness.

If you plan on spending some time in the Long Beach area, consider staying the night in one of the staterooms. The Hotel Queen Mary's rooms start around $119 per night for an inside stateroom, and rates go up to $660 a night for a royalty suite. A stay includes a self-guided tour of the ship, and children 17 and under stay free. Several package deals are also available. Check the Web site or call for more information. AAA members can save up to 25% on room rates.

Hollywood

Hollywood can be a lot of fun, especially for families with older children and those interested in the entertainment industry. You can make this a part of your vacation or even a vacation in itself.

The El Capitan Theatre

6838 Hollywood Boulevard
800/347–6396
www.elcapitantickets.com

First opened in 1926, the El Capitan was one of Hollywood's premier stage theaters. Designed with a Spanish colonial exterior and an East Indian interior, the theater showed a great number of plays until 1936, when it became a movie theater. In 1941 *Citizen Kane* made its world premiere at the El Capitan. Later the theater was remodeled and reopened as the Hollywood Paramount. Then in 1989 Disney purchased it and restored the theater to its original glory with state-of-the-art special-effects equipment. The theater now hosts both live performances and movies, boasting an entirely digital movie system. In addition to showing the latest Disney features, the theater hosts special productions, such as Disney sing-alongs. For most of the big Disney box office releases, you're treated to additional entertainment prior to the movie, such as a live-action Disney character show or admission to an interactive-exhibit fun house next to the theater.

Tickets vary in price from $16 for general admission to $26 for VIP tickets that include a reserved seat (close to the center of the theater), popcorn, and a drink. Check the theater's Web site for the schedule. If you can fit this into your vacation,

Insider's Tip

If you'll be in Hollywood during a Disney movie premier and want to take part in the celebration and fun, be sure to order your tickets early—the premiers usually sell out quickly.

it's a reasonable way (especially if you see a matinee) to experience the glory of Hollywood. Before or after the show, stop by the Disney Soda Fountain and Studio Store right next door. This shop offers a variety of old-time ice cream treats as well as DVDs and other Walt Disney Studios merchandise.

Grauman's Chinese Theatre

6925 Hollywood Boulevard
323/464–8111
www.manntheatres.com

This theater is one of the Hollywood classics from the industry's golden age. Its main claim to fame began in 1927, when actress Norma Talmadge accidentally stepped into wet concrete. Since that time, more than 200 stars have stepped into immortality by making hand- or footprints here. There's no charge to browse through the area.

The Walk of Fame

Hollywood Boulevard

The sidewalks along Hollywood Boulevard, between Gower Street and La Brea Avenue, as well as a portion of Vine Street south of Hollywood Boulevard, contain large metal stars with the names of celebs from the entertainment industry. This attraction is a free and fun activity while you're touring Hollywood Boulevard.

Kodak Theatre

6801 Hollywood Boulevard
323/308–6300
www.kodaktheatre.com

The site of the Academy Awards ceremony, this is one of the most televised theaters in America. Guided tours are available every day from 10:30 AM to 2:30 PM. On the tour, you'll see an actual Oscar statuette, learn where this year's nominees sat, and see how the entire production is made from a behind-the-scenes view. Admission is $15 for adults and $10 for senior citizens and children 3 to 12. The theater also features a num-

Helpful Hint

Hollywood Boulevard contains a number of classic and historic buildings. Even if you're visiting the area for only one of its attractions, if you have the time, walk along the boulevard and just look around to see how many famous places you can recognize.

ber of performances throughout the year. Check the Web site for current events and tour discounts.

Studio Tours

Many television and movie studios are in the Los Angeles area. Several offer tours of their facilities, and some allow guests to view live tapings of their shows. Before you plan on visiting these places, be sure to check age requirements. Some tours have a minimum age of 10 years, and tapings can require 16 years or older.

Helpful Hint

Of the studio tours, the Warner Bros. Studio VIP Tour is the best—and the most expensive. It runs $45 for a tour lasting a little over two hours. However, none of these tours are as entertaining as a day at Universal Studios theme park, which also features rides and shows.

NBC Studio Tours

3000 W. Alameda Avenue, Burbank
818/840–3537

Sony Pictures Studios

10202 W. Washington Boulevard, Culver City
310/244–8687
www.sonypicturesstudiostours.com

The Warner Bros. Studio VIP Tour

Olive Avenue and Hollywood Way, Burbank
818/972–8687
wbsf.warnerbros.com

Watching a Taping

If you're in the area and have the time, it's fun to watch a show taping. There are a number of ways to get free tickets for tapings. Tickets for NBC shows are available at the NBC ticket counter at the studios. You can call 818/840–3537 for more information, and you can also request tickets by mail.

Audiences Unlimited offers tickets at its booths at Universal Studios, Universal CityWalk, Mann's Chinese Theatre in Hollywood, and the Los Angeles Convention and Visitors Bureau Information Centers in Hollywood and downtown Los Angeles. Check out the Web site at www.audiencesunlimited. com, where you'll find tickets for the taping of some Disney Channel shows.

Several other Web sites offer schedules as well as information on obtaining tickets. Some of the better sites are www. studioaudiences.com, www.1iota.com, and www.tvtix.com. If you would like to see a taping, be sure to get your tickets early. Some popular shows give out all of their tickets a month or more in advance. Also, plan on arriving at least an hour early to wait in line. Just because you have a ticket does not mean you will get in.

Most tapings do not allow children under 16, so this is not a good idea for families with young children.

Los Angeles Museums and Parks

Los Angeles has several museums throughout the city, as well as some large and remarkable parks that are attractions in themselves.

Exposition Park

Exposition Boulevard and Figueroa Street

This park contains two museums and is near the L.A. Memorial Coliseum. While visiting these museums, be sure to stop by the 7-acre sunken rose garden. There are 16,000 specimens in 190 different varieties.

California Science Center

700 State Drive, Exposition Park
323/724–3623
www.californiasciencecenter.org

This science-based museum features exhibits covering health, space, physics, and the environment. Many of the exhibits are interactive and let children experience science firsthand. There's a Digital Jam Session, where visitors can play a number of instruments. Body Works features a 50-foot human figure that explains how the various parts of a body function. The space simulator's changing exhibits let you experience space flight. There's also an IMAX theater showing both 2-D and 3-D movies.

Admission to the museum is free. However, there's a charge for the IMAX movies, ranging between $5 and $8. If you have the time, this is a great educational attraction, and children from elementary to high school will enjoy seeing scientific principles put into action. It's also one of the best bargains in town.

Natural History Museum of Los Angeles County

900 Exposition Boulevard, Exposition Park
213/763–3466
www.nhm.org

This is an impressive museum with several different types of exhibits. Two large halls show African and North American mammals in their natural habitats. The Marine Hall features dioramas of California sea life. There's also a hall of birds. The Discovery Center is a great interactive area where children can check out "discovery boxes" filled with educational activities.

They can also take fossil rubbings from a rock wall, look at a drop of water under a microscope, and observe live animals, including snakes, lizards, and fish. The Insect Zoo hosts a variety of creepy crawlies. However, most kids' favorite exhibit is the dinosaurs. Skeletons of a Tyrannosaurus rex and a triceratops, ready to do battle, highlight the exhibit, which also includes a cast of a complete Mamenchisaurus skeleton, the longest-necked dinosaur ever discovered.

Admission to the museum is $9 for adults, $6.50 for senior citizens and children 13–17, and $2 for children 5–12. Everyone can get in free on the first Tuesday of every month. Hours are 9:30 AM to 5 PM daily; the museum is closed on most major holidays. This is a great museum and a super place to spend several hours if you can fit it into your plans.

Griffith Park

Said to be the largest urban municipal park in the United States, Griffith Park covers more than 4,000 acres. Bordered by Interstate 5 on the east and the 134 Freeway on the north, this park contains the Los Angeles Zoo and a number of other museums and attractions. There's a miniature railroad, a motion simulator ride, a merry-go-round, hiking trails, and much more. Park admission is free; the rides run from $1 to $2.

Fun Fact

Walt Disney used to take his daughters to the merry-go-round at Griffith Park when they were little. During these visits he came up with the idea of Disneyland as a place for families, with something to do for everyone.

Autry National Center of the American West

4700 Western Heritage Way, Griffith Park
323/667–2000
www.autrynationalcenter.org

Formerly known as the Museum of the American West, this museum was started by Gene Autry, one of Hollywood's most popular Western stars. However, the museum focuses on the American West as it really was. Children will enjoy the Family Discovery Gallery, where they can learn about history through a number of games and workshops. This gallery is completely hands on, letting kids touch and feel history rather than just look at it through glass. They can even try the same games kids from 100 years ago played. Other exhibits illustrate the real life of a cowboy on the cattle drive. Of course, there are also displays of artifacts from television shows and movies, including one of the Lone Ranger's masks and his silver-inlaid saddle.

Admission is $9 for adults, $5 for senior citizens and teens 13–18, $3 for children 3–12, and free to the public on the second Tuesday of every month. It's open Tuesday through Sunday from 10 AM to 5 PM.

Los Angeles Zoo

5333 Zoo Drive, Griffith Park
323/644–4200
www.lazoo.org

The Los Angeles Zoo contains more than 1,200 animals from around the world. You can see a variety of primates, such as monkeys and gorillas, as well as elephants, giraffes, lions, tigers, and bears—oh my! For a complete list of animals, check the zoo's Web site. Several shows play throughout the day, and the Animal Encounters Program is a favorite among many children because they're allowed to get up close and even touch some of the zoo's residents. Kids also enjoy Adventure Island, which is a zoo just for young children.

The zoo is spread out, so bring comfortable shoes for walking and a stroller for small children. Although the Safari Shuttle runs about the zoo, it costs adults $4 to ride, $1.50 for senior citizens, and $2 for children ages 2 to 12. Admission to the zoo is $13 for adults, $10 for senior citizens, and $8 for children 2 to 12. The zoo is open daily (except Dec. 25) from 10 AM to 5 PM.

La Brea Tar Pits (The Page Museum)

5801 Wilshire Boulevard, Los Angeles
323/934–7243
www.tarpits.org

This museum features one of the world's most famous finds of fossils from the Ice Age. Mammals, birds, and plants were caught from 10,000 to 40,000 years ago in the sticky asphalt, commonly called tar, where their bones fossilized. More than a million bones have been uncovered at this site, including the remains of mammoths and saber-toothed cats. Even insects were caught and preserved. Skeletons of these creatures have been assembled for viewing.

Many of the exhibits here are designed with children in mind. Kids can touch bones of long-extinct animals or test their strength against the pull of asphalt to see if they would have been able to escape from the tar pits. Because the site is still being excavated, you can observe fossils being cleaned and prepared for display. Outside the museum are viewing areas and life-size replicas of animals such as mammoths that lived during the Ice Age. In fact, the area is landscaped with plants from species that were around during the Ice Age; such plants were found preserved as fossils in the asphalt. In summer, you can see paleontologists working in Pit 91.

You can visit the park area for free, but admission to the museum is $7 for adults, $4.50 for senior citizens and students with an ID, and $2 for children 5 to 12 years of age. Admission is free the first Tuesday of every month. It is open daily (except for holidays) from 9:30 AM to 5 PM. Children usually enjoy seeing the replicas in the tar pits as well as the fossilized skeletons, and this is a good place to visit after the Natural History Museum. However, warn your children in advance not to expect any dinosaurs—during the age of the dinosaurs, Los Angeles was under the ocean.

Beaches

Southern California offers some of the most famous beaches in the world, and many families try to visit at least one of them during their vacation. The Los Angeles area has more than 100 miles of beaches—too many to cover within the scope of this book.

If you're staying in the Anaheim area, there are several great beaches nearby. Driving south on Harbor Boulevard and then the 55 Freeway south will take you to Newport Beach. This city has a nice 6-mile-long beach, Newport Beach Municipal Beach, which includes access to a pier. There's a metered parking lot as well as street parking. For more information, call 714/644–3044.

Driving Beach Boulevard south takes you to Huntington Beach, a city with more than 8 miles of beaches. The State

Helpful Hint

If you're interested in hitting the beaches during your vacation, there are some great Web sites that provide helpful information on the various beaches in the area. Check out www.beachcalifornia.com. This site lists beaches by city and includes information on local things to do.

Insider's Secret

If your family wants to swim or just have fun in the water, it's usually a good idea to do this at your hotel's pool or at a water park. Swimming in the ocean can be dangerous for adults as well as children, especially if they're not accustomed to the waves and currents. The Pacific Ocean can be quite rough at times with dangerous riptides at some places, which can carry a person away from the shore quite rapidly. No matter which beach you choose to visit, be sure to read and heed all warnings.

Beach (714/536–1454) has a $5 entrance fee per vehicle; the Municipal Beach (714/536–5280) costs $6 per vehicle and includes a pier.

Long Beach also offers several nice beaches if you plan on visiting other attractions in the area. Call 562/594–0951 or visit www.longbeach.gov/park for more information.

Many of the beaches have playgrounds for children as well as changing facilities, so you do not have to wear beach attire to and from the beach. You can also rent surfboards, Boogie boards, bikes, Jet Skis, and small boats at some beaches. Call ahead or check online to see what's available.

Although most public beaches have lifeguards, they're usually on duty only in summer and on some weekends. If you're going to the beach with children, don't expect the lifeguards to babysit them. They're there for emergencies only. Beaches can be quite busy, especially when the weather is warm, and all types of people come to the ocean to cool off. Be aware of beach closings caused by contamination and other problems. When swimming, stay away from piers and storm drains, which can be dangerous.

CHAPTER

14

San Diego
Area
Attractions

San Diego Attractions

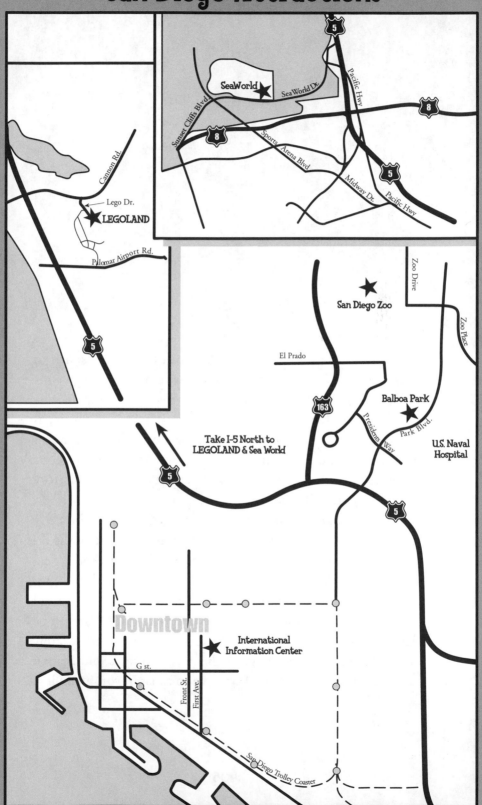

About two hours south of Los Angeles and 90 minutes from Anaheim, San Diego contains a number of interesting places to visit. This was the first European settlement in Alta California (Upper California, as opposed to Baja California, or Lower California, which is down south) and the location of the first of a string of missions founded by Father Junípero Serra. There's a great deal of history as well as entertainment here.

While San Diego is close enough to Anaheim for a day trip, if you plan on spending time at more than one of the attractions in or near San Diego, including LEGOLAND, SeaWorld, and the San Diego Zoo and Wild Animal Park, we suggest staying at least one night or more in the area instead of commuting back and forth. The hotels in San Diego can be less expensive than some of those in the area immediately around the Disneyland Resort. Chapter 2 contains information on a few hotels in the San Diego area to assist in your planning.

Money-Saving Tip

If you're planning to add SeaWorld and the San Diego Zoo to a trip to Disneyland, consider purchasing the Southern California CityPass. It includes a Three-Day Park Hopper ticket for Disneyland and Disney's California Adventure, a one-day ticket to Universal Studios Hollywood, and one-day tickets to both SeaWorld and the San Diego Zoo or Wild Animal Park. Adults pay $259 and children 3 to 9 pay $219, for savings of almost $95 per adult ticket. You can purchase these passes online or at any of the included attractions. For more information, check out the Web site at www.citypass.net and select Southern California. There's also a 3-for-1 ticket available that includes unlimited admission to SeaWorld, the San Diego Zoo, and the Wild Animal Park for five consecutive days; the passes cost about $115 for adults and $92 for children 3 to 9.

SeaWorld

500 Sea World Drive, San Diego
800/257–4268 or 619/226–3901
www.seaworldsandiego.com

SeaWorld is in Mission Bay, just north of San Diego and about 90 minutes from Anaheim. If traveling from the Los Angeles area, take Interstate 5 southbound, exit west onto SeaWorld Drive, and follow the signs to SeaWorld. Although it began as an animal park for marine life, SeaWorld has grown into a theme park that tries to make each of its attractions educational in some way.

Admission is $65 for adults and $55 for children 3 to 9. You can buy tickets at the park or in advance at some hotels or online. The park Web site usually offers some great deals, such as a second day free or discounted rates. AAA members also get discounts. Park hours range from 10 AM to 5 PM during the fall and winter months, and from 9 AM to 11 PM in spring and summer. Be sure to check the Web site for the date you plan on visiting.

Money-Saving Tip

You should never have to pay full price for admission. Discounts are available at most hotels. Also, check with your employer or a credit union for coupons or other discounts. To take advantage of these discounts, you usually have to purchase your tickets at the park. AAA members also receive discounts and can purchase their tickets at most AAA offices.

Attractions

SeaWorld offers a number of entertaining attractions. Many of them are educational as well.

Journey to Atlantis

SeaWorld's newest attraction takes you on a journey to the ancient lost city of Atlantis. You board Greek fishing boats and sail through the story of the famous city featuring special effects that include tremors, flooding, and water cannons. The flume ride turns into a roller coaster as the boats are lifted eight stories and then travel along a track, culminating in a 60-foot plunge into a lake. Passengers also get to see black-and-white Commerson dolphins, which are native to the waters off the coast of the southern tip of South America. The ride takes about six minutes and has a 42-inch minimum height requirement. A good gauge for determining whether kids will like this ride is Splash Mountain and the Matterhorn at Disneyland. If they're fine with both of these rides, they should have no trouble on this one.

Penguin Encounter

Watch penguins waddle and swim around in this Antarctic habitat, housing more than 350 penguins at a comfortable 25°F. Because the habitat is set to Antarctic time, the lights are often dimmed by afternoon to represent sunset, making it difficult to observe the penguins, so try to visit this attraction early to midday. The exhibit also houses puffins, murres, and other arctic birds as well as warm-weather penguins, which are housed outdoors.

Sesame Street Bay of Play

This new area includes three rides: Elmo's Flying Fish lets riders go up and down as they fly around in a circle; Oscar's Rocking Eel spins around as it rocks from side to side; and Abby's Sea Star Spin is a spinning teacup–style ride. This kids' activity center also contains slides, net climbs, fountains, a water maze, a two-story ship to climb on and in, and much more. This is a good place to hit during the middle of your visit to let the kids burn off some extra energy before seeing more shows and exhibits.

Shark Encounter

In this attraction, you walk through a 57-foot tube underwater to watch sharks and rays swim overhead and off to both sides. You'll feel as if you're in the water with them! Children usually like seeing the sharks.

Shipwreck Rapids

This is SeaWorld's version of the popular rafting rides. Passengers travel past waterfalls and creatures of the sea, through a dark tunnel into the interior of a ship's engine room, and into a near collision with a ship's propeller. The ride lasts about five minutes, and you can expect to get wet. There's a 42-inch minimum height requirement. The ride can be a bit scary as the rafts bump up and down in the rapids, and the dark parts can also be frightening. Six-year-olds will usually be fine, and younger children who are tall enough and really want to ride will probably enjoy it as well. If you're unsure, there are a few places where you can watch others on the ride. After watching, let your children determine whether they want to go or not.

Wild Arctic

This attraction combines a ride and an exhibit. You first board a "jet helicopter" that takes you on a simulated motion ride to an arctic research station. Along the way, the helicopter bumps up and down as well as to the side, avoiding obstacles and dangers during the flight. When you finally arrive at the research station, the fun is just beginning. You'll walk through an ice tunnel and observe polar bears, beluga whales, and walruses in almost natural environments. This is one of the park's most popular attractions. It has a 42-inch height requirement, and most kids who are tall enough will be fine on this ride.

Helpful Hint

For younger children and adults prone to motion sickness, nonmoving seats are available during the helicopter flight of Wild Arctic.

World of the Sea Aquarium

This exhibit features four large habitats housing sea life from local to tropical climes. Because it's just a walk-through attraction, you can spend as much or as little time as you want here.

Shows

Shows make up a large part of the SeaWorld Experience. You should schedule your day around the show times to ensure you do not miss any of these entertaining and often educational exhibits.

Believe—Shamu Show

Featuring SeaWorld's most famous mammal, this show features killer whales and their natural behaviors. This entertaining and educational show is a park trademark. In summer, SeaWorld also offers a night show featuring lighting effects and rock music.

Helpful Hint
The first several rows in the stadiums are marked as splash zones. If you sit in them, be prepared to get wet.

Cirque de la Mer

This is a new and exciting show at SeaWorld featuring acrobats performing on land as well as in and on the water. Set in a mythical land of Amphibia, this impressive show will be enjoyed by most guests.

Sea Lions LIVE

SeaWorld's entertaining sea lions, Clyde and Seamore, put on quite a show as they do their own versions of two popular TV shows. Expect a lot of fun as they stage "Sea Lion Idol" and "Dancing with the Pinnipeds." This is a great show for all ages.

Dolphin Discovery

This is another water show—this time, bottlenose dolphins and pilot whales perform. During the summer months, there's also a nighttime performance.

Pets Rule!

This show features household pets doing a variety of tricks and acts. It's a good choice for small children and pet lovers.

Insider's Secret

For all shows, it's a good idea to get there at least 15 minutes early. This helps ensure that you get not only a seat but also a good one.

Sesame Street presents Lights, Camera, Imagination! in 4-D
This 3-D movie incorporates special effects that make you feel as if you're a part of the show. Bert and Ernie, Elmo, Big Bird, and Cookie Monster, invite you to attend the Sesame Street Film Festival. However, when the projector stops working, everyone must use their imaginations to finish the show. The effects help make guests feel like they are swimming through an imaginary ocean or flying through the sky. While it is aimed at younger children, the entire family will enjoy the special effects.

Time-Saving Tip

Because you want to get to the shows early, use the time you're waiting for a show as well as during the show to have a meal or a snack. Just get the food before you head to the show, or send part of your family for the food while the rest hold the seats.

Interacting with Animals

SeaWorld offers many opportunities for you to get up close and personal with some of the resident animals. These exhibits are a terrific way for children, as well as adults, to gain a greater understanding of life under the sea.

California Tidepool

This exhibit allows guests to pick up live sea stars as well as touch other animals from the intertidal zone, including sea urchins, tube worms, and hermit crabs. Many children consider this one of their favorite parts of SeaWorld.

Forbidden Reef

You can reach into the water and touch bat rays as they swim by or even offer them a piece of squid to eat. Then you can look through observation windows at moray eels living and hiding in the underwater caverns.

Helpful Hint

After touching and feeding the various marine life, you may want to clean your hands and especially your children's. This is when having a few antibiotic wet wipes or towelettes can come in handy.

Rocky Point Preserve

This exhibit lets you watch and feed dolphins as well as observe sea otters as they dive for their food. There are also several interactive displays for you to learn more about these fascinating creatures.

Seal and Sea Lion Exhibit

What do seals and sea lions like for a snack? Let's just say that it's fishy. Children will enjoy feeding the animals here, but be sure to check the schedule for feeding times so you don't miss it!

Other Programs

SeaWorld offers a variety of personal programs for interacting with animals. Dining with Shamu is offered on most weekends and on some weekdays throughout the year. It features a meal with everyone's favorite killer whale. The poolside buffet runs around $39 for adults and $19 for children 3 to 9. You can also choose to have breakfast with Shamu. It's less expensive, at $26 and $16, respectively. You can book these online or call 800-25-SHAMU (74268) for dates and reservations.

The Dolphin Interaction Program lets you get in the water with dolphins and learn about training them. The Wild Arctic Interaction lets you interact with beluga whales, walruses, seals, and even polar bears. The costs for each is $170 per person. Call 800/257–4268 Ext. 7 for more information and to make reservations; you can also book both programs online.

San Diego Zoo

2920 Zoo Drive, Balboa Park, San Diego
619/231–1515
www.sandiegozoo.org

This is one of the largest zoos in the world, with more than 4,000 animals housed in exhibits that simulate their natural habitats. The zoo is also home to a number of endangered and rare animals not normally seen in captivity, such as koalas and pandas.

To get to the zoo from the Los Angeles and Anaheim areas, take I–5 south, then State Route 163 north. Take the Zoo/Museums exit at Richmond Street and follow the signs to the zoo. Admission is $24.50 for adults and $16.50 for children 3 to 11. You can usually find discounts at local hotels or through your employer or credit union. These can save you up to $5 per ticket. The Best Value package includes rides on the Bus Tour, Express Bus, and Skyfari aerial tram for $35 ($26 for children 3 to 11). Or you can add admission to the San Diego Zoo's Wild Animal Park for a total of $60 ($43 for children 3 to 11). This price includes the rides at the zoo. Although the admission may seem high for a zoo, it's one of the best in the world. Plus, parking is free.

The zoo is quite large and spread out, so plan on doing a lot of walking. For families with young children, that translates to "Bring a stroller." You can rent strollers at the zoo for $9.

Insider's Secret

If you choose to walk with small children, be sure either to keep them in a stroller or hold on to them tightly. Many of the walkways also serve as roads for the tour buses and are quite narrow. Use caution when walking along these areas, for the safety of your children.

Transportation

You can walk all over the zoo, but there are a few options to give your feet a rest. The Guided Bus Tour takes you around the zoo on a 40-minute trip while a host tells you about the various animals and habitats. This provides a good overview and can help you determine what you want to see. This is included in the Best Value admission package or can be purchased separately for $10 for adults and $7 for children. The Express Buses are more like shuttles, making five stops throughout the zoo, and are included with the Guided Bus Tour packages. Finally, the Skyfari Tram travels from one end of the zoo to the other. Deluxe admission includes this ride, or you can pay $3 per person for a one-way trip.

San Diego Zoo's Wild Animal Park

15500 San Pasqual Valley Road, Escondido
760/747–8702
www.sandiegozoo.org/wap

This 1,800-acre wildlife preserve allows you to view animals out in the open while the humans are confined within their modes of transportation. The park also includes a number of exhibits and displays that allow you to view animals in a closer, more zoolike way.

To get to the Wild Animal Park from the Los Angeles and Anaheim areas, take Interstate 5 south, then the State Route 78 east exit at Oceanside. Continue to Interstate 15 and take it south to the Via Rancho Parkway exit. Continue east and follow the signs to the park.

Admission is $28.50 for adults and $17.50 for children 3 to 11. The Best Value package includes admission, the Journey into Africa Tour, and the Conservation Carousel for $35 ($26 for children 3 to 11). You can also purchase two-park tickets, which include admission to the San Diego Zoo and Wild Animal Park, for $60 ($43 for children 3 to 11). Strollers are available for rent for $9. Parking is $9.

Plan on doing a lot of walking here. Probably hiking is a more accurate term, because you will be taking hikes of more than a mile at several of the habitats and exhibits at the park. Wear comfortable shoes, and be sure either to bring or rent a stroller for younger children so you do not end up having to carry them around the park.

Other San Diego Attractions

Balboa Park

> 1549 El Prado, San Diego
> 619/239–0512
> www.balboapark.org

Overlooking downtown and the Pacific Ocean, 1,200-acre Balboa Park is the cultural heart of San Diego. Ranked as one of the world's best parks by the Project for Public Spaces in 2004, it's the place where you can find most of the city's museums and its world-famous zoo. For $39 ($21 for children), you can buy a one-week passport that includes individual tickets to 13 of the museums and attractions in the park. Besides hosting these attractions, the park, boasting beautiful botanical gardens, is fun to explore in itself.

Reuben H. Fleet Science Center

1875 El Prado, Balboa Park, San Diego
619/238–1233
www.rhfleet.org

This museum features an IMAX theater, a motion simulation ride that takes you on a journey through the universe, and five galleries of hands-on science exhibits and demonstrations. The center is open daily. Admission is $10 for adults and $8.75 for children 3 to 12. Tickets for the theater and the ride are extra, or you can purchase them as part of a package with admission.

San Diego Aerospace Museum

Ford Building
Pan American Plaza, Balboa Park, San Diego
619/234–8291
www.aerospacemuseum.org

This museum houses more than 65 U.S. and foreign aircraft and spacecraft and brings to life the rich heritage of aviation in which Southern California had such a vital and important part. You can see replicas of the Wright Flyer and fighter planes from both world wars as well as the Korean and Vietnam wars, and there's also a Blackbird spy plane on display. The people who made aviation history are also featured, as well as exhibits on the physics and principles of flight. Replicas of spacecraft from the Mercury, Gemini, and Apollo missions are also on display, along with a moon rock, space suits, and other related items.

The museum is open daily except on Thanksgiving, Christmas, and New Year's Day. Admission is $15 for adults and $6 for children 3 to 11.

San Diego Natural History Museum

Park Boulevard and Village Place, Balboa Park, San Diego
619/232–3821
www.sdnhm.org

This museum is not as large as the one in Los Angeles but still offers a good variety of exhibits about the flora, fauna, and geology of the area as well as of Baja California. Check the museum's Web site for exhibits during your visit.

The museum is open daily except Thanksgiving, Christmas, and New Year's Day. Admission is $13 for adults, $8 for children 13 to 17, and $7 for children 3 to 12.

Old Town San Diego State Historic Park

Wallace Street and Juan Street, San Diego
619/220–5422
www.oldtownsandiego.org

This six-block area contains many of San Diego's original buildings that made up the first European settlement in California. Free guided tours of the area begin at 11 AM and 2 PM daily except for Thanksgiving and Christmas. You can also purchase a self-guided tour pamphlet for $2. There's no fee for admission to the area and the buildings. All of the buildings are minimuseums that feature artifacts and exhibits from various times in San Diego's history.

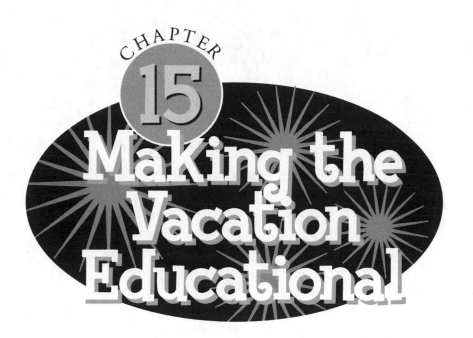

CHAPTER

15

Making the
Vacation
Educational

When most people think of a trip to Disneyland, they think of fun and entertainment. However, there are many ways to make your family vacation an educational trip as well as a fun experience for your children.

Taking Kids Out of School

If your children will miss school for the vacation, speak to their teachers at least a week or more in advance. Many schools offer an independent study program in which teachers provide lessons and work for the children to do that covers what they miss. When they return from the vacation, the children are up to speed and ready to continue with the rest of their class.

The earlier you get the schoolwork for your children, the earlier they can begin getting it done. In fact, you should encourage them to get as much of it completed as they can, if not all of it, prior to leaving. The last thing they will want to do immediately after getting home from the vacation is homework.

Let your children's teachers know where you'll be going, and ask if there are any special projects or reports your children

420

can do that will incorporate what they learn on vacation with what they're studying in school. Some teachers may be inclined to have the child do such projects instead of some of the schoolwork. The child can then present what he or she learned to the class when you return. If the teacher does not have any ideas in mind, you might suggest some listed in this chapter.

Writing Reports

In lieu of assigning normal schoolwork, some teachers may be interested in having children write reports about their trip. Kids could write about visits to museums and other related places or the history of Disneyland or Walt Disney. Children can include pictures they take or pamphlets they pick

> **Insider's Secret**
>
> Don't hit your children's teachers with the news of your vacation the day before you leave. This does not give the teachers enough time to prepare material for your children or to set up an independent study program. At least one week should be sufficient notice.

up during the vacation. Even younger children can do reports. These may consist of nothing more than an album of photos or postcards with captions written or dictated by the child.

Educational Attractions

Most families try to add some education to their vacations by visiting learning-related attractions such as museums and zoos. Southern California has a number of these attractions, many of which are designed to be interactive and fun for kids.

Zoos, aquariums, and animal parks teach about the variety of life on our planet as well as how we can help take care of it. Children usually enjoy seeing the different animals and how they live. There are also theme parks designed around animals, such as SeaWorld in San Diego. These places combine rides with animal experiences.

Learning in Other Ways

Whether you decide to include educational attractions in your vacation or not, you can still teach your children while you're away from home.

Helpful Hint

Unless you're planning to surprise your children with a vacation, let them take part in the planning. Depending on the size of your family, and the number of days you will be on vacation, you may want to allow each child to be king or queen for the day—or half-day. During their royal tenure, they can plan some of the activities the family will do or even where they eat one of the meals.

Preparing for the Vacation

It's important to allow your children, especially as they grow older, to take part in planning the vacation. Ask each child to come up with a list of places he or she would like to visit. Then during a family meeting, each can make a short presentation of why the family should go to these places. Older children should be encouraged to do some research for their presentations, using this book and possibly the Internet. This exercise will help them with public speaking as well as learning how to re-search.

Once your family has decided where to go, ask the children to come up with a schedule for each day of the vacation. The older the children, the more detailed the schedules can be.

Preschoolers may just list a couple of rides at Disneyland, whereas older children could list times to see shows as well as strategize the best times to hit popular rides.

Older children can also help with travel arrangements. If your family is driving, ask them to plan your route, calculating the distance to travel and how long it will take to get there. They might also find good places to stop along the way for meals or restroom breaks. For families that are flying or making other travel arrangements, let older children call for quotes or check prices on the Internet. An adult should help them as they find the best rates.

In the days leading up to the vacation, children can help get ready by doing some packing, checking on the weather in Southern California, and even assisting in getting the car ready if the family is driving. Younger children can make a paper chain (see Chapter 3 for details) or use a calendar to count the number of days left until you leave.

Helpful Hint

Google Earth is a great educational resource when planning a vacation. Using this free computer application, you can view satellite images of the entire earth. You can see the Disneyland Resort in fairly high resolution and can use tools such as the distance ruler to determine how far you must travel to get to your vacation destination. Check out earth. google.com for this fascinating program.

While Traveling

Whether you're driving, flying, or taking some other type of transportation to Southern California, there's always something to do on the way. When driving, let older children navigate.

Provide a map, watch, pad of paper, and pen and let them guide you to Disneyland. They can practice their math by determining at various points along the trip how long you've been driving, how far you've traveled, how far you still have to go, and what time they think you'll arrive. They can even calculate the miles per gallon of gas your vehicle is using. Although they can use the pen and paper to do the math, encourage them to estimate the answers in their head before doing the calculations on paper.

Younger children can also join in the learning. Have them count cars or keep a running total of the number of cars by color or make. Playing an alphabet game is also fun for kids. This involves searching for letters, starting with A. They can use license plates and road signs to find each letter in the alphabet in order.

While in flight or at the airport, children can learn about the various parts of an airplane or look for landmarks on the ground below. You can also have them trace your flight using a map of your own or one in the airline magazines.

At the Resort

Once you're at the Disneyland Resort—or any other theme park, for that matter—the learning can still continue. Although younger children may not be able to use the map to help you navigate to Southern California, give them a daily schedule for a theme park, including a map, and let them determine where different attractions are located. Then they can lead the family to the attractions. For children learning to read, encourage them to read everything they can, from shop signs to ride-related notices.

There's also a lot of math that children can do at a theme park. They can count how many Dumbos are on the ride, add up what a meal for the family would cost, or estimate how many people could ride an attraction within an hour's time.

While you're in line for an attraction, keep them thinking. This will also make the time pass more quickly.

Disneyland has a few attractions that are specifically educational. Innoventions contains several exhibits that teach about topics ranging from the human body to computer animation. The sailing ship *Columbia* has a small museum below deck. In fact, a report on the actual ship and its voyage around the world could be accompanied by ship photos taken at Disneyland. The attraction Great Moments with Mr. Lincoln is located in the Main Street Opera House. This attraction gives a brief history of the Civil War and features the 16th president giving the Gettysburg Address.

California Adventure has several attractions that are designed to be educational and entertaining. All in the Golden State, they include tours of the bakery and tortilla factory, the Bountiful Valley Farm, and the Walt Disney Imagineering Blue Sky Cellar. Also, don't forget to visit Disney Animation. This attraction covers the art of animation and lets guests create their own.

Insider's Secret

Be sure to try out the Animation Academy inside Disney Animation at Disney's California Adventure. A Disney animator shows you how to draw characters such as Mickey, Goofy, and Winnie the Pooh. Our kids love learning the basics of drawing and like to go to this more than once. Ask the cast member at the entrance what times and which characters are being drawn throughout the day so you can try different ones. The shop inside Disney Animation, Off the Page, sells Disney character drawing books. You can also find these books at the World of Disney in Downtown Disney.

Other theme parks also offer educational fun. The Studio Tour, Special Effects Stage, and other attractions at Universal Studios teach about the ways movies are made and the effects used during the process. The Ghost Town area at Knott's Berry Farm also has several exhibits where you can learn how people lived more than a century ago.

Index